Environmental Politics

edited by
Stuart S. Nagel

Published in cooperation with
the Policy Studies Organization

The Praeger Special Studies program—
utilizing the most modern and efficient book
production techniques and a selective
worldwide distribution network—makes
available to the academic, government, and
business communities significant, timely
research in U.S. and international economic, social, and political development.

Environmental Politics

PRAEGER SPECIAL STUDIES IN U.S. ECONOMIC, SOCIAL, AND POLITICAL ISSUES

Praeger Publishers   New York   Washington   London

Library of Congress Cataloging in Publication Data

Nagel, Stuart S   1934-
    Environmental politics.

    (Praeger special studies in U.S. economic, social,
and political issues)
    "Published in cooperation with the Policy Studies
Organization."
    1. Environmental policy—Addresses, essays, lectures.
2. Environmental policy—International cooperation—
Addresses, essays, lectures.   3. Environmental protec-
tion—Addresses, essays, lectures.   I. Title.
HC79.E5N33   301.31'0973   74-3138
ISBN 0-275-09030-2

PRAEGER PUBLISHERS
111 Fourth Avenue, New York, N.Y. 10003, U.S.A.
5, Cromwell Place, London SW7 2JL, England

Published in the United States of America in 1974
by Praeger Publishers, Inc.

Printed in the United States of America

PREFACE
Stuart S. Nagel

Within the last few years there has been a tremendous increase in the public's concern for environmental problems. There are a number of explanations for this increase and they can be separated into those relating to the problems of pollution and land use planning in general and those relating to specific forms of pollution or to specific types of land use planning.

General explanations include increased pollution due to industrialization and population increases. The increased concentration of people in cities has also made them more subject to pollution. Not only has pollution and subjection to it increased, but the American public has also become more sensitive to pollution even if the pollution level and individual contact with pollution were held constant. This increased sensitivity is due in part to increased education as to the dangers of pollution, increased leisure time for outdoor recreational activities, and increased affluence that enables people to be more concerned with environmental matters rather than just basic food, shelter, and clothing. Another general factor that helps explain the timing of the environmental movement in the early 1970s is the ending of the civil rights, poverty, and antiwar movements, the need for alternative societal concerns, and the advent of the energy shortage.

Factors relating to specific forms of pollution include the increased use of automobiles, electrical energy, and sulfur dioxide coal, which have generated increased air pollution. Likewise, increased water pollution can be attributed to developments in the chemical, paper, and food processing industries, developments in agriculture regarding chemical fertilizers and the housing of livestock, and developments relating to energy sources such as oil transportation, acid runoff from strip mining, and thermal pollution from atomic energy plants. Solid waste problems have increased as a result of abandoned automobiles, throwaway bottles and cans, and the decreased market for scrap metals. Concern for radiation pollution is clearly a recent development due to nuclear energy expansion. Noise pollution and land use problems both have increased as a result of transportation developments.

Along with the increased concern for environmental problems has come an increased turning to government to do

something about these problems. Governmental action has increased because the problems have generally become too technical, too geographically widespread, and too connected with
large business enterprises to be capable of resolution by
individuals pursuing their private interests under such
common-law notions as nuisance, trespass, and negligence.
As the government's role in promoting the quality of the environment has increased, there have been important trends
regarding which governmental bodies are increasingly bearing
the burden of protecting the environment. A key trend has
been the shift from local to state regulation and to federal
regulation in recognition of the intergovernmental nature of
the problems and in recognition of the need to deal with the
problems at the source point where the various products responsible, like automobiles, are manufactured.

     Within the federal government (or for that matter
within the state or local governments as well) there has
been an increasing trend toward shifting antipollution activity from the courts to the legislatures and also to administrative agencies that have both quasi-legislative and
quasi-judicial power. This shift reflects the need for
broader standard setting and the need for.more full-time
expertise to deal with the problems involved. Along with
the standard setting has come versatile experimentation
with various incentives designed to encourage greater compliance with the standards set. These incentives have included discharge taxes, injunctions, tax rewards, civil
penalties, adverse publicity, selective buying, fines, jail
sentences, and conference persuasion.

     As government involvement in environmental protection
has increased, it has logically followed that the interest
of political scientists in this kind of governmental activity would also increase. This increased political science
interest has manifested itself in a number of scattered
articles, original research books, conference papers, unpublished research projects, and theses. The main purpose
of this present book is to bring together an analysis of
that fugitive literature and the issues to which the literature is addressed.

     It is interesting to note that the literature cuts
across all fields of political science including normative
political philosophy, empirical political analysis, international relations, comparative government, American national government, state and local government, political
dynamics, legislative behavior, the judicial process, and
public administration. It is for that reason that this
book is organized by fields within political science. Such
an organization should help stimulate further political

science research on environmental matters, and it should help reveal to other scholars, policy makers, policy appliers, and the general public how political science can be used in promoting environmental protection.

The chapters vary in the depth to which they review the issues involved in their respective fields of political science. Some of the chapters are mainly designed to discuss basic issues and references in their respective fields without presenting any in-depth examples. Those chapters largely stem from a 1973 symposium, "Environmental Policy and Political Science Fields," sponsored by the Policy Studies Organization and the <u>Policy Studies Journal</u>. Many of those papers have been expanded to include additional details. The symposium has also been supplemented by longer studies that further bring out the relevance of the political science fields involved to environmental protection.

One underlying theme of most of the chapters is the orientation to environmental problems that recognizes that although it is important to develop antipollution technologies, these developments are not very likely to be adopted by industrial or commercial concerns without governmental incentives. This seems true since antipollution devices do add to a business firm's expenses but do not add to its income. Likewise, even municipal governments (which are responsible for a good deal of water pollution and other forms of pollution) are not so likely to adopt improved technological devices without financial help from the federal government since such devices may be more expensive than politically feasible local taxes can support.

Related to that political theme is the orientation to environmental problems that recognizes that although individual efforts to decrease pollution are also desirable, large-scall pollution reduction must probably come mainly from governmental efforts. This is partly so because individuals rather than large business firms and municipalities are not responsible for most of the pollution that occurs. Such an orientation also seems to make sense in view of the fact that where individuals are responsible for certain forms of pollution (such as solid waste littering of nondecomposable plastic containers, cans, and bottles), those forms of pollution can generally be more meaningfully reduced through legislation that gets at the source of their existence (such as legislation prohibiting nondecomposable plastics and nonreturnable bottles and cans).

These two political realities both emphasize the importance of the role of governmental activity in minimizing pollution, maximizing environmental quality, and in foresightful land use planning. As such, they help justify the

importance of a book like <u>Environmental Politics</u>. It is
hoped the book will further clarify some of the problems involved in developing and applying environmental policies at
various governmental levels and within various governmental
institutions. The stakes from having more effective environmental policies are at least the quality, if not the survival, of life itself.

CONTENTS

LIST OF TABLES AND FIGURES

Section

1

ENVIRONMENTAL POLITICS: WHAT ROLE FOR POLITICAL SCIENTISTS?

Harold and Margaret Sprout

A great deal has been said about the accelerative depletion, pollution, and spoliation of the earth and the consequent disruption of ecological processes and systems. Tens of millions of words have been written describing and predicting the adverse impacts of these events on the human condition and prospect. The predominant theme running through this expanding literature is the mess that Americans (along with the rest of humankind) have blundered into through activities that are making our planet a less congenial habitat and may be insidiously making it less habitable for our children and their posterity.

Future events may or may not confirm pessimistic predictions that spreading industrialism, gluttonous consumption of resources derived from our physical habitat, unchecked population growth, and worsening pollutions are likely to bring about a collapse of modern industrial society within a century or so.[1] There is a large speculative element in still more somber predictions that continuation of present disruptive trends may destroy the earth's habitability within an even shorter period.[2] But such warnings from reputable scientists and others serve the useful purpose of focusing attention on the kinds of degenerative changes that are already seriously disturbing the complex ecology of our terrestrial habitat. Hence, it is only common-sense prudence to put these issues upon the agenda of every relevant science and discipline. The function of this chapter is to demonstrate the relevance of political science and to preview some of the issues that will be dealt with in various fruitful ways by other contributors to this book.

POLITICAL CONTEXT: THE MISSING DIMENSION

Plenty of research money and professional talent have been devoted to the threat of instant catastrophe from thermonuclear war and other techniques of mass destruction that might render much or all of the earth uninhabitable or so disrupt the biosphere as to make recovery questionable, to say the least.[3] Much less, though currently expanding, attention has been devoted to the consequences of incremental depletion and spoliation of the earth, which are beginning to be perceived as a comparably dangerous threat to the human future.[4]

Increasingly, physical scientists and engineers--in government and in private industry as well as in academia-- are directing their research to ways and means of curbing pollutions, raising the efficiency of energy utilization, and other problems deriving from a depreciating physical habitat.[5] While some may query whether a good deal of this environmental engineering may not produce "cures" that merely aggravate the malaise,[6] relatively few appear to challenge in principle the essential role of scientific and engineering research and development if the drift toward ruination of our habitat is to be arrested.

Economists are also getting into the act, and most of them are bringing along the well-known presuppositions and biases of their orthodoxy. With some exceptions, economists approach environmental problems with a strong antigovernmental bias. A few even appear to view public authority as an enemy to be contained as narrowly as possible. The prevailing view among economists who have uttered on environmental problems is that physical scientists and engineers can be counted on to devise technical solutions to environmental disorders: for example, inventing substitutes for increasingly scarce natural materials. They contend that abatement of pollutions by governmental regulation and punitive enforcement is inefficient, oppressive, and incurably prone to corruption. Their prescription is to deal with environmental problems in the marketplace, with as little governmental meddling as possible. Their chosen method is to charge polluters the cost of repairing the damage they cause. They contend that this method will discourage pollution, or at least provide funds for cleaning up polluted air, water, and land. They assume that pollution charges will be passed along to consumers in higher prices for necessities as well as for luxuries. They admit that combating pollutions and other environmental disorders in this manner is as regressive as flat-rate sales taxes. But with notable exceptions, they shrug off the

4

additional burdens that this mode of financing imposes upon less affluent members of the society. When they meet this issue at all, they are wont to invoke the magic recipe of economic growth, insisting that a rising per capita production of goods and services will trickle down sufficiently to the poor and near poor without seriously eroding the amenities of the affluent or otherwise seriously disrupting the economic-social status quo.[7]

Transmuting an old maxim about the danger of leaving the conduct of war to military specialists, it might be argued that dealing with the worsening environmental crisis involves a good deal that is lacking in the professional equipment of most natural scientists, engineers, and economists. More specifically, without minimizing in the slightest the relevance of formal ecological models, innovative technology, and economic formulas, something else is manifestly needed. The largely missing ingredient, we submit, is sophisticated knowledge of the political system and the social order to which it is responsive and which imposes constraints on political programs and operations.

Here is an intellectual landscape ready-made for students of government. It is a landscape formerly left, largely by default, to nonpolitically oriented specialists. It is good news to be able to report that political scientists, especially younger political scientists, are beginning to penetrate deeply and percipiently into the problems of environmental politics. Every environmental problem, we repeat, has salient engineering and economic dimensions. But each one also exhibits comparably salient political and social parameters. Even the regressive pollution charges advocated by economists require exercise of public authority to impose and enforce. And enforcement will inevitably involve some exercise of the police power of government. Indeed, we are inclined to believe that most of the technical and economic aspects of environmental repair and protection may turn out to be easier to deal with than the hard, often harsh, realities of the political system and constraints imposed by the social order.

PARAMETERS OF ENVIRONMENTAL POLITICS

We recognize that there is, and will likely continue to be, some disagreement about these parameters of environmental politics. Hopefully, a brief summary of our own findings will evoke debate and further research and thereby contribute to clarification of a core of fundamental issues implicit in the processes of policy making and the substance of environmental policies.

5

1. Our point of entry is the historical generalization that today's environmental crisis is largely attributable to human activities associated with technological-
economic development as such development has unfolded to
date. This is a historical process characterized by, among
other things, largely unplanned industrial expansion, gluttonous consumption of natural resources, accelerative population increase, and concomitant accelerative depletion,
pollution, and spoliation of our terrestrial habitat.
2. This pattern of technological-economic development
has been widely rationalized and defended by a technocratic
perspective and ethic that posits <u>Homo sapiens</u> as conqueror
and master of nature rather than as a link in the complex
ecology of the biosphere.[8]
3. The higher the level of a community's technological-
economic development, the larger and more diverse its output.
Also, the higher the ratio of its population to usable space,
the heavier becomes its "ecological demand." By ecological
demand is meant its consumption of earth-derived resources
and its consequent production of wastes that pollute air,
water, and land, which was estimated in 1970 to be doubling
every 13-14 years.[9]
4. Technological-economic development entails specialization, and specialization multiplies interdependencies
that in turn proliferate vulnerabilities to attack, intimidation, or other kinds of damage.
5. The higher the level of technological-economic development, with concomitant increase of human density, the
more vulnerable a community becomes to a multiplicity of
disruptive conditions and events both inside and outside
its geographic space and legal jurisdiction.
6. Proliferation and severity of vulnerabilities derive from many sources, in addition to accelerative dys-
functional changes in the physical habitat:

(a) Disruption of essential services from such
causes as work stoppages: lockouts, slowdowns, strikes,
etc.;[10] illicit interventions: sabotage, hijacking, blackmail, etc.;[11] and accidental breakdowns, from human error
or mechanical failure, to which complex technical systems
are increasingly prone;[12]

(b) Erosion of the community as a viable going concern from such causes as civic alienation, attrition of mo-
rale, and other by-products of modern industrial society as
presently constituted;[13]

(c) Disruptive intrusions of foreign origin from
such causes as military intimidation and attack, including
possibly irreversible catastrophe of thermonuclear war;
disruption of economic and other activities by embargoes
and other foreign interference with international trade and

finance; adverse psychological penetration from abroad; and insidious migratory intruders, including air- and waterborne pollutants, and invasive organisms that damage or destroy plants, animals, and humans.[14]

7. The more densely inhabited, technologically advanced, and economically and otherwise complex a society becomes, the larger the proportion of its output must be allocated to keeping it a functional going concern.

8. Proliferating demands and rising costs in virtually every sector of society are, in the aggregate, outrunning resources disposable within the constraints imposed by the prevailing social order, resulting in a crisis of priorities that has far-reaching impacts on military budgets, civic services, overdue and increasingly urgent social reforms, in addition to repair and protection of the physical environment and still other expanding claims on resources.[15]

9. The crisis of priorities intensifies demands for major redistribution of income and wealth and other reforms that seriously threaten the economic and social status quo.

10. Resulting pressure on the economic-social status quo intensifies resistances to new claims that include, among others, expensive programs for the repair and future protection of the physical habitat.

11. The crisis of priorities both from multiplying vulnerabilities and rising costs, and from the rigidity of the existing distribution of income and wealth, inexorably expands the role of government, including demands for tougher "law and order" and consequent erosion of civil liberties and heightened risk of insidious growth of arbitrary rule.

12. The spreading and worsening environmental crisis transcends the capability of any single government, since none can unilaterally protect even its own citizens from the consequences of environmentally disruptive practices and policies in other countries and in the international oceans and atmosphere; that is to say, environmental politics does not end "at the water's edge" but entails concerted international action on a scale without precedent except possibly during World War II.

The central theme running through the above summation is the multiplicity of vulnerabilities to which modern societies, especially industrialized urban societies, are exposed and to which accelerative disruption of the physical habitat and consequently of the ecology of the earth adds still another congeries of risks that, in the aggregate, may well prove to be as ominous as the catastrophe of thermonuclear war.

Concurrent peaking of multiple vulnerabilities, escalating costs of coping effectively with them, and the insuf-
ficiency of disposable resources to do so confront students
of government as well as elected policy makers and appointed
officials with a cluster of problems that hitherto (again
one must note exceptions) have been swept under the carpet
or dealt with gingerly or peripherally to other aspects of
politics and administration.[16]

SHORT- VERSUS LONG-TERM STRATEGIES

At the threshold of environmental politics one also
confronts still another neglected complication. With very
few exceptions, elected policy makers opt for publicly acceptable short-run solutions without much regard for possibly long-run damaging, even catastrophic, consequences.
They are especially prone to do so if disagreement among
experts provides a plausible excuse for parsimony or procrastination. The entrepreneurial perspective that pervades our society--and others too--influences policy in the
same direction: a bird in hand is generally worth ten in
the bush, especially when there is some uncertainty whether
anything is in the bush. Thus environmental politics, like
all politics, is rigged against long-range risks that impose or threaten short-run losses, inconveniences, or other
deprivations. The normal strategy at all levels of government in such cases is to wait and see--"who knows what the
future may bring?" Hence, delay and procrastination until
disaster strikes--a course perfectly typified in the current energy crisis that percipient experts were predicting
at least as early as the middle 1950s.
The strategy of short-term gains, parsimony, and procrastination worked after a fashion in the past, largely
because adverse consequences resulting from inaction or
palliative action could be rectified. The introduction of
nuclear weapons posed the novel possibility of global catastrophe from which there could be no recovery. Accelerative
environmental deterioration by incremental piecemeal disruption poses a comparable threat, but in more subtle form.
We say subtle, because the drift toward possible irreversible disruption of the biosphere has crept up on humankind
insidiously.
We perceive several additional obstacles to dealing
effectively with the ultimate possibility of irreversible
catastrophe. One is implicit in the above paragraph:
namely, the reluctance of people to believe unpleasant
forecasts. Another is the propensity to leave the future

to future generations, summed up in the cynical question: "What has posterity ever done for me?"[17] A third obstacle is the time-honored legal doctrine that the "burden of proof" calls upon the complainant. This doctrine has been repeatedly invoked in legislative bodies and in other contexts to "legitimize" inaction or palliative therapy--despite the near certainty that no conclusive proof can be established until catastrophe has occurred.[18] A fourth obstacle, to which we have alluded several times, is the difficulty if not impossibility of allocating large resources to environmental repair and protection by whatever means without seriously disturbing the existing distribution of income and wealth. Put another way, advocating large allocations to environmental programs immediately evokes questions regarding priorities assigned to military budgets, exploration of outer space, social security, public assistance, highway building, nonmilitary international relations, and other categories of claims that will come to mind.

We have reviewed all too briefly our conception of the social and political context in which environmental programs are hammered into shape and carried into operation. No short survey can possibly offer a really comprehensive picture. It is hopefully sufficient, however, to put some flesh on the overarching questions that political scientists are beginning to move higher upon their research and teaching agendas. We would express these questions as follows: How, and how well, does the political system respond, or can be made to respond, to the kinds and magnitudes of risks implicit in continuing accelerative depletion, pollution, and spoliation of our physical habitat? Is the response vigorous, informed, imaginative, and courageous? Or is it negative, timid, ambiguous, or simply niggardly and palliative? And if the latter, what can and should be done about it?

FURTHER QUESTIONS FOR POLITICAL SCIENTISTS

These questions suggest more specific areas for investigation, analysis, and speculation. In our view, the more obvious ones include (1) reexamination of the philosophical presuppositions, perspectives, and ethics that permeate theorizing about the role of government and the nature and substance of political action; (2) modes of setting standards of environmental quality; (3) alternative strategies for obtaining public compliance with prescribed standards; (4) criteria for estimating costs of alternative strategies; (5) distribution of burdens in a society exhibiting wide

extremes of poverty and affluence; (6) alternative strategies for balancing demands and disposable resources; (7) de-
termination of priorities; (8) building public support for
policies that are certain to entail unpleasant changes in
personal lifestyles, especially among the more affluent
members of the society; (9) criteria for legislative assessment of future consequences, especially in the presence of
conflicting expert testimony.

We recognize, of course, that there is no "best" way
to categorize problem areas of environmental politics. Indeed, at this stage, a plurality of conceptualizations and
approaches seems not only certain but desirable. Whether
one opts for a distinct "field" of environmental politics
or fits the problems of environmental repair and protection
into established fields of political science seems to us a
minor issue. Far more important is the accumulating evidence, to which this volume contributes, that environment
problems, and the public policies that evolve from these,
are receiving increasing attention from professional students of politics who can provide an additional salient dimension to this widening sector of governmental action.

NOTES

1. The principal reference here is to Jay Forrester,
World Dynamics (Cambridge, Mass.: Wright-Allen Press,
1971); Donella H. Meadows et al., The Limits to Growth (New
York: Universe Books, 1972); and "A Blueprint for Survival," in The Ecologist (London), January 1972.

2. See, for example, the introductory chapter by Yale
biologist C. E. Hutchinson in The Biosphere (San Francisco:
W. H. Freeman, 1970), esp. p. 11.

3. The numerous writings of geochemist Harrison Brown
immediately come to mind, especially the concluding chapter
of The Challenge of Man's Future (New York: Viking, 1954).

4. This possibility was anticipated over a century
ago by George Perkins Marsh (New England businessman, lawyer, and diplomat, in addition to being a dedicated geographer and naturalist). See his Man and Nature: Or Geography as Modified by Man, originally published in 1864 and
reprinted in 1965 by Harvard University Press. Other
largely unheeded warnings came from Fairfield Osborn, Our
Plundered Planet and The Limits of the Earth (Boston:
Little, Brown, 1948 and 1953); William Vogt, Road to Survival (New York: William Sloane Associates, 1948); Aldo
Leopold, A Sand County Almanac (New York: Oxford University Press, 1949). More recently the warnings have multi-

plied: among others, Barry Commoner, <u>Science and Survival</u> (New York: Viking Press, 1963) and <u>The Closing Circle</u> (New York: Alfred A. Knopf, 1971); Paul R. Ehrlich and Anne H. Ehrlich, <u>Population, Resources, Environment: Issues in Human Ecology</u> (San Francisco: W. H. Freeman, 1970). Early warnings from political scientists include R. A. Falk, <u>This Endangered Planet: Prospects and Proposals for Human Survival</u> (New York: Random House, 1971); R. R. and L. T. Rienow, <u>Moment in the Sun</u> (New York: Dial Press, 1967).

    5. A long list of scientific and engineering works could be cited. Some of the less technical ones are being included in accumulating anthologies: among others, John Harte and R. H. Sokolow et al., <u>Patient Earth</u> (New York: Holt, Rinehart and Winston, 1971); R. H. Wagner et al., <u>Environment and Man</u> (New York: W. W. Norton, 1971); T. R. Detwyler et al., <u>Man's Impact on Environment</u> (New York: McGraw-Hill, 1971). Anyone interested in this rapidly expanding scientific and engineering literature should consult <u>Science and Public Affairs</u> (formerly <u>Bulletin of the Atomic Scientists</u>), <u>Science</u> (weekly journal of the American Association for the Advancement of Science), <u>Scientific American</u>, and the more technical journals of the natural and engineering sciences.

    6. See, for example, K. R. Stunkel, "The Technological Solution," <u>Science and Public Affairs</u>, September 1973, pp. 42ff.

    7. For examples of the "orthodox" economic position, see E. L. Dale, "The Economics of Pollution," <u>New York Times Magazine</u>, April 19, 1970; H. C. Wallich, "A World Without Growth," New York <u>Times</u>, op. ed. page, February 12, 1972; S. H. Schurr, <u>Energy, Economic Growth, and the Environment</u> (Baltimore: Johns Hopkins University Press, 1972); Peter Passell and Leonard Ross, <u>The Retreat from Riches: The Gross National Product and Its Enemies</u> (New York: Viking Press, 1972); and critique of the Forrester-Meadowes model, by Peter Passell, Leonard Ross, and Marc Roberts, <u>New York Times Book Review</u>, April 2, 1972. Many other books and journal articles argue the conventional economic thesis. As stated in the text, there are important dissenting views among economists: among others, H. E. Daly, "Toward a Stationary Economy," in Harte and Sokolow, op. cit.; A. V. Kneese, "The Faustian Bargain," <u>Resources</u>, September 1973; K. E. Boulding, "The Economics of the Coming Spaceship Earth," in <u>Environmental Quality in a Growing Economy</u>, ed. Henry Barnett (Baltimore: Johns Hopkins University Press, 1966), pp. 3-14; B. G. Murray, Jr., "Continuous Growth or No Growth: What the Ecologists Can Teach the Economists," <u>New York Times Magazine</u>, December 10, 1972; Nicholas

Georgescu-Roegen, "Energy and Economic Myths," a lecture delivered at the School of Forestry and Environmental Studies,
Yale University, to be published in Growth Limits and the
Quality of Life, ed. W. Burch and F. H. Bormann (San Francisco: W. H. Freeman, 1974).

8. In the early 1930s the American geographer, Isaiah
Bowman, summed up the technocratic ethic in one sentence:
"Most men take the view that the world is their oyster [and]
they are out for conquest." Geography in Relation to the
Social Sciences (New York: Charles Scribners Sons, 1934),
p. 7. On this issue, see also William Leiss, The Domination
of Nature (New York: Braziller, 1972).

9. For further exposition of the concept of "ecological demand," see Man's Impact on the Global Environment, a
Report of the Study of Critical Environmental Problems,
sponsored by Massachusetts Institute of Technology, 1970,
pp. 117ff.

10. On societal vulnerability to work stoppages and
slowdowns, see, for example, R. L. Heilbroner, "Phase II of
the Capitalist System," New York Times Magazine, November 29,
1970, p. 90; also C. L. Sulzberger, "New Society and Old
State," New York Times, op. ed. page, December 18, 1970;
J. C. Giddings, "World Population, Human Disaster, and Nuclear Holocaust," Science and Public Affairs, September
1973, p. 46.

11. On societal vulnerability to illicit interven-
tions, see, for example, Giddings, op. cit.; also D. V.
Segre and J. H. Adler, "The Ecology of Terrorism," Survival
(London), July/August 1973, pp. 178ff, esp. p. 183; R. E.
Lapp, "The Ultimate Blackmail," New York Times Magazine,
February 4, 1973.

12. On societal vulnerability to accidental break-
downs, see, for example, René Dubos, "The Roots of Counter-
culture," New York Times, op. ed. page, September 24, 1972;
Giddings, op. cit.; James Reston, "The Impotence of Power,"
New York Times, September 11, 1970; and editorial, "The
Vulnerability of Systems," New York Times, March 13, 1972.

13. On community erosion, see, for example, R. G.
Wilkinson, Poverty and Progress (New York: Praeger, 1973),
esp. p. 188; W. A. Weisskopf, Alienation and Economics (New
York: Dutton, 1971); John Gardner, No Easy Victories (New
York: Harper & Row, 1968), esp. p. 145; Irving Goffman,
Relations in Public (New York: Harper & Row, 1971), esp.
pp. 189-90; Marshall McLuhan and B. Nevitt, "Everybody into
Nobody," op. ed. page, New York Times, July 16, 1972; Ivan
Illich, Tools for Conviviality (New York: Harper & Row,
1973). A similar theme is implicit in Aldo Leopold, "A
Land Ethic," in A Sand County Almanac (New York: Sierra

Club/Ballantine Books, 1966), pp. 237-64; and in Garrett
Hardin, "The Tragedy of the Commons," originally published
in Science 162 (1968): 1243-48 and now available in numerous anthologies.

14. External sources of societal vulnerability are
dealt with in Harold and Margaret Sprout, Toward a Politics
of the Planet Earth (New York: Van Nostrand Reinhold,
1971), Chapter 17; and in Chapter 15 of The Structure of the
International Environment, Vol. 4 of The Future of the International Legal Order, ed. C. E. Black and R. A. Falk
(Princeton, N.J.: Princeton University Press, 1973).

15. For the authors' previous development of the hypothesis of "The Dilemma of Rising Demands and Insufficient
Resources," see World Politics 20 (1968): 660-93; and "National Priorities: Demands, Resources, Dilemmas," World
Politics 24 (1972): 293-317.

16. Pioneering work in this and related areas of environmental politics has been done by Lynton Caldwell and a
few other political scientists. Caldwell's series of environmental studies (Lynton E. Caldwell, ed., Environmental
Studies: Papers on the Politics and Public Administration
of Man-Environment Relationships, 4 vols. (Bloomington:
Indiana University, Institute of Public Administration,
1967) and his numerous books and shorter writings are land-
marks in the development of a field of environmental studies
in political science. We wish that space permitted listing
here the accumulating assortment of books and journal papers, including many by younger members of the profession,
dealing with various legislative, administrative, and judicial aspects of environmental repair and protection. It is
notable also that much of this significant new work is coming not only from a few recognized centers of research but
also from a broad cross-section of colleges and universities.

17. Quoted by K. E. Boulding in Environmental Quality
in a Growing Economy, op. cit., p. 11.

18. For legal aspects of the doctrine of "burden of
proof" in environmental litigation, see J. L. Sax, Defending the Environment (New York: Alfred A. Knopf, 1971),
esp. pp. 176, 201-05.

2

BASIC REFERENCES IN
ENVIRONMENTAL
POLICY STUDIES
Dean Mann

THE PROBLEM OF DEFINITION

The very term "environmental policy" suggests the difficulty of defining this field of policy analysis. Inevitably, the researcher in this field confronts the problem
of establishing boundaries between environmental policy and
urban, welfare, health, international, and virtually every
other field of public policy. On neither technical, economic, or political criteria is it possible to make entirely satisfactory distinctions because of the interpene-
tration of environmental policy with other fields of policy
analysis.

A further complexity is added by the fact that political scientists have probably done more in the area of natural resources policy than in any other field of public
policy except foreign and military policy. The focus has
been on the management of and public investments in natural
resources, especially water resources, but seldom with an
environmental focus in the sense of concern for the ecological balance and quality of life issues that are explicitly
involved in current concern for the environment. Thus, an
excellent little study, Natural Resources and the Political
Struggle by Norman Wengert[1] suggests the earlier orientation toward issues of costs and benefits, conservation of
scarce resources and public versus private development, and
the relative lack of concern for ecology, aesthetics, and
recreation. Pollution, for example, is virtually ignored.

Perhaps the best approach to a definition for political scientists is expressed in the movement away from a
concern only for development, for man's economic well-
being, and exclusively "natural" resources to a concern for

protection, avoidance of economic and social "bads," and a recognition of man and his relationship to the environment --both natural and man-made.

A recent volume produced by the Environmental Protection Agency (EPA) recognizes the difficulties of defining the quality of the environment.[2] The contributions produced for a conference sponsored by EPA, deal with varying approaches to the concept of the "quality of life" from a variety of disciplinary perspectives. The results cast doubt on the possibility of achieving aggregate measures of such a concept but suggest promising areas of research.

These difficulties of definition are mitigated by the fact that very little research has been done by political scientists on environmental policy. Much of what constitutes the best literature on environmental policy has been produced by economists, lawyers, planners, and activists in the environmental movement. Whether political scientists can improve on their policy analysis remains largely to be demonstrated.

The focus of this chapter is on what political scientists have done on environmental policy, while briefly tracing--where relevant--the scholarly antecedents in the study of natural resources.

INSTITUTIONAL ANALYSIS

Institutional analysis has long been a strong suit for political scientists although one can't argue so strongly that the perceptions have been particularly acute or the recommendations especially relevant. In reviewing environmental policy analysis for the past decade it is clear that some of the best work has been done by people who may best be styled political economists. Most are in fact economists who recognize the institutional character of most environmental problems and limitations of economic analysis. The names of Allen Kneese, Myrick Freeman, Marc Roberts, Edwin Haefele, Ralph D'Arge, and Robert Haveman come quickly to mind. A quick reference to The Economics of Environmental Policy by A. Myrick Freeman III, Robert H. Haveman, and Allen V. Kneese will display an integrated treatment drawing on the two disciplines.[3]

Among political scientists Lynton Caldwell has established himself as perhaps the leading figure in the discussion of public organization for environmental management. His Environment: A Challenge to Modern Society[4] represents both his philosophy with respect to environmental policy and his analysis of the political steps required to achieve a higher-quality environment. It is a reasonable, thoughtful, and sensitive approach to the manifold values involved. It is not a particularly <u>political</u> book in the sense that it seldom suggests the reality of the political conflict and the technological and economic character of the issues that make the issues often intractable. His institutional analysis tends strongly toward the rational, comprehensive model as the means of achieving a higher quality.

More closely related to the political economists is the work of two political scientists studying environmental problems: Vincent Ostrom and Matthew Holden. Ostrom's article, "Water Resource Development: Some Problems in Economic and Political Analysis of Public Policy"[5] states some assumptions of the political system, analyzes consequences of various institutional forms, and challenges the rational-comprehensive model of decision making with his own model of decentralized decision making by public entrepreneurs. This work has recently been expanded into a much fuller statement of this position for the National Water Commission. In his <u>Pollution Control as a Bargaining Process: An Essay on Regulatory Decision-Making</u>[6] Holden raises important questions concerning the application of effluent charges or the utilization of systems analysis in dealing with pollution, concluding that elements of bargaining among continuing participants in the decision-making process would lead to substantial divergence from the results anticipated by those espousing those techniques as the solutions for environmental problems.

POLITICS AND THE ENVIRONMENT

Two recent texts on environmental policy display both comprehensiveness and care in their treatment of various aspects of environmental policy. Gerald Garvey's <u>Energy, Ecology, Economy</u>[7] is more explicitly interested in the integration of political and economic analysis and with the development of a strategy that combines both public control and management and economic incentives. <u>Politics of Environmental Concern</u> by Walter A. Rosenbaum[8] covers somewhat more territory and is more exclusively political in its analysis of the manner in which American political institutions have responded to the environmental challenge.

For an empirical and descriptive look at the pollution control efforts in the United States, one should turn to <u>The Politics of Pollution</u> by J. Clarence Davies.[9] Written from an insider's viewpoint and stressing water and air pollution control this book covers in a traditional way the participants and institutions in the pollution control policy process, but adds interesting and insightful chapters on standard setting and compliance. James McCamy has written a small book for laymen covering the principal areas of pollution and then dealing with such subjects as the relationships of the professions, business, and the bureaucracy to the environmental problem. He makes a useful effort at establishing principles and guidelines for action.[10]

Congress takes its usual lumps as a policy-making institution from the only scholars who have seriously looked at Congress and its role in cleaning up the environment. Richard Cooley and Geoffrey Wandesforde-Smith have compiled in Congress and the Environment[11] a set of case studies that describe the manner in which Congress has dealt with environmental issues. The authors conclude that Congress has dragged its feet, in considerable part because of its alleged archaic structure. In the opinion of this writer, the cases do not always support the critical tone of the authors unless one assumes that the only values worth achieving are wilderness and scenic rivers.

ADMINISTRATIVE POLITICS

With new agencies proliferating in the environmental field, we should look for careful studies of the manner in which they carry on their business. Until those are forthcoming we shall have to examine the implications of some excellent treatments that have been given at least two of the most important resource agencies: the Forest Service and the Bureau of Land Management. Herbert Kaufman's The Forest Ranger[12] and Ashley Schiff's Fire and Water: Scientific Heresy in the Forest Service[13] demonstrate the orthodoxy and virtual ideology that infuse the Forest Service, the means used to ensure the persistence of that orthodoxy, and the perils associated with it. Philip Foss has recorded for us the battles over grazing district administration in his Politics and Grass: The Administration of Grazing on the Public Domain,[14] and Robert Morgan examined the record of the Soil Conservation Service in Governing Soil Conservation: Thirty Years of the New Decentralization.[15]

STATE-LEVEL STUDIES

Studies by political scientists of the administration of the environment at the state level are seldom to be found as yet. The most recent and comprehensive study is by Elizabeth H. Haskell, Managing the Environment: Nine States

Look for New Answers.[16] Haskell examines the responses of
nine states in terms of public organization and policy
change to accommodate the demands for higher quality environment. Elizabeth Haskell and Victoria S. Price have built
on this study in their State Environmental Management: Case
Studies of Nine States.[17] In the field of water resources,
Daniel Hoggan, an engineer, surveyed State Organization Patterns for Comprehensive Planning of Water Resources Development.[18]

LEGAL INSTITUTIONS

The courts and their utility in dealing with environmental problems have been examined to some extent by the
lawyers but little by political scientists. Joseph Sax has
done some of the work most relevant for political scientists
who are not concerned with the strictly legal institutional
questions. His Water Law, Planning and Policy: Cases and
Materials[19] and especially his Defending the Environment[20]
display his sanguine view about the ability of the courts to
counter skullduggery in the bureaucracy, although he is less
convincing that the judicial route provides an avenue for
altering the basic processes for decision making with respect to environmental issues. More generally concerned
with priorities, intergovernmental relations, and enforcement and control techniques within the context of American
legal institutions is Environmental Control: Priorities,
Policies and the Law by Frank P. Grad, George W. Rathjens,
and Albert J. Rosenthal.[21] The first thoroughgoing study
of the impact of the National Environmental Protection Act
is found in Frederick R. Anderson's NEPA in the Courts: A
Legal Analysis of the National Environmental Policy Act.[22]
Anderson examines how suits reach courts, circumstances requiring an impact statement, their preparation and content
and their impact on federal decision making. Harmon Henkin,
Martin Merta, and James Staples have written an account of
the legal attack on continued use of DDT before a hearing
examiner in Wisconsin.[23]

WATER POLICY

Turning now to examinations of specific policy sectors
within environmental policy, one finds that water resources
have been the most studied of all resources. The enduring
questions of the past--costs and benefits, federal organization, river basin organization, state functions--have tended
to dominate the analyses. Arthur Maass' Muddy Waters[24] is a

classic example of this genre and William H. Stewart's <u>The Tennessee-Tombigbee Waterway: A Case Study in the Politics of Water Transportation</u>[25] is a more recent example that strangely almost entirely ignores the environmental issues that are clearly involved in the project proposal described in the book. The works of Charles McKinley, Henry Hart, Norman Wengert, Ernest Englebert, Hubert Marshall, and Albert Lepawsky all deserve praise in this field of study. Unfortunately few have continued this good work with respect to the broader issues of water--both quantity and quality-- and environmental concerns. Among recent political science writings, perhaps the study by Roscoe Martin et al., <u>River Basin Administration and the Delaware</u>[26] was an initial effort to deal with what was both a quantity and quality problem in the Delaware River System. This was followed by Edward J. Cleary's study of Orsanco, the compact covering the Ohio River basin.[27] Both studies revealed the favorable prospects for the interstate compact device--which now has been applied to both the Delaware and the Susquehanna--for dealing with the critical problems of water quality management.

Helen Ingram has written an extremely insightful study of the politics of Western water development in her analysis of the Colorado River Basin Bill from the perspective of the State of New Mexico. Her explication of coalition building and the rules that govern it are very useful.[28] Some of the best recent work has been done under the auspices of Ralph Nader's Center for Study of Responsive Law. Despite shortcomings of analysis and oversimplification in their recommendations for change, these investigators have taken the lead in revealing the truly monumental failures of our water pollution control program. <u>Water Wasteland</u> by David Zwick and Marcy Benstock[29] is a broad attack on the entire water pollution control program, while <u>The Water Lords</u> by James M. Fallows[30] provides the detailed case study of the Savannah River and the unwillingness of regulatory agencies to grab hold of this problem. Another sector of water pollution-- oil in coastal waters--has been examined by A. E. Keir Nash, Dean E. Mann, and Phil G. Olsen in their study of the Santa Barbara oil spill.[31] The authors place emphasis on the institutional complexity, the diverse attitudes, and the legal framework within which the spill was treated.

AIR POLLUTION

Political scientists have paid far less attention to air pollution. The most perceptive analytical study is by a planner, George H. Hagevik, entitled <u>Decision-Making in</u>

Air Pollution Control.[32] Hagevik stresses alternative
strategies for achieving improved air quality, including
bargaining, and raises important questions about the decision framework involving regional entities, states, the federal agencies and a multiplicity of local units of government. Utilizing a community power framework of analysis,
Matthew A. Crenson has examined The Un-Politics of Air Pollution: A Study of Non-Decision-Making in the Cities.[33] He
concludes that the power structure has prevented solutions
to air quality problems by preventing these problems from
having a place on the political agenda. The Ralph Nader
Center also examined air pollution in its devastatingly
critical way in Vanishing Air by John C. Esposito.[34]

                          RECREATION

     The Cooley and Wandesforde-Smith volume contains case
studies dealing with outdoor recreation, but political
scientists have not done much more empirical work in this
area. One notable exception is the lengthy analysis by
Daniel M. Ogden in "Outdoor Recreation: Policy and Politics" in The Political Economy of Environmental Control,
edited by Joe S. Bain and Warren F. Ilchman,[35] He examines
outdoor recreation policy in the context of "power cluster"
politics, which is very reminiscent of Douglass Cater's
"subgovernments."

                 INTERNATIONAL INSTITUTIONS

     The concept of the "spaceship" earth and the perceived
worldwide dangers of ecological destruction have made the
adoption of an ecological framework a natural thing for
students of international politics. Several books worthy
of note have made their appearance in the last several
years. Lynton Caldwell's In Defense of Earth: International Protection of the Biosphere[36] reflects his experience with the International Union for the Conservation of
Nature and Natural Resources and the National Academy of
Sciences Committee for Environmental Programs. It is a
careful and scholarly examination of the institutional
problems of international environmental management and it
provides recommendations for strengthening both national
and international institutions for environmental control.
A reader giving attention to the same problems is David A.
Kay and Eugene B. Skonikoff, World Eco-Crisis: International Organizations in Response.[37] Specific strategies

and institutions are examined by a variety of experts and administrators. Harold and Margaret Sprout's Toward a Politics of the Planet Earth[38] tends toward the traditional text in international politics with an environmental gloss. In contrast, Richard A. Falk has written a book on international politics that makes a more thoroughgoing effort to suggest the distinctive character of the ecological imperatives for the international political system.[39] The solutions recommended, however, do not suggest anything remarkably new in international politics as means of achieving a balanced political and ecological order. A recent study by a geographer, William M. Ross, looks at the oil pollution problem in its international context through a case study of the oil pollution threat in the Puget Sound region.[40]

ATTITUDES AND PERCEPTIONS

Another area of potentially great concern to political scientists is the perceptions and attitudes of both elites and masses concerning environmental conditions and policy. Geographers have perhaps done the most extensive work in this area--Gilbert White, W. R. Derrick Sewell, David Lowenthal, Frank Quinn, Tom Saarinen are names that stand out. Various articles and polls are available on public perceptions and attitudes, some done by political scientists, but the most comprehensive collection is probably Perceptions and Attitudes in Resources Management, edited by W. R. Derrick Sewell and Ian Burton.[41] This collection draws on both Canadian and U.S. experience with respect to public attitudes and participation of publics and elites in the decision-making process.

CONCEPTS AND IDEOLOGY

The concepts of the environmental movement have been little investigated by political scientists in terms of relating them to broader political thought. The historians of political ideas have been helpful, however. Two notable examples are Samuel P. Hayes, Conservation and the Gospel of Efficiency[42] and Roderick Nash, Wilderness and the American Mind.[43] Among political scientists, perhaps Grant McConnell has been most insightful with his analysis of the relationship between the ideology of decentralization and disaggregation of power and the consequences for the conservation movement. This is to be found most fully in his Private Power and American Democracy.[44]

FUTURE EFFORTS

Obviously, there is much to be done by political scientists in the area of environmental policy. Whole areas of environmental concerns such as pesticides, nuclear power plant effluents and radiation dangers, power plant siting, and aesthetics are almost virgin territory. Moreover, political scientists ought to be endeavoring to meet the challenge of designing political institutions that will achieve the public purposes embodied in law but so often disemboweled in administration. This probably means considerable boning up on the economics of environmental control but it also means careful examination of the incentives created by public law and organization and the consequences of the adoption of alternative strategies to the various publics involved. These implications may be examined in both political and economic terms and neither should be ignored in undertaking such policy analysis.

NOTES

1. Garden City, N.Y.: Doubleday, 1955.
2. EPA, The Quality of Life Concept: A Potential New Tool for Decision-Makers (Washington, D.C.: EPA, Office of Research and Monitoring, Environmental Studies Division, 1973).
3. New York: John Wiley, 1973.
4. Garden City, N.Y.: Doubleday, 1971.
5. Ostrom in Political Science and Public Policy, ed. Austin Ranney (Chicago: Markham, 1968).
6. Ithaca, N.Y.: Cornell University, Water Resources Center, 1966.
7. New York: W. W. Norton, 1972.
8. The Politics of Environmental Concern (New York: Praeger, 1973).
9. Indianapolis: Bobbs-Merrill, 1970.
10. James L. McCamy, The Quality of the Environment (New York: The Free Press, 1973).
11. Seattle: University of Washington Press, 1970.
12. Baltimore: Johns Hopkins University Press, 1960.
13. Cambridge, Mass.: Harvard University Press, 1962.
14. Seattle: University of Washington Press, 1960.
15. Baltimore: Johns Hopkins University Press, 1965.
16. Washington, D.C.: The Smithsonian Institution, 1971.
17. New York: Praeger, 1973.
18. Logan: Utah State University, June 1969.

19. Indianapolis: Bobbs-Merrill, 1968.
20. New York: Alfred A. Knopf, 1971.
21. New York: Columbia University Press, 1971.
22. Baltimore: Resources for the Future, 1973.
23. The Environment, the Establishment and the Law (Boston: Houghton Mifflin, 1971).
24. Cambridge, Mass.: Harvard University Press, 1951.
25. University, Ala.: University of Alabama, Bureau of Public Administration, 1971.
26. Syracuse, N.Y.: Syracuse University Press, 1960.
27. The Orsanco Story: Water Quality Management in the Ohio Valley Under an Interstate Compact (Baltimore: Johns Hopkins University Press, 1967).
28. Patterns of Politics in Water Resource Development: A Case Study of New Mexico's Role in the Colorado River Basin Bill, Publication no. 79 (Albuquerque: University of New Mexico, Division of Government Research, 1969).
29. New York: Grossman, 1971.
30. New York: Grossman, 1971.
31. Oil Pollution and the Public Interest: A Study of the Santa Barbara Oil Spill (Berkeley: University of California, Institute of Governmental Studies, 1972).
32. New York: Praeger, 1970.
33. Baltimore: Johns Hopkins University Press, 1971.
34. New York: Grossman, 1970.
35. Berkeley: University of California, Institute of Business and Economic Research, 1972.
36. Bloomington: Indiana University Press, 1972.
37. Madison: University of Wisconsin Press, 1972.
38. New York: Van Nostrand Reinhold, 1971.
39. This Endangered Planet: Prospects and Proposals for Human Survival (New York: Random House, 1971).
40. Oil Pollution as an International Problem (Seattle: University of Washington Press, 1973).
41. Ottawa: Department of Energy, Mines and Resources, Policy Research and Coordination Branch, Resource Paper No. 2, 1971.
42. Cambridge, Mass.: Harvard University Press, 1959.
43. New Haven, Conn.: Yale University Press, 1967.
44. New York: Alfred A. Knopf, 1966.

CHAPTER

3

**FACILITIES FOR THE
STUDY OF
ENVIRONMENTAL POLICY**
Dean Mann and
Geoffrey Wandesforde-Smith

        In a recent review of contributions to the literature
of environmental policy analysis, Charles Jones posits the
existence of a pattern of policy response.[1] Of interest
here is the pattern that Jones perceives developing outside
government, as scholars and publicists shift the focus of
their energies to come to grips with a new issue. Incrementalism is the order of the day. Information is exchanged
haphazardly, research proposals and results lack coordination and integration, and it is very difficult to discover
just what is known about the issue that might serve as the
basis for improving public policy. Whether these conditions
prevail only for a short time, before rationality and comprehensiveness in research design, execution, and application become possible, is a question that Jones does not address. A look at the steady proliferation of sources for
the study of environmental policy over the last few years,
however, suggests that serendipity must remain a hallmark
of the informed student.

UNIVERSITY PROGRAMS: SOURCES FOR STUDENTS

        In 1969 the Office of Science and Technology published
a report on the response of universities to problems of

        Preparation of this chapter was supported in part by a
grant from the California Water Resources Center under the
matching grant program of the Water Resources Research Act
of 1964, and in part by a grant to the Tahoe Research Group
from the division on Research Applied to National Needs of
the National Science Foundation. The assistance of Ms. Pat
Farid is also acknowledged.

environmental quality.[2] The findings of the report, based
upon a detailed analysis of multidisciplinary programs at
six leading institutions,* tend to confirm the incrementalism hypothesized by Jones. University resources for the
study of environmental issues had initially clustered around
programs that were already established and funded, notably
programs in environmental science and engineering. Attention to the social science aspects of environmental problems
had been added on to these programs, but the report argued
that the increment was insufficient to yield much that was
worthwhile. The need for more research on the policy implications of specific environmental problems was emphasized in
the report.

A similar pattern was revealed in a more extensive
study by the Environmental Policy Division of the Legislative Reference Service (now the Congressional Research Service) for the House Committee on Science and Astronautics.[3]
Analysis of questionnaire responses from persons involved in
environmental studies programs at 106 colleges and universities showed that the social sciences were poorly represented.
The report observed that environmental studies centers had
been originated most usually by departments in engineering,
the physical and biological sciences, and medicine and public health. Greater emphasis on the social sciences was
deemed to be essential, the report suggesting that this development could be expected as research and teaching became
more strongly focused on the interrelationship of man and
his environment, particularly the behavior of man in both
natural and artificial surroundings. The House report
showed that in 1969 most environmental studies programs concentrated on graduate and postgraduate instruction and research. The expansion of undergraduate programs was encouraged, as it was in the Office of Science and Technology
study, and at the 1969 meeting of the American Association
for the Advancement of Science, undergraduate study of environmental problems was the subject of a lively symposium.[4]

Since 1969, opportunities for students to acquire training in environmental policy studies, either as a specialty
or as part of a more general program in political science
and public administration, have shown an increase. This is
reflected in a second report from the House Science and Astronautics Committee published in 1972.[5] The committee has
sustained a long-term effort to relate federal science policy to issues of environmental quality, and as part of this

---

*The University of Southern California, Cornell Univer-
sity, Harvard University, University of Michigan, Massachusetts Institute of Technology, and Johns Hopkins University.

effort undertook a survey of teaching and research on the relationship between science, technology, and society, including teaching and research in such special fields as marine affairs, biology and society, pollution and environmental management, and energy use. From 302 completed questionnaires information was compiled about programs at more than 150 institutions. The responses from each institution are uneven in the amount of detail provided. Nevertheless, it is clear that the social sciences, and political science in particular, are much better represented than previously.

Some notable developments have occurred at institutions with long-standing reputations for natural resources policy analysis. These programs now provide opportunities for students to pursue work under the contemporary rubric of environmental policy analysis at both the graduate and undergraduate levels. Examples that come readily to mind are the Institute for Environmental Quality, formerly the School of Natural Resources, at the University of Michigan, and the Department of Political Science and cognate departments in the College of Forestry and Natural Resources at Colorado State University.

Other developments take the form of new programs in environmental studies that either have very flexible undergraduate degree requirements, allowing students to acquire some training in political science, or have a more structured curriculum based in the sciences but drawing upon the talents of associated faculty with environmental policy interests. Programs at the University of Massachusetts at Amherst, Williams College, Dartmouth College, Purdue University, the University of Wisconsin at Green Bay, the State University of New York at Albany, and the University of California campuses at Davis, Santa Cruz, and Santa Barbara exemplify one or another of these mixes. In some cases the standard academic curriculum is supplemented by programs allowing students to participate in environmental policy activities off-campus. At the University of California at Davis, for example, internships are arranged with government agencies, legislative committees, and interest groups engaged in environmental policy formulation and implementation. Internships are required for the bachelor's degree in Political Science: Public Service, which has an optional specialization in environmental quality control, and they are also provided for students emphasizing environmental policy analysis in the nondegree programs of the Division of Environmental Studies.

At the graduate level, environmental policy studies can be pursued within established programs, such as those of the Graduate School of Public Affairs at the University of

Washington and the Graduate School of Administration at the
University of California at Riverside, and through new programs, such as that of the School of Public and Environmental Affairs at Indiana University. Graduate-level environmental research and teaching are also associated with specialized schools, centers, and institutes, such as the Water
Resources and Marine Sciences Center at Cornell University,
the water resources centers at many land-grant universities,
the School of Forestry at Yale University, and the Center
for Urban Studies at the University of Southern California.
The increasing array of graduate programs undoubtedly reflects the growing needs of local, state, and federal entities for persons who have combined training in the natural
and physical sciences with training in the social sciences.
It also reflects the opportunities for contract consulting
work that have arisen as states have imposed environmental
impact statement requirements on state and local agencies
and private developers. This latter set of opportunities
has created interest among students in programs that combine
training in planning with training in environmental politics
and administration. No review of such programs will be attempted here, although they are clearly attractive to students who see consulting work in environmental planning and
management as an alternative to entering an oversupplied
academic market.

There are not many special sources of funding for graduate students interested in environmental policy. Most financial assistance is associated with research grants awarded
to faculty members. However, mention should be made of the
prestigious fellowships awarded by Resources for the Future
and of the new fellowship program initiated by the National
Wildlife Federation. The generous postdoctoral fellowship
program recently started by the Center for the Study of Environmental Policy at Pennsylvania State University should
also be noted.

Of course students do not have to be in a program of
study that allows some degree of specialization in environmental policy analysis in order to discover something about
the subject. At many colleges and universities there are
faculty members and courses that deal in a limited way with
various aspects of environmental policy. Preliminary surveys conducted by the authors in conjunction with the Policy
Studies Organization and the Western Political Science Association have shown that interest and activity is very widespread.[6]

Finally, mention should be made of the role of law
schools. For several years law school has seemed an attractive possibility to students completing their undergraduate

work in a variety of disciplines. Environmental studies students have found law school particularly appealing because the small but growing number of environmental lawyers have made a dramatic impact on environmental policy in the United States. Many students believe that as members of the legal profession they can have more impact on policy than in any other capacity, and some have diligently attempted to heed the many calls to be interdisciplinary in approaching environmental issues by going to law school after undergraduate work in the physical and biological sciences. The number of courses in environmental law has increased very rapidly and, according to a report by Frances Irwin based on survey responses from 64 institutions, continues to increase.[7] It is clear from a reading of environmental law texts and articles in legal periodicals that the research interests of lawyers are often very similar to those of political scientists. Indeed some of the best case-study literature is to be found in law school publications.

Thus, while it has not been possible to provide here a complete and up-to-date inventory of college and university programs that deal with environmental policy analysis and can be seen as sources and resources to which students can turn, it seems clear that the incremental development foreseen by Jones has produced a rich diversity of opportunities. We turn now to a different category of sources.

JOURNALS AND OTHER SOURCES FOR THE RESEARCHER

With the burgeoning interest in environmental policy there has been an explosion in the number of publications dedicated to a concern for the environment. Moreover, other journals that had somewhat narrower orientations have altered their perspective to include the broader considerations of environmental quality. The following discussion is not intended to be exhaustive but it may provide some awareness of the literature now available to the student of environmental policy.

Given the central concerns of political scientists generally it is hardly to be expected that their major journals would prove to be significant outlets for articles on environmental politics. During the years 1969-72 one article appeared in the <u>American Political Science Review</u>.[8] The period 1969-72 was chosen simply because one might have expected that environmental concerns that became prominent in the late 1960s might have found scholarly expression by that time period. A quick survey of the other leading journals--

Journal of Politics, Midwest Journal of Political Science, Western Political Quarterly, Political Science Quarterly and Polity--revealed not a single article that remotely concerned environmental or natural resource policy during that period. Public Administration Review did publish several articles during the period and appeared to be the only political science journal of more or less general circulation that was attractive to or responsive to those interested in research and writing on the environment. Some highly descriptive papers have appeared in Public Opinion Quarterly, a journal of more limited circulation than those already mentioned.

As we move away from journals of interest principally to professional political scientists and toward journals having more of a policy focus, we find more interest in and concern for the environment. Public Interest and Public Policy are two journals that publish the results of research related to a broad range of public policy issues. Both have recently published important articles dealing with ecology as a public issue, water pollution control, and population policy.[9] Environmental policy has also received limited treatment in Policy Sciences.

More clearly in the environmental field but having a strong scholarly and interdisciplinary character are six excellent journals. For more than a decade political scientists and other social scientists have found The Natural Resources Journal, published by the School of Law at the University of New Mexico, to be important reading in the resource field. Of considerable interest to, but seldom the outlet for articles by, political scientists is Land Economics, which has a broad concern for land use and land use planning. Three new additions are Environment and Behavior, a Sage Publication, which describes itself as "an interdisciplinary journal concerned with the study, design, and control of the physical environment and its interaction with human behavioral systems." Even more recent is Environmental Affairs, published by the Environmental Law Center of Boston College. Its articles cover a broad range of environmental topics. Their authors include lawyers, scientists, publicists, economists, and other academic types, although no political scientists appear in its columns. Beginning also in 1971 was the Journal of Environmental Systems, edited at Brooklyn Polytechnic Institute, which devotes itself to "the analysis and solution of problems which relate to the system-complexes which make up our total societal environment." The journal clearly emphasizes conceptual approaches and models and appears to focus on the urban environment. Finally, there is the International Journal of

Environmental Studies, published in England and devoted to a broad range of topics of interest and understandable to political scientists. The emphasis appears to be on social policy rather than technical subjects.

The most impressive of the journals providing more popular, but nevertheless authoritative, discussions of the entire range of environmental issues is Environment, published by the Committee for Environmental Information at St. Louis. It dedicates itself to the publication of "information about the effects of technology on the environment and about the peaceful and military uses of nuclear energy." Other journals are more concerned with providing current information or with inciting their readers to do battle with the enemy. The Environmental Monthly tends toward the former, providing highlights of current issues and events. Not Man Apart, published by Friends of the Earth, the John Muir Institute for Environmental Studies, and the League of Conservation Voters, provides more in-depth treatment but is fully committed to action on the specific issues it highlights such as Mineral King or nuclear power plant safety. Far more propagandistic and less scholarly are such publications as Ecology Action, which calls itself a "Journal of Cultural Transformation" and Environmental Action.

In a legalistic society, lawyers are quick to mobilize informational resources and they have done so with respect to the environment. The most authoritative law journal is the Ecology Law Quarterly, published by the School of Law, University of California, Berkeley. Beginning in winter 1971, this journal has published lengthy treatises and comments on a wide range of issues of importance to environmental policy. Northwestern Law School at Lewis and Clark College in Portland, Oregon publishes Environmental Law. While emphasizing legal matters, this journal tends to be more eclectic in its approach and less exhaustive in its treatment.

In a somewhat different category are the environmental law reporting publications. Two are noteworthy: the Environmental Reporter published by the Bureau of National Affairs, provides a weekly report on such topics as federal and state laws, federal regulations, air, water, solid waste, and land use laws, and judicial decisions. Providing more exhaustive and analytical treatment of these issues while reporting current happenings is the Environmental Law Reporter published by the Environmental Law Institute. Its authoritative treatment has been cited by the courts in rendering decisions on such matters as the interpretation of the National Environmental Policy Act.

For those interested in particular environmental issues, there are journals that deal with selected elements in the environment. The Journal of the Air Pollution Control Association and the Journal of the Water Pollution Control Federation contain mainly technical articles but there are a considerable number of thoughtful articles on such topics as environmental planning, strategies of control, research, training, and other matters. Air and Water News supplies current information on what is happening with respect to "the law, markets, technology." Water Resources Research is heavily weighted toward technical discussions but has an occasional article on water policy and institutions of interest to the political scientists. Other journals that have been around a long time such as the Journal of Forestry and Soil and Water Conservation contain articles that make relevant their principal concerns to environmental issues. Last but not least, there is even a publication entitled Shore and Beach that has been around a long time and seems concerned with preserving shoreline values by means of technology.

Among other valuable sources the CF Letter, published by the Conservation Foundation each month, and the Conservation Report, published weekly while Congress is in session by the National Wildlife Federation, are worthy of special note. Each issue of the former is devoted to a discussion of a particular policy issue. Although the emphasis is on filling in the background to recent developments in Congress and the administration, occasional issues deal with state and local problems and with attempts to come to grips with environmental issues on a global scale. The occasional special publications of the Conservation Foundation are also useful. The Conservation Report faithfully records the introduction of legislation and reports on the debates and discussions that take place at congressional hearings. Each year one issue is devoted to a review of congressional accomplishments and failures. The Sierra Club's National News Report is less thorough and more selective in its coverage of national policy developments.

There is no single authoritative guide to the literature on environmental policy analysis, which is reviewed elsewhere in this volume. The closest approximation is probably the three-volume work prepared by Lynton Caldwell and several collaborators at Indiana University.[10] Nor is there a guide for students who want to study at close quarters the administrative, regulatory, and legislative bodies with environmental responsibilities. However, the guide to participatory education in political science recently published by John Bollens and Dale Marshall is an excellent general introduction to the vagaries of field work and how to avoid them.[11] Those unfamiliar with government documents will find a beginner's guide to library research using these sources in <u>Congress and the Environment</u>.[12] One additional source emanating from the Government Printing Office should be noted, namely the <u>102 Monitor</u> issued by the Council on Environmental Quality. This publication contains a complete month-by-month listing of environmental impact statements prepared subsequent to the National Environmental Policy Act (NEPA). It also contains from time to time a listing of significant federal court cases involving interpretation of NEPA, as well as the text of court decisions and federal agency regulations affecting environmental programs.

Clearly there are other sources of value to the researcher. Although we have mentioned those that we have found especially helpful, the concerned student of environmental policy will presumably become acquainted with others having something important to say on environmental matters.

NOTES

1. Charles O. Jones, "From Gold to Garbage: A Bibliographic Essay on Politics and the Environment," <u>American Political Science Review</u> 66 (June 1972): 588. See also Anthony Downs, "Up and Down with Ecology--The 'Issue-Attention Cycle,'" <u>The Public Interest</u> 28 (Summer 1972): 38-50.
2. Executive Office of the President, Office of Science and Technology, <u>The Universities and Environmental Quality: Commitment to Problem Focused Education</u> (Washington, D.C.: Government Printing Office, September 1969).
3. U.S. Congress, House, Committee on Science and Astronautics, <u>Environmental Science Centers at Institutions of Higher Education</u>, 91st Cong., 1st sess., Committee Print, December 1969.
4. A summary of the symposium proceedings was published by Everett M. Hafner, John M. Fowler, and Curtis A. Williams, <u>Environmental Education 1970</u> (New York: Scientists' Institute for Public Information, 1970).
5. U.S. Congress, House, Committee on Science and Astronautics, <u>Teaching and Research in the Field of Science Policy--A Survey</u>, 92d Cong., 2d sess., Committee Print, December 1972.
6. Dean Mann and Geoffrey Wandesforde-Smith, <u>Political Scientists and Environmental Studies: A Preliminary Directory</u> (Davis: University of California, Department of Political Science, February 1973, mimeo.), and Geoffrey Wandesforde-Smith, "The Study of Environmental Public Policy: A Preliminary Directory," <u>Human Ecology</u> 2 (January 1974): 45-62.

7. Frances Irwin, "The Law School and the Environment," Natural Resources Journal 12 (April 1972): 278-85.

8. Jones, op. cit., 588-95.

9. See the winter 1972 issue of Public Interest and the winter 1971 issue of Public Policy.

10. Lynton K. Caldwell, ed., Science, Technology, and Public Policy: A Selected and Annotated Bibliography (Bloomington: Indiana University, Department of Government, 1969), 2 vols., and Lynton K. Caldwell and Toufiq A. Siddiqi, Science, Technology, and Public Policy: A Guide to Advanced Study (Bloomington: Indiana University, School of Public and Environmental Affairs, April 1972).

11. John C. Bollens and Dale Rogers Marshall, A Guide to Participation: Field Work, Role Playing Cases, and Other Forms (Englewood Cliffs, N.J.: Prentice-Hall, 1973), Chapters 1-6.

12. Richard A. Cooley and Geoffrey Wandesforde-Smith, eds., Congress and the Environment (Seattle: University of Washington Press, 1970), pp. 261-68.

4

REVERSAL IS THE LAW OF TAO: THE IMMINENT RESURRECTION OF POLITICAL PHILOSOPHY

William Ophuls

My thesis is very simple. We are about to enter one of those eras of great crisis and transition that have in the past inspired the great works of political philosophy. To be more specific, although one may legitimately argue about the time scale, we are clearly moving toward the kind of society that human ecologists call a "steady-state society"—that is, one in which a population is in a state of long-term dynamic equilibrium with the environment that provides its life support. The difficulties we are having with current energy shortages provide a small foretaste of the kinds of awkward dilemmas that will become increasingly common in the future, as we are swept further into the vortex of the environmental crisis. Business as usual will become impossible, and we shall of necessity change radically our whole way of life as we respond to the exigencies of the new era. We shall therefore be forced to overhaul completely our political values and institutions as we formulate a political theory suitable for the steady-state society. In fact, the construction of a new political philosophy and a new political order is likely to be the task of the next several decades.

Why we are about to enter an era of ecological crisis is a story that is simple in its essentials but highly complex and controverted in its details. Because I have made this detailed argument elsewhere[1] and numerous other authoritative accounts are available,[2] I shall confine myself to a simple statement of the essentials of the environmentalist argument so that I can devote most of the chapter to an exposition of some of the political philosophical issues buried in it.

MAN, THE HEEDLESS COTTAGER

Although afflicted by methodological flaws, the Club of Rome study reported in The Limits to Growth[3] nevertheless provides the best capsule summary of how great increases in population and demand have put us on a collision course with ecological limits and of how present and projected "solutions" to various environmental problems either provoke worse problems elsewhere in the system (DDT is a classic example) or depend on resources (like cheap, abundant, ecologically safe energy) that are themselves subject to limits. Actually, The Limits to Growth is but a more glamorous, computerized version of an argument made by several generations of human ecologists. In 1954, for example, Harrison Brown published The Challenge of Man's Future, which differs from current writings only in detail.[4] Nearly a century earlier, George Perkins Marsh described mankind metaphorically as a heedless cottager tearing down his earthly abode for kindling in order to keep a lively but evanescent fire blazing in the hearth.[5] Indeed, concern over man's misuse of the earth can be found in Plato and Mencius, among other ancient thinkers. What is happening is not, therefore, a new story. Rather, it is a very old story that is just now verging on an explosive denouement, pushed there by many interrelated factors that make a painful outcome almost inevitable—the near total implementation of a particular kind of technological system; the rapid growth in human numbers due to "death control" (that is, public health measures) without birth control; the more recent impact of high-consumption, resource-devouring, "modern" economies; and so on. Reasonable men will, of course, still differ on the time, intensity, and nature of our final collision with natural limits. For one thing, too much is yet uncertain about the exact location of these limits, but much also depends on how we respond to various subcrises along the way or on what impact various indirect negative feedback effects (such as steeply rising prices of energy and materials) will have on our behavior. But among those knowledgeable about the problems—not excluding some of the severest critics of the so-called doomsday literature[6]—there is virtual unanimity that (1) the crisis is real; (2) without effective human intervention the worst fears of the "doomsdayers" will be realized; (3) at least some actions must be undertaken now, for time is our scarcest resource in dealing with exponential growth; and (4) no matter what, major changes in our lives, values, and institutions will eventually be required.

ECOLOGICAL SCARCITY

As implied above, the basic message of ecology is limits, and this means that we must once again come to terms
with scarcity, a specter we thought we had banished once and
for all with perpetual economic growth and technological
wizardry. Indeed, ecological scarcity is in many ways much
harder to cope with than classical scarcity. It is not just
that many of those best things in life that once were free,
like fresh water and clean air, have become exceedingly
scarce goods that must now be allocated by centralized political decision making. Rather, the problem is that we
must come to terms politically with the exigencies of what
Kenneth Boulding calls a "spaceman economy,"[7] which will be
one of the essential components of the steady-state society.
In a spaceman economy, human welfare does not depend upon
rapid consumption or more and more consumers--these are potentially fatal--but on the extent to which we can wring the
maximum richness and amenity for a reasonable population
from minimum resources. Boulding tells us that a good, perhaps even affluent, life is possible, but

> it will have to be combined with a curious
> parsimony; [in fact] far from scarcity dis-
> appearing, it will be the most dominant as-
> pect of the society; every grain of sand
> will have to be treasured, and the waste
> and profligacy of our own day will seem so
> horrible that our descendents will hardly
> be able to think about us. . . .[8]

I hardly need to say that the reemergence of scarcity
has potentially grave consequences for our political values
and institutions. In effect, it portends the end of a
three-centuries-old age of abnormal abundance. The bonanza
of the New World and other founts of virgin resources, the
take-off and rapid-growth stages of science and technology,
the availability of "free" ecological resources like air and
water to absorb the by-products of economic activities, and
other lesser factors allowed our ancestors to fantasize endless material growth. Many thinkers were so carried away by
this golden prospect that they forecast infinite abundance
and the eventual elevation of the common man to the economic
nobility, where he could enjoy the use of a private carriage,
foreign travel, and all the other traditional perquisites of
the aristocratic style of life. And with the abolition of
scarcity would come a withering away not only of poverty but
also of inequality, injustice, and numerous other age-old

evils alleged to have their roots in scarcity. Outside of
William Blake and a few other disgruntled romantics or the
occasional pessimist like Thomas Malthus, the basic progress
ideology was shared by all in the West. (Marxists tended to
be more extreme optimists than non-Marxists, but they differed fundamentally only on how the drive to utopia was to
be organized.) One cannot, for example, read the works of
John Locke and Adam Smith, the two thinkers who gave modern
bourgeois political economy its fundamental direction, without being impressed by their cornucopian assumption that
there is always going to be more.[9] In other words, virtually all the philosophies, values, and institutions typical of
modern society--the legitimacy of self-interest, the primacy
of the individual and his inalienable rights, economic laissez faire, and democracy as we know it--were a response to
this waning era of unparalleled abundance. We must therefore question whether they can continue to exist in their
current form once we return to the more normal condition of
scarcity.

Let us explore briefly some of the political problems
created by ecological scarcity. Although I analyze the
problems in terms of doctrinal answers proposed by several
of the great theorists of politics (and state their conclusions in the baldest possible form), this is only a device
for making clear the profound nature of the political issues
involved and for showing that the crisis reraises almost all
the classic questions of political philosophy in an acute
form, above all the question "How is the common interest of
the collectivity to be achieved when men throughout history
have shown themselves to be passionate creatures prey to
greed, selfishness, and violence?" More specifically, I
hope to point out the particular issues that seem likely to
dominate our political agenda during the decades to come in
the way that the relationship of church and state or the
grounds of justified rebellion have been the overriding issues on the agenda of times past. Again, because I have
published relatively detailed arguments elsewhere,[10] I will
confine myself to brief sketches of three problems--"the
tragedy of the commons," the competence of the common man to
make ecological decisions, and the feasibility of continuing
to "muddle through" with incremental decision making--before
attempting to suggest, equally briefly, some dimensionf of a
political philosophy of ecology. I shall then conclude by
considering what the discipline of political science can
contribute to the resolution of the crisis in general and
to the formulation of a new political philosophy suitable
for a steady-state society in particular.

THE TRAGEDY OF THE COMMONS

The tragedy of the commons[11] occurs when the herdsmen using a common pasture land are not subject to controls. Each herdsman reasons that it would be in his interest to increase his flock, even if the result of grazing more animals damages the commons. Why? Because all the benefit from the extra animals will accrue to him, while the damage his animals do to the commons is shared by all. Worse, even if an individual herdsman is willing to restrain himself, he fears that others will not do so and that they will gain from increasing their flocks while he shares equally in the resulting deterioration of the commons. But, of course, each herdsman reaches the same conclusion, and the result is competitive overexploitation of the resource that leads to its degradation or destruction.

Ocean fisheries, especially the whaling industry, provide classic examples of the tragedy of the commons in operation. Other abound. Pollution, for example, reverses the dynamic without altering it: If he can get away with it, it will always be rational for a producer to pollute, because the cost to him of controlling his effluents is so much greater than his share of the environmental costs; besides, any attempt to introduce a cleaner (and therefore costlier) production process would lead to competitive disadvantage in the market. The logic of the commons that produces tragedy in fact pervades modern life. Francis Carney's analysis of the Los Angeles smog problem well illustrates how all our daily acts trap us in this insidious and tragic logic:

> But the automobiles are also the bearers of
> our greatest curse, the smog. Every person
> who lives in this basin knows that for
> twenty-five years he has been living through
> a disaster. We have all watched it happen,
> have participated in it with full knowledge
> just as men and women once went knowingly
> and willingly into the "dark Satanic mills."
> The smog is the result of ten million indi-
> vidual pursuits of private gratification.
> But there is absolutely nothing that any in-
> dividual can do to stop its spread. Each
> Angeleno is totally powerless to end what he
> hates. An individual act of renunciation is
> now nearly impossible, and, in any case,
> would be meaningless unless everyone else
> did the same thing. But he has no way of
> getting everyone else to do it. He does

not even have any way to talk about such a
course. He does not know how or where he
would do it or what language he would use.[12]

THE ANSWERS OF HOBBES AND ROUSSEAU

It is clear that we have here a version of the Hobbes-
ian state of nature.[13] Where men desire gain and the desired goods are scarcer than men's wants, they are likely to
fall to fighting. They each know individually that all
would be better off if they abstained from fighting and
found some way of equitably sharing the desired goods. However, they also realize that they cannot alter the dynamics
of the situation by their own behavior. Personal pacifism
merely makes them a prey to others. Unless all men can be
persuaded or forced to lay down their arms, nothing can prevent the war of all against all. The crucial problem in the
state of nature is thus to make it safe for men to be reasonable, rather than merely "rational," and thereby share
peacefully in what the environment has to offer. Hobbes's
solution, of course, was the erection of a sovereign power
by a majority that would constrain all men to be reasonable
and peaceful.
The commons situation also exemplifies Rousseau's distinction between the "general will" and the "will of all."
The former represents what reasonable men leaving aside
their self-interest would regard as the right and proper
course of action; the latter is the mere addition of the
particular wills of the individuals forming the polity,
based not on a conception of the common good, but only on
what serves their own self-interest. In essence, Rousseau's
answer in The Social Contract was not all that different
from Hobbes's in Leviathan: man must be "forced to be
free"--that is, made obedient to his real self-interest,
which is the common good or general will. The problem that
the tragedy of the commons forces us to confront is, in
fact, the core issue of political philosophy: how to protect or advance the interests of the collectivity as a whole
when the individuals that make it up (or enough of them to
create a problem) behave (or are impelled to behave) in a
selfish, greedy, and quarrelsome fashion. The only answer
is a sufficient measure of coercion. Following Hobbes, a
certain minimum level of ecological order or peace must be
established; following Rousseau, a certain minimum level of
ecological virtue must be imposed by our political institutions.
It need hardly be said that these conclusions about the
tragedy of the commons call into question fundamental American

values. In a situation of ecological scarcity, the individual, possessing an inalienable right to pursue happiness as he defines it and exercising his liberty in a basically laissez-faire system, will inevitably produce the ruin of the commons. Accordingly, the individualistic basis of society, the concept of inalienable rights, the purely self-defined pursuit of happiness, liberty as maximum freedom of action, and laissez faire itself all require abandonment or major modification if we wish to avoid inexorable environmental degradation and perhaps extinction as a civilization. We must thus question whether democracy as we know it can survive.

COMPETENCE, DEMOCRACY, AND PLATO

The presumption against democracy is strengthened when we consider the issue of competence. Even the most staunchly democratic theorist will agree that decisions on issues beyond the personal competence of the average man must be delegated to those who are competent and that, where highly significant differences in competence exist, effective rule may even require the sacrifice of political equality. Robert Dahl, for example, says that, where the members of a political association "differ crucially in their competence [as is clearly the case with respect to hospitals and passenger ships], a reasonable man will want the most competent people to have authority over the matters on which they are most competent."[14] Thus, the closer you are to the situation of a vessel embarked on a dangerous voyage, the greater the rationale for the rule of the competent few. But, as the earth and its various territories approach more and more closely to a realization of the spaceship metaphor with each step toward the ultimate ecological limits, the highest degree of competence will become indispensible for effective rule, and even a democratic theorist might have to begin to echo Plato's Republic: The polity is a ship of state that must be commanded by the best pilots, or it will founder.

TECHNOLOGY'S UNWANTED "SOCIAL FIX"

The profoundly antidemocratic and antilibertarian implications of the environmental crisis may persuade many to put their faith in salvation by technology, as technologists urge. After all, better technological hope, however forlorn, than such repugnant political solutions. Alas, salvation by technology turns out to be a double-edged sword. It may

40

indeed succeed in pushing back certain of the limits to growth, but only at a price, and this price is well described by Alvin Weinberg, one of the foremost spokesmen for nuclear power as the solution to our energy problems:

> We nuclear people have made a Faustian bargain with society. On the one hand, we offer . . . an inexhaustible source of energy [the breeder reactor]. . . . But the price that we demand of society for this magical energy is both a vigilance and a longevity of our social institutions that we are quite unaccustomed to.[15]

Thus, the "technological fixes" offered as the answer to our environmental crisis will involve some rather major "social fixes" as well, and Weinberg tells us that one imperative is "the creation of a permanent cadre or priesthood of responsible technologists who will guard the reactors and the wastes so as to assure their continued safety over millennia."[16]

The wider implications are apparent. In a crowded world where only the most exquisite care will avoid the collapse of the technological leviathan we are well on the way to creating, the grip of planning and social control will of necessity become more and more complete. Accidents cannot be permitted, much less the random behavior of individuals, and the technocrat pilots will run the ship in accordance with technological imperatives. Thus, Weinberg's Faustian bargain looks to be more like a pact with the Devil that will lead us inexorably down the path to total domination by technique and the machine and therefore toward a society that may at best resemble Aldous Huxley's Brave New World. C. S. Lewis once said that "what we call Man's power over Nature turns out to be a power exercised by some men over other men with Nature as its instrument,"[17] and it appears that the greater our technological power over nature, the more absolute the political power that must be yielded up to some men by others. It thus matters little whether we are successful in finding technological solutions to environmental imperatives, for the social fixes attached to technology will push us toward a version of the steady-state or spaceman society--characterized by the most scrupulous husbanding of resources, by extreme vigilance against the ever-present possibility of disaster should breakdown occur, and therefore by tight controls on human action--that human ecologists have all along said would be necessary. In other words, ecological scarcity is a classic dilemma. It may be possible for us to avoid crashing into the physical limits, but only by adopting radical and unpalatable measures that, paradoxically, are little different in their ultimate political and social implications than the policies proposed by the so-called doomsdayers.

RETURN TO CLASSICAL POLITICS

At the very least, it is crystal clear that "muddling through" in a basically laissez-faire socioeconomic system-- using "disjointed incrementalism," the decision-making system described and even glorified by Charles Lindblom to make policy[18]--is no longer tolerable or even possible. The necessities of survival in an age of renewed scarcity impose a certain "common interest" on us if we wish to survive, at least in reasonable order and dignity. Without prejudging what political measures would be needed to achieve this goal--for if we act soon, we still have a wide latitude of political response available to us--it is evident that our political future will inevitably be much less libertarian and much more authoritarian, and much less individualistic and much more communalistic than at present. Indeed, the likely result of the reemergence of scarcity appears to be the resurrection in modern dress of the classical polity, in which the few govern the many and in which government is no longer of or by the people (with the resulting risk that it will no longer be for them either).

To say this much is already to point us toward the past for guidance on our political future, and the political theorists who will build the new order seem likely to be creative reactionaries. Indeed, human ecology as a social doctrine or philosophy--exemplified, for example, in the works of Rene Dubos and Ian McHarg among others[19]--bears an uncanny resemblance to earlier modes of thought, in particular the conservatism of Edmund Burke. For example, the major tenet of both human ecology and Burke is trusteeship, or better yet, stewardship. Burke talked mainly about man's social patrimony rather than his natural heritage, but from the nature of his reasoning, it is clear that he meant both. The current generation holds the present as a patrimony in moral entail from our ancestors and must pass it on to posterity--improved, if possible, but at all costs undiminished. Beyond this general overriding imperative, human ecologists echo other tenets of Burke. The general skepticism about the possibility of "progress"; the awareness that the solution to one problem generates a new set of problems; the acceptance of human limits and imperfections; the need for organic change in order to preserve balance and harmony in

the social order; the interdependence and thus mutual moral
bondage of society; the need to check aggressive self-
interest; the contingent and situational nature of morality;
the inevitability and desirability of the diversity of mankind both within societies and among societies; progress as
a gradual evolution toward what is immanent in a historical
society; the social order as part of or as the outgrowth of
the natural order; politics as the balancing off of many
conflicting and equally legitimate claims to achieve the
best possible state of man considering the objective situation; and many other features are common to the two sets of
ideas. Ecology broadly defined thus turns out to be a fundamentally conservative orientation to the world. Indeed,
it is almost a feudalistic orientation to the world. The
natural order into which we must learn to fit harmoniously
is in many ways feudalistic, as a modern biologist's description of the climax stage of ecological succession, the
"goal" toward which nature is tending in the biosphere,
makes explicit:

> In all these cases, the trend of changes
> seems toward some final, more or less
> settled state. In this "climax" condition,
> changes still occur, but normally they are
> the stable rhythms of maturity: the steady
> income and outgo, the quietness of main-
> tenance, . . . balanced manufacture and con-
> sumption. Such a natural community knows
> where it is going. Such a natural community
> is a perennial feudal society, with all the
> rich tapestry of contrast and vividness that
> feudalism implies. Deaths of individuals
> occur in it, of course, but there can be
> little doubt as to successors. Only catas-
> trophe in the form of climatic change or
> overwhelming human interference or earth-
> quake can destroy its relative equilibrium.[20]

Since Burke was the last great spokesman for the premodern,
medieval point of view, which stressed the organic and corporate nature of society, perhaps we should carefully reflect on his thought in the new light of ecology.

It by no means follows, however, from the conservatism
of ecology that we must adopt Burke's political doctrines.
Rule by a landed aristocracy is now anachronistic at best
and reactionary (in the pejorative sense) at worst.[21] Yet
we must give Burke his due. He saw much more deeply into
the implications of his age than he usually gets credit for.

He is not, as some say, a mere writer of brilliant political tracts. We now realize that in many ways the collapse of organic community was a great loss and that many of our modern ills derive from the atomization of society. We now know too what some of the consequences of turning the direction of society over to "sophisters, economists, and calculators," Burke's epithets for the amoral capitalistic men who typified the new dispensation, can be. Thus, to read Burke and to see in his works only a political defense of privilege fails to do his thought justice. In our search for a set of social and political ideas that correspond to an ecological world view, Burke will have much to teach us.

Ecology has resonance with even older bodies of thought, like the classical tradition. Take, for example, Plato's Republic. In Book Two, Plato says in essence that while men need tools, some division of labor, and the like--in other words, a modest level of "development"--in order to live a civilized and humane life, they do not seem to know when to stop. Thus, they overdevelop, and the consequence is luxury, vice, class struggle, war, and other ills. To prevent this, we have to restrain men with wise rule by philosophers who know that what men desire is not always desirable for them and that true justice requires the establishment of controls, so that the balance and harmony of the whole are served. The classical tradition also distrusts technology. Just as excessive or uncontrolled economic development threatens to turn the direction of society over to money and the vagaries of the market, so too uncontrolled technological change undermines politics, the rational direction of human affairs, by turning social decisions over to mere things.[22]

The irony is, of course, that the ideas of human ecology, despite their resemblance to older conservative ideas, will not be interpreted as conservative at all by most Americans, but as revolutionary in the most profound and radical way. Compared to them, Marxism, which merely asks that "progress" be given central direction in the interest of social justice, seems like an old friend. Human ecology is, after all, against the conquest of nature, against growth as we think of it, against the isolation of thought and action, against individualism as an ideology, and against moral absolutes like the inalienable rights of man. The "subversive science" thus seems like a pitifully weak soubriquet for ecology, which demands only that our current political, social, economic, and moral order be stood on its head.

ARISTOTELEAN POLITICS AND THE ECOLOGICAL CONTRAST

All this means that we are about to undergo a more profound revolution in values than the one that established our
independence. If so, the appropriate response to environmental problems is not policy analysis but rather politics
in the Aristotelean sense (which, of course, includes the
former). That is, the crucial issues involved in environmental policy have to do primarily with ends, such as the
nature of the good life and the definition of the common interest, rather than means designed to achieve tacit goals.
The question for us is the Aristotelean one: How does man-
the-political-animal--possessing neither the instinct of the
beasts nor the infallible, spontaneous right action of the
Gods--design and create institutions that insure the survival of the city of man and some measure of the good life
within it? Specifically, just as it was the task of the political theorists of the seventeenth and eighteenth centu-
ries to create the "social contract" theory of government,
so it will be the task of the next several generations of
theorists to create an "ecological contract" theory that
will promote harmony not just between man and man, but also
between man and nature.
This reversion to Aristotelean politics is clearly going to be a novel and rather awkward turn of events for the
discipline of political science, which in the postwar era
has deliberately tried to purge itself of all taint of phi-
losophy--and with such success that many speak the word
"wisdom" only with contempt (as in "wisdom literature"). It
is perhaps to be expected that the common man should have
little or no feeling for the relativity and transitoriness
of all political values and institutions. But that our profession, the heir of the great tradition of political discourse, should have assumed that our particular historical
situation was somehow the permanent culmination of history
itself and that philosophy could therefore be banished is a
matter for deep regret, not to say chagrin. The plain truth
is that, as "scientists," we have nothing to say to anybody
about value questions, yet these are the questions that need
to be answered. We are thus sadly unprepared to give intellectual or moral leadership to the American people during
the coming era of crisis and transition. We must even ask
ourselves if the profession as it exists today is fit to
educate a new generation of citizens and, above all, leaders
for life in a vastly different cultural and political
milieu.

An era of crisis is also an era of grand opportunity--
in this case, for political science to regain its lost heritage and become once again the "master science." In its mad
rush to be scientifically respectable, the discipline forgot
its true calling. For us to continue to hew to a narrow
scientific line (moreover to a brand of science no longer
practiced by the natural sciences, which left Newton and
exact-law physics to the engineers several generations ago)
would be little short of disastrous from any point of view.
Only as an Aristotelean master science can political science
hope to contribute to the solution of the political and social difficulties that confront us, while living up to the
highest professional ideals, which require scholars fear-
lessly to determine and teach the truths men need for their
survival and well-being here on earth.

NOTES

1. William Ophuls, "Prologue to a Political Theory of
the Steady State: An Investigation of the Political and
Philosophical Implications of the Environmental Crisis,"
Ph.D. dissertation, Yale University, 1973 (available from
University Microfilms, Inc., Ann Arbor, Mich.). See also
idem., "Locke's Paradigm Lost: The Environmental Crisis and
the Collapse of Laissez-Faire Politics," a paper delivered
to the 1973 Annual Meeting of the American Political Science
Association, New Orleans (available in the Proceedings of
that meeting from University Microfilms, Inc., Ann Arbor,
Mich), which presents part of the argument of the longer
work.
2. Eugene P. Odum, Fundamentals of Ecology, 3d ed.
(Philadelphia: W. B. Saunders, 1971) and Paul R. Ehrlich
and Anne H. Ehrlich, Population, Resources, Environment:
Issues in Human Ecology, 2d ed. (San Francisco: W. H.
Freeman, 1972).
3. Donella H. Meadows et al., The Limits to Growth
(New York: Universe Books, 1972).
4. Harrison Brown, The Challenge of Man's Future (New
York: Viking, 1954).
5. George P. Marsh, Man and Nature: Or Geography as
Modified by Man, ed. David Lowenthal (Cambridge, Mass.:
Harvard University Press, 1965; originally published in
1864).
6. One example is Robert U. Ayres and Allen V. Kneese,
"Economic and Ecological Effects of a Stationary Economy,"
Reprint No. 99 [from Annual Review of Ecology and System-
atics 2 (1971)] (Washington, D.C.: Resources for the Future, December 1972).

7. Kenneth E. Boulding, "Is Scarcity Dead?," _Public Interest_ 5 (Fall 1966): 42-43.

8. Ibid.

9. See in particular the discussion of property in Chapter V of Locke's _Second Treatise._

10. In addition to the works cited in note 1, see William Ophuls, "Leviathan or Oblivion?," in _Toward a Steady-State Economy_, ed. Herman E. Daly (San Francisco: W. H. Freeman, 1973), pp. 215-30.

11. Garrett Hardin, "The Tragedy of the Commons," _Science_ 162 (December 17, 1968): 1243-48.

12. Francis Carney, "Schlockology," _New York Review of Books_, June 1, 1972, pp. 28-29. See also Thomas C. Schelling, "On the Ecology of Micromotives," _Public Interest_ 25 (Fall 1971), pp. 61-98, which provides dozens of homely examples.

13. Ophuls, "Leviathan or Oblivion?," op. cit., outlines the virtual identity of argument between Hobbes and Hardin.

14. Robert A. Dahl, _After the Revolution?: Authority in a Good Society_ (New Haven, Conn.: Yale University Press, 1970), p. 58. (Emphasis added.)

15. Alvin M. Weinberg, "Social Institutions and Nuclear Energy," _Science_ 177 (July 7, 1972): 33.

16. Alvin M. Weinberg, "Technology and Ecology--Is There a Need for Confrontation?," _BioScience_ 23, no. 1 (January 1973): 43.

17. C. S. Lewis, _The Abolition of Man_ (New York: Macmillan, 1965), p. 69.

18. Charles E. Lindblom, _The Intelligence of Democracy: Decision Making Through Mutual Adjustment_ (New York: The Free Press, 1965).

19. Rene Dubos, _So Human an Animal_ (New York: Scribner, 1968); Ian McHarg, _Design With Nature_ (Garden City, N.Y.: Natural History Press, 1971). See also the collection edited by Paul Shepard and Daniel McKinley, _The Subversive Science: Essays Toward an Ecology of Man_ (Boston: Houghton Mifflin, 1969), as well as the works by Odum and the Ehrlichs, op. cit.

20. Daniel McKinley, "Lichens--Mirror to the Universe," _Audubon_ 72, no. 6 (November 1970): 53-54.

21. However, see Warren A. Johnson, "Paths Out of the Corner," an interesting proposal for a "new feudalism." Available from the author, Department of Geography, California State University, San Diego.

22. Much more could be said about the relevance of the classical tradition to modern problems, and a first-rate essay that does this is Mulford Q. Sibley, "The Relevance of Classical Political Theory for Economy, Technology, and

Ecology," a paper presented to the 1972 Annual Meeting of
the American Political Science Association, Washington,
D.C., and reprinted with minor revisions in _Alternatives_ 2,
no. 2 (Winter 1973):   14-35.

5

ECOLOGICAL PROBLEMS,
POLITICAL THEORY,
AND PUBLIC POLICY
Peter G. Stillman

Over the past decade there has been a new and wide-spread concern with ecological problems: too much pollution, too many people, and too great a demand for energy, food, and industrial output. With this concern has come some awareness that the real problems raised by the environmental and population crises are not mere technical problems. For the techniques are available to "solve" these crises, to whatever degree required--even if one of the techniques is to return to the life- and consumption-style of the 1920s and 1930s or earlier. Rather, these crises raise moral, ethical, and philosophical questions: What kind of society is desirable and reasonable? What changes in life-style, in the economic system, and in the political order would such a society require? What values would such a society stress and foster? Ecological studies that describe technical problems and point out the techniques for their solutions play an important and essential role. As Ecologists become aware of the problems and the variety of possible ways to mitigate or ameliorate them, however, they must then start to consider the kind of society--in structure and culture--that is ecologically sound and humanly desirable. In other words, ecologists must begin to consider the questions of normative political theory.

The consideration of political theory takes on an added importance because questions of political theory and political values underlie, explicitly or implicitly, public policy

The author would like to thank Michael E. Kraft for his assistance and encouragement. He kindly discussed at length the issues raised in this chapter and offered many ideas and suggestions. He is, of course, not culpable for the final product.

decisions. Recent policy decisions--for example, to build the Alaska pipeline, to lower standards to allow utilities to burn highly polluting fuel--have been based in varying degrees on the value that ecological matters are substantially less important that high mass consumption of energy to satisfy the consumer's whims about his travel and his heating his house. Thus, as ecologists become concerned about policies with an ecological impact, it is understandable and necessary that they also become concerned with questions of values and political theory.

Furthermore, ecological policies are in one crucial way different from other public policy issues. Whereas most public policy issues deal with the distribution and redistribution of values and utilities, ecological policy issues ultimately also relate to the survival of people and civilizations. The standard administrative policy of "muddling through" can be allowed for issues of less moment, where the costs of muddling along with an eventually unsatisfactory policy are neither great nor irreversible. But incremental decision making--"muddling through"--is, at even its proponents realize, inherently stagnant in that it tends to be bound by the logic of past decisions and not to consider nor strike out in new directions:

> the method is without a built-in safeguard
> for all relevant values, and it also may
> lead the decision maker to overlook excel-
> lent policies for no other reason than that
> they are not suggested by the chain of suc-
> cessive policy steps leading up to the
> present. Hence, . . . policies will con-
> tinue to be as foolish as they are wise.[1]

Because it is narrow and backward-looking, "muddling through" tends not to be a good method for the formation of ecological policies, especially since it is "muddling through" with present policies that has gotten us into so much of the mess we are in. Instead, the approach to ecological policy questions ought to include as much examination of as wide a range of policy alternatives as possible. In this type of overview of various options, political theory can define and illuminate the alternatives and can provide a comprehensive framework from which policy decisions can be made and judged.

ECOLOGICAL POLITICAL THEORY

Recognizing how central questions of political theory are to ecological issues and policies, some ecologists and other social scientists have turned their attention to developing an ecological political theory. In the theoretical statements proposed thus far is much that lays the basis for an intelligent discussion of some issues and for a reasonable orientation of policy. Nonetheless, the main tendency of current theorizing suffers from some serious problems.

Most proposals for an ecologically sound political order stress the need for increased governmental power, intervention, and planning.[2] The government is seen as the only or the major repository of power that can coerce nonecologically minded political actors; it alone can consistently intervene in social and economic life in a legitimate and--presumably--effective way; and it alone has the ability to assemble the expertise and the power and ability to act to carry out the conclusions of the experts. Especially when the issue is population, but usually for almost all particular ecological issues, ecological political theorists recommend more government and more governmental coercion as the primary or the only means to attain the goal of an ecologically sound society. Ehrlich, Commoner, Hardin, Daly, Ophuls, Davies, Nader, Rosenbaum--the list could be extended beyond the capacity of the page to hold the footnote citations.[3]

To focus on governmental coercion as the chief answer to our ecological problems is an approach that has some plausibility in the contemporary world, where much ecological damage is done by corporations befouling the air, land, and water, and by individuals producing large numbers of babies and pollutants. But most ecological theories of governmental intervention have some serious drawbacks: Too frequently, important norms and values are ignored, and crucial political variables and findings are omitted. Many of these weaknesses derive, of course, from the overspecialization of academic disciplines and from other, more mundane causes--like lack of space in a publication. But political science and political theory contain many relevant and important--and too frequently ignored--writings and ideas that have a direct bearing on ecological theories of governmental intervention and that suggest the limits to the predominant political theory for achieving sound ecological policies.

THE INADEQUATE TREATMENT OF NORMATIVE ISSUES

Theorists of governmental coercion fail adequately to treat normative issues. When they seriously handle normative matters, they do look at the one important value on which coercion bears directly: freedom. But their treatments of values are usually defective because they rarely examine any important normative value other than freedom.

For instance, in the theorists' visions of ecologically
sound societies, what will be the concept of justice and how
will it be put into effect? What will be the idea of human
fulfillment or satisfaction: Which aspects and characteristics of human beings are to be called forth, emphasized, and
esteemed? How, if at all, will the society meet the human
desire for community, that is, "the wish to live in trust
and fraternal cooperation with one's fellows in a total and
visible collective entity"?[4] What will happen to the idea
that an individual should have some control or influence
over some decisions that affect his life? How will compromise and conflict-resolution, goals of pluralism, be attained when there is increased planning? These and other
questions relate to the central issues of individual life
and of social and political interaction; along with freedom,
they are basic questions about human existence.

These philosophical and theoretical questions are important to ask of any design for a new society; but they may
well be particularly important questions to ask of a design
that stresses an increase of governmental control and coercion and therefore--implicitly--an expansion of modern bureaucracy. For Max Weber, the great sociological theorist
of bureaucracy, perceived the normative bankruptcy of a
highly bureaucratized society; without new prophets or a
"great rebirth of old ideas and ideals," he foresaw a dreary
future:

> No one knows who will live in this cage in
> the future . . . [of] mechanized petrifica-
> tion, embellished with a sort of convulsive
> self-importance. For of the last stage of
> this cultural development, it might well be
> truly said: "Specialists without spirit,
> sensualists without heart; this nullity im-
> agines that it has attained a level of civili-
> zation never before achieved."[5]

If Weber's premonition is even partially correct, concern
with values other than freedom is essential.

Yet most ecological theorists ignore the wide range of
normative issues. The few, like Commoner and Ophuls, who do
mention them usually do so without much attention to detail
or to the crucial questions of the mutual compatibility, the
mutual viability, the interactions, and the necessary relationships among the many values and the institutions within
which these values are embedded.[6] But these issues are important, for how they are handled will determine one major
aspect of the "quality of life" for future generations.

THE DUBIOUS ASSUMPTIONS

Too narrow in their treatment of normative issues and values generally, ecological theorists of governmental coercion also overlook many problems directly connected with their proposed solution. In general, the theorists make a number of assumptions about strong, interventionist government. First, they assume that it will be expert, or at least expert enough to be able to solve or mitigate ecological crises or problems. Second, they assume that it will be well-intentioned, that is, that it wish and try to use its expertise to solve these problems. Third, they assume that the expert, well-intentioned government will be effective, that is, that it will be able, through laws and regulations, to reverse, avert, or minimize ecologically unsound practices. Fourth, they assume that an expert, well-intentioned, and effective government will also be able to maintain popular consent or cooperation in its endeavors. These assumptions, essential to ecological theories of governmental coercion, are rarely made explicit; even when they are mentioned, usually no way of attaining them is proposed.

Merely to state these four assumptions is enough to indicate how crucial they are, how they need explicit analysis, and how--if governmental coercion is to remain a viable solution--they need extensive justification. Certainly, at present the evidence indicates that none of these four assumptions is accurate.

The first assumption is that the government can or does have the expertise needed to formulate ecological policy. There is no doubt that successful intervention and coercion require expertise, and that government is alone in the position to be able to assemble and coordinate all available experts on any particular issue. But, with the possible exception of military technology, where the enemy is clearly and obviously defined, and where expertise is applied purely to questions of hardware, there seems to be little reason to expect the assembled and coordinated experts to arrive at a reasonably correct answer. The results of the application of expertise to housing problems, urban renewal, and economic issues should at least give pause to anyone relying on governmental expertise. Moreover, in ecological matters there is a critical lack of knowledge in some areas. At a most obvious level, the definition of the severity of the current ecological crisis needs careful attention--even though the expert assessments may ultimately disagree; for the requisite governmental actions may depend on the severity of the problem. At a basic level, concepts like "ecological survival" need careful treatment; what is "survival," its chief components, the chief variables? Not enough work has been done in these areas for ecological experts even to claim to have requisite expertise for policy making.[7]

Nor can anyone be confident that an expert government would be well-intentioned, the second assumption. It seems to be a matter of faith among ecological theorists that the strong government would be headed by altruistic ecologists. But it is hard to know what facts sustain this faith. At present, ecologists have little political power and little access to decision making; it is difficult to imagine that a stronger government would give ecologists this power and access, and it is even more difficult to imagine a stronger government run by altruistic ecologists. Further, if ecologists' influence does not increase, it seems most likely that the government will roughly continue its historical role of damaging or destroying more of the environment than it aids or saves.[8]

It is equally hard to know what theory sustains the faith that the strong central government would be ecologically well-intentioned. As all analyses of the "tragedy of the commons" are careful to point out,[9] the problem of the commons cannot be solved by the people acting in their individual capacities; as Mancur Olsen argues, "rational, self-interested individuals will not act to achieve their common or group interests."[10] Therefore, most analyzers of the commons assert, what is required is a strong government with a strong ruler. But these analyzers conveniently overlook that the ruler, if he is (like everyone in the society) "a rational, self-interested individual," will probably not act to solve ecological problems. He will probably not act because ecological reforms run counter to the attitudes, whims, and rational self-interest of the populace; and thus for the ruler to impose ecological policies would be for him to act contrary to his own rational self-interest by increasing popular discontent, undermining consent, and reducing popular obligation. Just as economic calculations that assume rational, self-interested individuals produce continual economic optima at all points of growth until just before environmental costs become infinite and the system is on the verge of collapse,[11] so too the rational, self-interested ruler is better off by allowing people to satisfy their desires and thus consent to his rule until just before environmental costs become infinite and the system is on the verge of collapse. Because of the difficulties and the costs of meeting ecological requirements, a rational, self-interested ruler would avoid action as long as possible. (It is perhaps unnecessary to add that a democratically elected ruler would have a similar difficulty, exacerbated by his need to be reelected periodically.) There are, in sum, both theoretical and practical reasons to doubt that a strong government would or could be ecologically well-intentioned.

Even if these compelling practical and theoretical problems could be overcome, two further problems facing the assumption of a well-intentioned strong government might be noted. One is that planners are frequently out of touch with their constituency, even when the planners do try to be in touch.[12] In other words, the government must have not only good intentions but the means by which those intentions can be given a popularly and ecologically sound content.

The second is that the commentaries and controversies surrounding the Watergate investigations have reopened the crucial question whether any strong government could or would be ecologically well-intentioned. Certainly it is clear that many lawyers in Nixon's government disobeyed the law, and that many of their actions were not legally well-intentioned, that is, were not in keeping with the spirit of the law and the constitution. Would ecologists do better than lawyers? In general, the many abuses--by many presidents and both parties--that have been disclosed as a result of the Watergate investigations should lead to a serious re-thinking of the effects of strong government and the uses to which governmental power can be--and would be--put. In short, it is imperative again to examine the idea that power corrupts, and to face the possibility that ecologists may not have divine dispensation from Lord Acton's dictum about the corrupting effects of power.

The third assumption--that an expert, well-intentioned government could act effectively against ecologically un-sound practices--is equally tenuous. Independent government agencies have not been noted for their effective action in the pursuit of policies opposed by powerful local or private groups. As the past history of some independent agencies, like the Tennessee Valley Authority (TVA), indicates, even well-intentioned bodies seem unable to withstand severe po-litical pressure. As Philip Selznick's classic study of the TVA amply documents, the TVA, with its stated conservation goals, was co-opted by the Farm Bureau Federation (the farm-ing equivalent of the National Association of Manufacturers), with the result that the TVA found itself supporting the opinions of local (white) farmers over the technical conclu-sions of its own experts and over any notions of participa-tion or rewards for Negroes; the TVA, co-opted, conserved, and strengthened both the existing social and political sys-tem and the existing (nonconservationist) goals.[13] What holds for independent agencies like the TVA is also true for

the so-called regulatory agencies, whose co-optation by existing organized groups has been amply documented by Theodore
Lowi and Ralph Nader's "raiders."[14]

The fourth assumption, that an ecologically sound government can maintain popular consent, also needs much analysis. Many theorists ignore the question of consent.[15] But
consent and compliance would surely be a problem that an effective, well-intentioned, strong, ecologically active government would face. For it is apparent that, at least in
the short run, ecologically sound policies by an effective
and strong government would limit freedom as currently defined, the scope of democratic decision making and political
compromise, the ever-increasing consumption of goods, and
the hope that the benefits of a rising GNP will "trickle
down" to everyone so that everyone can look to the future as
a time when he will be better off. And, to limit freedom,
democracy, consumption, and hope is to limit major factors
that produce consent among citizens of this country and thus
produce legitimacy for the government. At the level of specific laws, it seems apparent that people tend not to do
things nor to obey laws they don't like: Prohibition of
liquor is one example, current drug laws are another, but
even some seemingly simple and beneficial actions--like
wearing seatbelts--are ignored by many.[16] Furthermore, drug
education and traffic safety education programs--as currently carried out--seem to have little effect. Consent to
ecologically sound laws and to an ecologically oriented government is necessary in order for the government and its
laws to be effective.[17] But ecological policies will probably reduce citizen consent to laws and government.

Moreover, as a very few ecological theorists correctly
realize, more than mere popular consent is necessary; some
ecological reforms require active citizen support and--as
one theorist has termed it--"moral growth" among citizens.
It is clear that a long-term ecological solution, like a
steady-state economic order, will make a strong demand on
the citizens' moral resources; so will any coercive solution to the population problem, including even those solutions that try to maximize individual choice, like Boulding's "green stamp" proposal.[18] These theorists have made
the important first step of recognizing the significance of
popular attitudes; but they have not made the next step, of
analyzing how these popular attitudes can be developed.
This next step, however, is essential. Indeed, it is highly likely that the necessary popular attitudes cannot be developed in the context of a powerful, expert, interventionist government operating through modern bureaucratic administration. A government of experts, intervening frequently,

and working through modern bureaucracy tends to reduce popular activity and "moral growth." It tends to make the citizens passive, since it "acts on" them without having to consult them; it tends to reduce the social rationality--the general social intelligence and efficacy--of the people, since it leaves all important choices in the hands of someone other than the people.[19] In sum, there is a contradiction in those ecological theories that call both for a strong central government and for citizen support and moral growth. It is not necessarily an irremedial contradiction; but it is a contradiction that needs much analysis and study before it can be resolved.

Because of the difficulties involved in the four assumptions that underlie the theory of increased governmental intervention, a further problem with the theory arises: the practical, political problem of gaining support for ecological policies. The theory that advocates increased governmental power is clearly a liberal theory, "liberal" as that term has been defined in twentieth-century United States. To insist on a liberal solution to ecological problems is to write off the possibility of gaining political support from many: those whose opposition to liberalism is more deep-seated and salient than their ecological concerns, as well as those whose opposition to liberalism is based on their perception that liberal solutions are inefficacious and impossible, even though they may feel strongly about ecological issues. Of course, if it were clear that the liberal approach of governmental intervention were the only possible or feasible ecological solution, then insistence on strong government, even to the extent of losing political support, would be justified. Since, however, the validity and viability of a liberal ecological theory is thrown in doubt because of the problems involved in its underlying assumptions, such cavalier ignoring of potential political support is a disservice to the cause of an ecologically sound society.

CONCLUSION

In short, ecological political theories that propose increased governmental power and activity are based on many assumptions whose validity is seriously in doubt; and the dubiousness of the assumptions leads to doubt about the theory as a valid and exclusive theory for ecological well-being. Yet governmental intervention cannot, of course, be discarded, for there are many areas where it will be beneficial ecologically: certainly, for instance, nationwide pollution and population standards are necessary in order to prevent one state from trying to reap an economic gain at the expense of another, more ecologically minded state.

The problems of the current predominant theory do mean that a renewed and critical attention to questions of political theory is necessary. Governmental intervention must be considered as one theory, but not as the sole theory, nor as a panacea even where effectively applied. Other topics must be seriously considered as well. In what areas should governmental intervention apply? In those areas, what should be the scope of governmental activity, and how should an appeals process work? How can limits be set on a government made more powerful in some respects in order to deal with ecological problems? How can the problems of citizen consent and "moral growth" be met? What alternatives are available in current society to develop a responsible citizen body? How can such responsibility be institutionally organized, or must it exist outside of institutional structures? Furthermore, theorists must consider values other than freedom, values like justice, human fulfillment, and community. It is to these varied and difficult questions and to the full range of important political values that ecological political theorists must address themselves. And, as theorists provide some tentative answers, these answers may be incorporated, to varying extents, as component parts of policy decisions and will exist as criteria against which to measure and evaluate existing policies and their implications.

NOTES

1. Charles E. Lindblom, "The Science of 'Muddling Through,'" Public Administration Review 19, no. 2 (Spring 1959): 87-88. For a detailed criticism of incremental decision making, see William Ophuls, "Locke's Paradigm Lost: The Environmental Crisis and the Collapse of Laissez-Faire Politics," a paper delivered at the 1973 Annual Meeting of the American Political Science Association, New Orleans, esp. pp. 12-15.

2. There are many minority proposals. Some stress the need to change attitudes, for example, E. F. Schumacher, "Buddhist Economics," in Toward a Steady-State Economy, ed. Herman E. Daly (San Francisco: W. H. Freeman, 1973); others see revolution as the only possible answer, for example, Richard England and Barry Bluestone, "Ecology and Social Conflict," in Daly, op. cit.; and yet others advocate a return to a type of communitarianism, for example, "A Blueprint for Survival," The Ecologist, January 1972, reprinted

in the Congressional Record (daily edition), January 21, 1972, pp. H 209-H 232. But revolution of an ecologically sound sort is surely unlikely in modern America; change of attitudes in itself is inefficacious (as the ecological troubles in Buddhist lands indicates); and communitarianism as an exclusive solution has many problems, which are outlined in some detail in Michael E. Kraft and Peter G. Stillman, "Toward a Political Theory of Ecological Survival," a paper delivered at the 1973 Annual Meeting of the American Political Science Association, New Orleans, esp. pp. 15-21.

3. See, for example, Paul R. Ehrlich and Richard L. Harriman, How to be a Survivor (New York: Ballantine Books, 1971), esp. pp. 33, 47, and 66; Barry Commoner, The Closing Circle (New York: Alfred A. Knopf, 1971), Chapters 10-13; Garrett Hardin, "The Tragedy of the Commons," in Daly, op. cit.; Herman E. Daly, "The Steady-State Economy," in Daly, op. cit.; William Ophuls, "Leviathan or Oblivion?," in Daly, op. cit.; J. Clarence Davies III, The Politics of Pollution (New York: Pegasus, 1970); Ralph Nader, "Corporations and Pollution," The Progressive, April 1970, esp. pp. 19-21; and Walter A. Rosenbaum, The Politics of Environmental Concern (New York: Praeger, 1973), esp. Chapter 10.

4. Philip Slater, The Pursuit of Loneliness (Boston: Beacon Press, 1970), p. 5.

5. Max Weber, The Protestant Ethic and the Spirit of Capitalism (New York: Scribner, 1958), p. 182.

6. Ophuls, for instance, outlines what he sees as a desirable, humane, and ecologically sound political order, but he makes no suggestions about how or why a strong central government might, would, or could establish such an order; see Ophuls, "Leviathan or Oblivion?," op. cit. See also Commoner, op. cit., p. 195 and Chapter 12.

7. For a beginning, see Peter A. Corning, "Comparative Survival Strategies," a paper delivered at the 1973 Annual Meeting of the American Political Science Association, New Orleans.

8. There are many examples; for one, see Charles R. Ross, "The Federal Government as an Inadvertent Advocate of Environmental Degradation," in The Environmental Crisis, ed. Harold W. Helfrich, Jr. (New Haven, Conn.: Yale University Press, 1970).

9. The classic statement is, of course, Hardin, "The Tragedy of the Commons," op. cit.; his analysis has been extended and elucidated by Ophuls, "Leviathan or Oblivion?," op. cit.

10. Mancur Olson, Jr., The Logic of Collective Action (New York: Schocken, 1968), p. 2, and the works cited in note 9.

11. David Pearce, "Is Ecology Elitist?," The Ecologist 3 (February 1973): 61-63.

12. Robert Arvill, Man and Environment (Baltimore: Penguin, 1967), esp. p. 225.

13. See Philip Selznick, TVA and the Grass Roots (Berkeley: University of California Press, 1949); TVA is still a major polluter and consumer of strip-mined coal.

14. See Theodore J. Lowi, The End of Liberalism (New York: W. W. Norton, 1969); and any book by Ralph Nader or his "Study Groups" at the Center for the Study of Responsive Law.

15. See, for example, Ehrlich and Harriman, How to be a Survivor, op. cit., p. 47; and Garrett Hardin, "Preserving Quality on Spaceship Earth," Transactions of the 37th North American Wildlife and Natural Resources Conference, 12-15 March 1972, p. 174, where Hardin asks rhetorically "how can the passengers on a spaceship [earth] accept special privilege and unfairness?" and has no answer other than "Plainly they must. We must."

16. See, for example, New York Times, September 9, 1973, sec. 4, p. 12.

17. For this assertion defended, see H. L. A. Hart, The Concept of Law (Oxford: Clarendon Press, 1961), esp. pp. 196-97 and Hannah Arendt, "What is Authority?" in her Between Past and Future (New York: Viking, 1968 [1961]).

18. See Herman E. Daly, "Introduction," p. 19 and Daly, "The Steady-State Economy," pp. 158-60, in Daly, op. cit.

19. For the classic statement, see Karl Mannheim, Man and Society in an Age of Reconstruction (New York: Harcourt, Brace, and World, 1940), pp. 58-60.

6

HUMAN FALLIBILITY,
POLITICAL THEORY,
AND THE ENVIRONMENT
Vincent Ostrom

Policy study, in the sense that analytical tools and skills are "applied" to practical problems, is an "applied science." The applied nature of policy analysis does not diminish the importance of theory as explanatory language that specifies elemental terms, identifies constants and variables, and postulates relational rules. Such an explanatory language enables its users to reason through problems and reach conclusions about consequences likely to follow from specifiable conditions. Applied analysis, however, places a substantial burden upon the analyst to be extraordinarily careful in the use of his language in a way that is consistent with the empirical circumstances that are subject to analysis. The application of rules of reason to hypothetical conditions that have little or no congruences with empirical conditions will enable an analyst to derive logically correct but empirically irrelevant inferences.

OMNISCIENT OBSERVERS AS POLICY ANALYSTS

Few problem areas of policy analysis involve greater difficulty in relating explanatory language and intellectual discourse to empirical referents than problems of environmental policy. The language of discourse is likely to be holistic, global, and universal in nature. Everything is related to everything else. Environmental policy from this perspective requires consideration of the total needs of the total man in the total environment.

Language systems that purport to deal with total needs of total man in the total environment carry a correlative burden for authors who use such language to assume the perspective of an omniscient observer. An omniscient observer presumes that he has access to perfect information in the sense of having complete foresight and complete hindsight, and an ability to comprehend all events and relationships and to see the whole picture in the total environment.

The difficulty inherent in scholars taking the posture of omniscient observers and presuming perfect information is indicated when it becomes apparent that a presumption of perfect information forecloses any need to expend time and effort either on learning or upon scholarship. An omniscient observer presumes to know everything and has no need to learn anything.

If human knowledge is incomplete then extensive areas of uncertainty will exist in relation to events in the environment. The total needs of total man in the total environment cannot be known. The interaction of all events in the total environment cannot be comprehended by finite minds. Whenever men take on the perspectives of omniscient observers, the probability of error deriving from such a presumption is great and risks to the credibility of scholarship based upon presumptions of omniscience are equally great.

NEW KNOWLEDGE

Learning implies that new knowledge can be acquired. The human capability to acquire new knowledge and to organize that knowledge in language systems further implies that knowledge can be accumulated through time and be aggregated into very large bodies of organized knowledge.

New knowledge also gives rise to new possibilities for action. When acted upon, these new possibilities manifest themselves as new events, relationships, and occurrences within "the total environment." Where new knowledge creates new possibilities and new possibilities could not have been anticipated without reference to that new knowledge, substantial limits are interposed upon any effort to control environmental conditions through time. Under conditions of rapidly expanding knowledge and technological development, long-term comprehensive planning thus becomes an impossibility.

The development of new knowledge and the creation of new possibilities necessarily implies that human efforts to anticipate the future course of events will always be subject to limited time horizons. Thus, all human planning and developmental efforts will be subject to obsolescence as old knowledge and techniques give way to new. Under conditions of rapidly expanding knowledge and technological development, forecasts are subject to an increasing magnitude of error the further projections are extended into the future.

Long-term plans that are designed to be "master plans" in the sense that they can provide a "blueprint" to predetermine the future course of events will be futile endeavors. Planning can be an essential strategy for organizing information in an assessment of alternative possibilities so long as time horizons are clearly indicated. A crude magnitude of uncertainty can then be specified in relation to the obsolescence of old knowledge and the generation of new knowledge.

Comprehensive planning in the sense of taking account of all variables in the total environment is also an impossibility. Planning that considers a limited range of alternatives in relation to ecosystems with specifiable boundaries and limited time horizons are within the realm of possibility. A limited degree of comprehensiveness can accrue through the method of successive approximation by using partially redundant or overlapping planning sets. However, all planning is beclouded by uncertainty in the presence of changing knowledge.

INCREASING RELATIVE IGNORANCE OF
INDIVIDUAL DECISION MAKERS

Rapid growth in the aggregate pool of human knowledge and in the generation of new knowledge is also the source of increasing difficulty for those who function as decision makers and policy analysts in an increasingly complex society. The Spanish philosopher José Ortega y Gassett in The Revolt of the Masses advanced the thesis that specialization of knowledge produces a "new barbarian" whom he characterized as a "learned ignoramus." As the aggregate pool of human knowledge increases there is a correlative increase in the relative ignorance of each individual in relation to that aggregate pool of knowledge.

No one can "see" or "know" the "whole picture." All decision makers are fallible. All decision making will occur under conditions of uncertainty. No decision maker will know all of the consequences that will flow from his choices or his actions. All decision making will be subject to error.

These relationships have been recognized by popular references to a specialist as one who knows more and more about less and less. The training of generalists as a strategy to overcome the limits of specialization is destined to failure. The generalist can be defined as one who

knows less and less about more and more. They are both subject to the paradox of the learned ignoramus.

Where all decision makers are assumed to be fallible,
error-proneness can be alleviated by the development of
error-correcting strategies as a part of the decision-making
process. Error-correcting strategies in decision making require that diverse forms of assessment representing different analytical skills be utilized to estimate the probable
consequences of alternative courses of action. Since inter-
personal comparisons of preferences or utilities are not
possible, mechanisms for the expression of preferences from
among diverse elements in the population of communities
sharing different environmental circumstances is also a
necessary condition for decision makers who are concerned
with the common wealth of environmental quality. Such efforts require substantial time and effort to be expended
upon due deliberation in the course of decision making.
Unfortunately, the increasing magnitude of interdependencies
associated with a rapidly changing technology will require
increasing expenditures of time and effort in decision making without any "guarantee" that errors will necessarily be
avoided. We design emission control systems that increase
fuel consumption and reduce the efficiency of automobiles
while claiming to reduce air pollution.

INSTITUTIONAL ANALYSIS

If long-term, comprehensive planning is an impossibility and if all decision makers confront a problem of increasing relative ignorance in relation to the aggregate
pool of human knowledge, then fallible decision makers are
confronted with substantial difficulties in dealing with
environmental conditions. No single set of central decision makers can control all events that affect the quality
of the environment. All forms of human productive efforts
involve the transformation of events that are elements in
environments. The knowledge relevant to such productive efforts is equivalent to the sum of all instrumental knowledge.
All human action affects environmental conditions. Since
central decision makers cannot directly control all events
that affect the quality of the environment, we are confronted with the task of moving to second-order solutions in
relying upon the environment and for introducing change into
those relationships. These second-order solutions will depend upon the development of an institutional analysis that
can identify the effect that different organizational or
institutional arrangements will have upon the choice of

strategies that individuals confront in the pursuit of opportunities inherent in different structures of events comprising ecosystems in the environment.

Most environmental problems will take on the characteristics associated with common-property resources and public
goods or will involve externalities that impose social costs
upon persons who are not directly involved in particular activities. In each of those circumstances communities of
people are implicated in relationships where market institutions will manifest serious weaknesses or institutional
failures.

The complexity of events occurring in various ecosystems of the environment further imply that the environment
affects many different communities of interest of different
sizes and shapes. The quality of the environment of urban
neighborhoods may implicate quite different communities of
relationships than the quality of environmental conditions
in the world's oceans. Oscar Newman's <u>Defensible Space</u> indicates some of the consequences that follow when environing
conditions are not organized so as to enable individuals to
exercise control in relation to properties subject to joint
use. The difficulties associated with the logic of collective action are apt to evoke the tragedy of the commons unless the relevant communities can be organized as a public
enterprise to take collective action to manage common properties. Purely voluntary arrangements will not suffice for
tending to common properties. Even units no larger than
families have recourse to coercive sanctions in their use of
common properties.

Organization for collective action to realize the advantage that accrues from quality environments raises all of
the fundamental issues in political theory. The realization
of common benefits requires reference to systems of rule
that enable individuals to pursue some opportunities while
constraining actions that evoke deleterious consequences.
If rules are to be effective they require mechanisms for enforcement. Mechanisms for enforcement necessarily imply
radical inequalities in decision-making capabilities. Radical inequalities imply that some may take advantage of those
inequalities to realize an advantage for themselves and to
impose deprivations upon others. The dispersion of authority so as to constrain the exercise of discretion by those
who act on behalf of the larger community of persons sharing
interests in common property systems raises the classical
issues of constitutional choice. The problems of human fallibility and the environment take us back to fundamental
issues in political theory where we share the concerns of
many classical thinkers such as Thomas Hobbes, Jean Jacques

Rousseau, John Locke, Alexander Hamilton, Thomas Jefferson, James Madison, Alexis de Toqueville and a multitude of others.

REFERENCES

Ashby, W. Ross. Design for a Brain: The Origin of Adaptive Behavior, 2d ed. New York: John Wiley, 1960.

Buchanan, James M. Cost and Choice: An Inquiry in Economic Theory. Chicago: Markham, 1969.

Cassirer, Ernst. The Myth of the State. New Haven, Conn.: Yale University Press, 1964.

Crozier, Michel. The Bureaucratic Phenomenon. Chicago: The University of Chicago Press, 1964.

Djilas, Milovan. The Unperfect Society. New York: Harcourt, Brace and World, 1969.

Hayek, Friedrick A. The Constitution of Liberty. Chicago: University of Chicago Press, 1960.

Newman, Oscar. Defensible Space. New York: Macmillan, 1972.

Olson, Mancur. The Logic of Collective Action. Cambridge, Mass.: Harvard University Press, 1965.

Ortega y Gassett, José. The Revolt of the Masses. New York: W. W. Norton, 1930.

Ostrom, Vincent. The Intellectual Crisis in American Public Administration. University, Ala.: University of Alabama Press, 1973.

Teilhard de Chardin, Pierre. The Phenomenon of Man. New York: Harper and Row, 1961. Originally published in 1955.

Tullock, Gordon. The Politics of Bureaucracy. Washington, D.C.: Public Affairs Press, 1965.

CHAPTER

7

RESEARCHING ENVIRONMENTAL POLICY: THE CROSS-SECTIONAL AND QUASI-EXPERIMENTAL PERSPECTIVE
Leslie L. Roos, Jr.

THE CROSS-SECTIONAL OR ONE-POINT-IN-TIME PERSPECTIVE

The importance of public sector activities is such that efforts to understand the determinants of public policy outputs have occupied the attention of a number of social scientists. Several previous studies have explored the relationships among factories, companies, state enforcement efforts, and water pollution.[1] This follow-up research was conducted as an effort to better fit together different variables that might influence government outputs. The research both related to an important policy problem and was intended to broaden the scope of the state and local government literature on policy outputs: the passage of legislation and the expenditure of funds. The basic model is presented below:

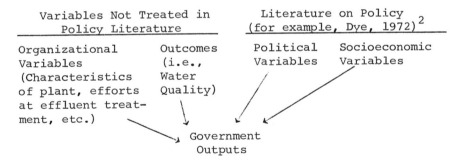

Variables Not Treated in Policy Literature		Literature on Policy (for example, Dye, 1972)[2]	
Organizational Variables (Characteristics of plant, efforts at effluent treatment, etc.)	Outcomes (i.e., Water Quality)	Political Variables	Socioeconomic Variables

Government Outputs

This chapter was facilitated by support from the University of Manitoba Research Board and Resources for the Future.

67

At the same time this research effort must be seen as preliminary. The policy literature has forwarded a number of
political and socioeconomic variables that might be considered. Only a few of these variables were used in this study.

This section is thus directed toward the "pure science"
of policy.[3] Particular variables may be shown to be important or unimportant regardless of whether or not they are
subject to alteration by policy makers. A more applied approach would emphasize those variables about which policy
decisions could be made; in this way, analysis would more
directly serve to help improve policy.

Two general tactics have been forwarded as useful for
analyzing the type of aggregate data typical of quantitative
correlational research on government outputs.[4] First of
all, size of the zero-order correlations provides a rationale for choice of independent variables. Such selection of
predictor variables from a pool of eligible variables raises
several general problems:

1. Selecting variables on this basis might also cap-
italize on measurement error. Random measurement error will
reduce the correlations among variables. Since some of the
variables eliminated from the analysis were probably measured with considerable error, this may have inflated the
perceived importance of variables measured with less error.

2. Some variables more theoretically interesting than
the independent variables chosen--and substantially correlated with them--may be eliminated from consideration for
the regression analysis on the basis of rather small differences in bivariate correlations.

One way to handle the above points is through cross-
validation, drawing a statistically independent sample and
analyzing it in a fashion similar to the original analysis.[5]
Substantive limitations of the data--that is, the fact that
a population rather than a sample is involved--do not permit
this. Data generated by a stronger research design--that is,
information from at least two points in time--would have permitted replication of the analysis and usefully contributed
to the discussion of measurement error. Unfortunately such
data were not available.

Another problem concerns the fact that the independent
variables involved are likely to be substantially intercorrelated. "Political" and "socioeconomic" variables associated with state governments are particularly likely to be
characterized by multicollinearity. According to J. L.
Sullivan, multicollinearity has sometimes been defined as a
particular level of zero-order correlation (.80) between two
supposedly independent variables, but a better definition is
that the zero-order correlation between the "independent"
variables exceeds their multiple correlation coefficient

with the dependent variable. To quote Sullivan directly, "multicollinearity is a problem because small errors of sampling or measurement (among the independent variables) can result in highly unreliable partial correlations, hence unreliable estimates of the 'independent effects' of various independent variables."[6]

One strategy proposed by Sullivan for dealing with multicollinearity is to look at the interrelationships between sets of predictors (political variables and socioeconomic variables in his example) and choose those having the lowest correlations with variables in the other set. Such a strategy may contradict the criterion of "highest magnitude of zero-order correlation" advanced earlier. Although the inter-set correlations are also subject to problems of measurement error, this strategy does seem of some utility. Unfortunately, the data set available in this preliminary study are not extensive enough to warrant using such a strategy.

Data Sources and Measurement

Questions of measurement are generally relevant. Information on water quality seems to be the weakest; correlations between two measures of water quality suggested by Wenner were quite low.[7] Factory and company-level variables concerning pollution were taken from a study by the Council on Economic Priorities.[8] The council's research appears to have been carefully carried out, but none of the standard statistical techniques for assessing reliability were used in its research. Estimates of certain variables were made and the researcher has no way to assess the reliability of the council's observations. Company financial reports provided the initial data base for _Forbes'_ analysis, which was in turn used here. Standard published and derived indices of socioeconomic and political variables were also utilized. The original sources are cited and the data discussed in Dye, Sharkansky and Hofferbert, and Walker.[9]

The indices of government output are derived from Wenner's study of water pollution control laws.[10] This study presented the indicators used to build the new indices; data on the reliability of Wenner's indices were not available. All indicators were converted to standard scores before being entered into the regression equations to make up the new indices. Weighting of indicators was based on factor analyses of indicators in the same issue area; more specific information is available on request. Information on the reliability of the new indices is presented in Table 7.1.

TABLE 7.1

Reliabilities of Indices of Government Outputs

	Number of Items	Split-Half Reliability*
Index of water quality standards	2	.61 (.44)
Index of legislative interest	2	.71 (.55)
Scale of strictness of law	5	.67
Scale of strictness of enforcement	5	.69
Scale of frequency of inspection	5	.73

Data from all 50 states were used to build these indices.

*The concept of split-half reliability is not really applicable when there are only two items on an index. Pearson product-moment correlations between the two variables are indicated in parentheses.

Source: M. L. Wenner, "Enforcement of Water Pollution Control Laws," Law and Society Review 6 (May 1972).

A second methodological question concerns the interrelationships among various measures of governmental outputs. As is seen in Table 7.2, intercorrelations among these indices are moderate, although the measures of legislative interest and strictness of enforcement is fairly substantial (.51). A principal factor analysis of this matrix indicated that the first factor (most highly correlated with legislative interest and strictness of enforcement) explained only 36 percent of the variance; the second factor explained an additional 24 percent. Thus, each of the indices will be treated as a separate dependent variable.

An analysis of the components of the indices and scales indicated that split-half reliability was roughly similar in the subsamples important for this research--those states having pulp and paper mills and states without such installations. There were, however, significant differences in mean scores between the two types of states. Such differences were particularly marked for the measure of strictness of laws, with laws being stricter in states with pulp and paper mills.

TABLE 7.2

Interrelationships among Indices of Government Outputs

	Index of Water Quality Standards	Index of Legislative Interest	Scale of Strictness of Laws	Scale of Strictness of Enforcement
Index of legislative interest	-.01	--		
Scale of strictness of laws	-.17	-.22	--	
Scale of strictness of enforcement	.07	.51*	-.38*	--
Scale of frequency of inspection	.05	.23	.06	.15

Pearson product-moment correlations are presented in this table; data from all 50 states were used.

*Indicates correlations are significant at the .05 level.

Source: M. L. Wenner, "Enforcement of Water Pollution Control Laws," Law and Society Review 6 (May 1972).

Substantive Analysis

Before discussing governmental outputs, the data produced from work on factory-level and company-level analysis can usefully be reviewed. A substantial amount of work was done on these variables, and more advanced analysis confirmed the earlier findings of weak relationships between factory-level and company characteristics on the one hand, and pollution control efforts on the other. It is worth speculating on why these relationships are so weak. Companies are making complicated decisions based on production facilities of widely differing types and ages. Available company data are at an aggregate level and do not provide an adequate picture of operations in particular areas.

Moreover, it may well be naive to expect that "good corporate citizens" can be identified relatively easily, particularly from the type of information that is available.

Turning to the work on governmental outputs, those variables not included in the analysis should be mentioned. These variables were rejected because of (1) weak relationships with the dependent variable(s) and (2) slight contribution to explaining variance in the dependent variable(s) when included in the regression equation. Not included in the final analysis were

1. factory-level variables relating to effluent treatment and residuals discharge—level of treatment (primary, secondary, or tertiary), BOD (biochemical oxygen demand) per day, BOD per ton of factory output. These data were from pulp and paper factories located in 26 states. Since the pulp and paper industry is such a significant source of residuals, these variables might have been important predictors of state government outputs, but this was not the case; and

2. amount of water quality change over time. This variable has been described by Wenner; essentially changes in four water quality measures in each state were measured between 1961 and 1969.

Turning now to the correlational analysis presented in Table 7.3, particularly noteworthy were

1. the consistent negative correlations between mean tons of paper per day per factory and various state-level policy outputs; and

2. the consistent positive correlations between state-level political and socioeconomic variables, on the one hand, and state-level policy outputs, on the other. These correlations are of roughly the same magnitude as those reported for other policy outputs.[11]

The reasons for political and socioeconomic variables being correlated with policy outputs have been discussed extensively elsewhere.[12] However, the negative correlations with the measure of average factory size—the tons of paper per day—bear discussion. There are several possible hypotheses here:

1. The correlation is spurious because of this variable's intercorrelation with such variables as degree of political competition. Partial correlation analysis does reveal that the factory size measure is significantly correlated with several of the policy variables, statistically controlling for the effects of other variables.

2. Smaller factories are more visible polluters; they do pollute more on a per ton basis.[13] Because of their visibility, states where such factories are located are likely to pass restrictive legislation.

TABLE 7.3

Interrelationships between Indices and Independent Variables
(N=26 states with pulp and paper factories)

	Tons of Paper Processed Per Day Per Factory[a]	Political Variables		Socioeconomic Variables	
		Political Competition[b]	Innovation[c]	Median Family Income[d]	Per Pupil Expenditure[d]
Index of water quality standards	-.46*	.57*	.49*	.56*	.54*
Index of legislative interest	-.63*	.28	.69*	.47*	.49*
Scale of strictness of laws	-.02	.06	.43*	.43*	.32
Scale of strictness of enforcement	-.58*	.52*	.58*	.63*	.39*
Scale of frequency of inspection	-.37	.33	.19	.32	.21

Pearson product-moment correlations are presented in this table.

*Indicates correlations are significant at the .05 level.

Sources: [a]Council on Economic Priorities, Paper Profits: Pollution in the Pulp and Paper Industry (New York: CEP, 1970).

[b]I. Sharshansky and R. I. Hofferbert, "Dimensions of State Politics, Economics and Public Policy," American Political Science Review 63 (September 1969).

[c]J. L. Walker, "The Diffusion of Innovations Among the American States," American Political Science Review 63 (September 1969).

[d]T. R. Dye, Understanding Public Policy (Englewood Cliffs, N.J.: Prentice-Hall, 1972).

3. Larger factories have more political clout and are able to prevent passage of legislation unfavorable to their interests. Additional data collection would be necessary to try to separate hypotheses two and three.

4. An underlying factor--such as degree of industrialization--is responsible for the results. There is some evidence in line with this possibility; mean tons of paper per day per factory is correlated .57 with level of industrialization.

Various efforts to construct multivariate regression and path models were undertaken. Multicollinearity presented definite problems; mean interitem correlations among "independent" variables ranged from .59 for political competition (with the other 4 variables) to .74 for median family income. As suggested by this multicollinearity and the bivariate correlations presented in Table 7.3, such models were difficult to work with. When standard techniques for "trimming" regression models were employed,[14] satisfactory models included just one or two of the predictors noted in Table 7.3. Of the five predictors presented in Table 7.3, innovativeness of state legislatures and mean tons of paper processed per day per factory were important for the strictness of laws measure. The two socioeconomic measures were significant predictors of strictness of enforcement. For the other dependent variables, models using one predictor proved appropriate.

These findings are of interest for public policy research for several reasons. Contrary to the author's earlier theorizing within the limits of the pollution problem in the United States several years ago,[15] magnitude of the problem does not seem to have markedly affected policy outputs in the water quality arena. The data on the small pulp and paper factories suggest that their visibility may affect policy, but only longitudinal evidence would permit stronger causal statements.

In summary, this cross-sectional study has explored a series of relationships between state-level variables, organizational variables, outcomes, and outputs. Identifying causal factors in such an analysis is hazardous, particularly when predictor variables are highly intercorrelated.

Discussion

The question of "where do we go from here" is very relevant. The data on the intercorrelations among variables and the problems in model building suggest that the causal relationships are still uncertain for environmental policy outputs. Efforts might be made to build more complex, multi-plicative models within the regression framework. However, these more complex models seem unlikely to reverse the substantive findings.

Considering additional "independent" variables and subjecting them to the screening procedures suggested by Sullivan may be useful. Level of industrialization seems to be a particularly "powerful" socioeconomic variable. Such techniques can be used, along with multiple-partial correlations, in an effort to further specify plausible causal relationships. The basic model presented below seems to fit some policy data,[16] but it certainly lacks theoretical interest:

Socioeconomic Variables ⟶ Political Variables
Policy Outputs

Some major questions of research strategy are involved. Arguments about the relative importance of variables that are based on minor differences in zero-order correlations seem particularly futile, especially given the possibilities for sampling error, measurement error, and so forth. Such discussions may also reflect weak theory and relatively unimaginative research strategies.

As an alternative strategy, I would propose the development and use of experimental and quasi-experimental approaches.[17] The substantive foundations of social science may not be as weak as Campbell has maintained,[18] but stronger efforts to identify causes and effects are clearly necessary. It is doubtful that significant progress will be made by pursuing the cross-sectional regression formulations characteristic of the state politics literature.

THE QUASI-EXPERIMENTAL OR OVER-TIME PERSPECTIVE

A recent review has noted several characteristics of evaluation research relevant for policy science.[19] Of particular interest for this chapter are the following points:

1. Uncovering the relationship between a policy and its factual scientific basis is critical, but "the policy social scientist has the added necessity of deciding among alternative policy choices."
2. Evaluation research for policy purposes requires an explicit statement of the time context of the findings.
3. Factors over which a policy maker has at least some control are of special concern.

Although values play a critical role in policy choice, policy-oriented research can significantly clarify the available options and evaluate the consequences of past decisions. One approach--that based on quasi-experimentation--seems suitable for dealing with the points raised by Levin and Dornbush.

The starting point for experimental and quasi-experimental designs is the basic pretest-posttest design:

$$O_1 \ X \ O_2$$

where O_1 and O_2 are the observations at times 1 and 2, respectively, and X is the experimental intervention--a treatment or event. As is discussed later, even if a strong difference is observed between O_1 and O_2, there are many plausible interpretations of such a difference. In an effort to better determine whether or not X (the treatment or event) actually caused the observed difference, a number of strategies have been suggested in standard works on research design:[20]

1. use of one or more control groups;
2. use of one or more additional experimental groups. Random assignment to experimental and control groups is often taken as a characteristic of true experimentation;
3. extension of the observations, both before and after the treatment (event) to provide more points in time. Such a series of data points is generally referred to as an "interrupted time-series" design.[21]

In quasi-experimental research, one basic technical feature of experimentation--an emphasis upon randomization and intervention--has been extended to deal with situations where these assumptions of experimentation must be stretched. The structuring of research problems in such terms, along with an effort to systematically eliminate plausible rival hypotheses, is the essence of quasi-experimental design. This section will deal with several issues relevant for policy research, using examples of particular importance for environmental studies. The topics include (1) developing a philosophy of quasi-experimentation, (2) highlighting useful quasi-experimental designs, and (3) discussing practical problems associated with the use of such designs.

The Philosophy of Quasi-Experimental Designs

Some general features of quasi-experimental designs need to be outlined. Quasi-experimental designs character-

istically revolve around interpretation of the effect of a
"treatment," conceived as an independent variable that may
or may not affect the dependent variable(s) being measured.
(This emphasis upon "treatment" or "event" is not found in
panel analysis, which presents a different approach to data
collected at two or more points in time.) A number of questions are raised by the above statement; the researcher needs
to know as much as possible about the nature of the treatment, when the treatment is applied, and to which units the
treatment is applied.

But in quasi-experimental situations, the questions
are harder to answer. First of all, "events" that take
place in the real, as compared with the experimental, world
are the usual "stimuli" in quasi-experimental designs. From
a theoretical point of view, such events are likely to be
multidimensional, incorporating several independent variables of interest. As will be discussed later, multiple
"experimental" and control groups are particularly useful in
interpreting quasi-experimental data. But developing such
relatively complex variations depends upon being able to say
which events are equivalent to which other events and the
important dimensions along which they differ.

There are further questions regarding events that need
to be discussed. An event is characteristically a "macro"
variable, a stimulus that must act through a complex chain
of behaviors in order to bring about a change in the dependent variable(s). (For example, one recent quasi-experimental study considers two types of "events" as independent
variables across 18 Black African countries: end of colo-
nial rule [self-rule or independence] and civil strife.[22]
Although careful and explicit measurement procedures were
used, a critic might still argue that civil strife in one
country was markedly different from such strife in another.)
To use an example from water quality research, a plausible
causal chain might be:

Change in Incentive Structure (i.e. change in laws, taxes, etc.)	→	Company Decision to Change its Effluent Discharge	→	Implementation of this Decision	→	Change in Effluent Discharged	→	Change in Water Quality (everything else being equal)

Many things can happen--or not happen--as an "event" or
"treatment" is reflected in such a causal chain. Coleman's
emphasis upon the "social audit" is essentially a call for a
micro-level examination of such chains:

> In a social audit, resource inputs initi-
> ated by policy are traced from the point at
> which they are disbursed to the point at
> which they are experienced by the ultimate

intended recipient of those resources. It
is then those resources as experienced that
are related to the outcomes in the research,
rather than the resources as disbursed.[23]

He has been particularly worried about an application in the
human resources area--the way resources intended to reach a
particular (deprived) group may be siphoned off in a bureaucracy.

At the micro-level, different treatments may be being
applied to different individual units or groups; the researcher must investigate in some detail to uncover the diversion of resources. Such a concern is obviously relevant
for pollution control. It is desirable to investigate the
micro-effects of each type of incentive program for pollution control.[24] Diversion of resources earmarked for pollution control is a widespread problem; Goldman has noted the
plant-level diversion of funds that were to prevent pulp and
paper waste from polluting Lake Baikal in the Soviet Union.[25]

An additional point concerns the need to thoroughly
document policy changes. Although most quasi-experimental
designs presume a sharp cutting point between "before" and
"after" conditions, policy changes do not occur overnight.
Specifying dates of change is full of dangers. In this
"gray period" when the policy change may or may not have occurred, some changes in one or more dependent variables may
begin. Since the basic statistical models for quasi experiments presume an abrupt shift between "before" and "after"
conditions, gradual changes can not be easily accommodated.
If data are collected frequently enough, and the "gray period" is long enough, the time period might be divided into
"before," "during," and "after" segments. Existing statistical models for long time series might be adapted fairly
easily to such a situation.

When the specific date of the relevant policy change is
in doubt, frequent data collection is valuable for several
other reasons. The more powerful statistical models are
based on a large number of measurements.[26] A short interval
between collection of the last "before" and the first "after"
data is also useful in reducing the plausibility of several
other rival hypotheses:

1. that these changes in the dependent variable(s)
were a normal pattern to be expected with the passage of
time ("maturation") regardless of the occurrence of absence
of a particular event.

2. that one or more other events occurring about the
same time were responsible ("history"). When there are multiple replications involving sites that differ in a number

of ways, the possibility of other events being regularly
linked with the "treatment" event is greatly diminished.
With specific regard to water quality, available data from
monitoring of U.S. rivers and lakes by the Environmental
Protection Agency are a rich source. Measures gathered on a
week-to-week or month-to-month basis are present for many
waterways and have been largely unexploited by policy researchers.

If complicated time lags can be ignored, a close correspondence between the implementation of a part of a new policy, on the one hand, and a shift in the value of the dependent variable, on the other, may provide clues as to which
elements of the policy are most important. Such a strategy
is risky because it can degenerate into "fudging" of the
before-after cutting point; one event rather than another
may be forwarded as important on a very ex post facto basis.
Without good theory to specify what part of the policy
change is critical, the data (that is, the dependent variables) may be relentlessly eyeballed in straining for substantive and statistical significance.

Problems of identifying the duration of an event have
been discussed above. A somewhat related question is "How
much of an event (or treatment) is necessary?" Both duration and intensity must be measured carefully to establish
the equivalence, or nonequivalence, of several seemingly
similar events. Only by comparing the impacts of a number
of events or treatments differing along measured dimensions
can important causal components of the treatment be isolated.
If effects are additive (that is, the more of an event or
treatment, the more effect), this may be highlighted by such
a strategy.

Measurement of dependent variables has characteristically received more attention than has measurement of
events, treatments, or other experimental variables. Measurement theory has concentrated on variables that may be
treated as ratio or interval scales. Campbell notes several
threats to validity that focus upon the dependent variable:

1. Instability: unrealiability of measures, fluctuations
    in sampling persons or components, autonomous instabil-
    ity of repeated or "equivalent" measures.
2. Instrumentation: in which changes in the calibration of
    a measuring instrument or changes in the observers or
    scores used may produce changes in the obtained measure-
    ments.
3. Testing: the effect of taking a test upon the scores of
    a second testing; the effect of publication of a social
    indicator upon subsequent readings of that indicator.[27]

The nature of environmental data suggests that most dependent variables are at least partially quantifiable. There are obviously difficulties in translating everything into a dollar figure suitable for cost-benefit analysis.[28] Although such setting of dollar values is useful for many purposes, it is not necessary for many quasi-experimental studies. Before-after studies using such nonfinancial indicators as amounts of various pollutants, numbers of visitors to a natural area, and so forth are valuable for many sorts of studies. Given the state of techniques for handling such quantitative indicators, it seems reasonable that one thrust of methodological work be directed toward better conceptualization of events and event-variable interaction.[29]

Relevant Quasi-Experimental Designs

One well-known quasi-experimental design, the interrupted time-series design, is especially suited for the analysis of environmental data. The author has used this design in two related studies of public policy and pollution.[30] A particular event or policy occurring at a specified time is posited as the independent variable; this event is measured in discontinuous terms. Either the event has not taken place (before) or it has (after). Essentially, a "burst of variance" in a variable (which may be defined at a very macro-level) is considered as the possible causal factor--the "treatment" or "event."[31] The dependent variable or variables are typically measured in ratio-scale fashion. The first step in probing the hypothesis that policy change or event is causally important in determining the dependent variable (perhaps level of effluent discharge) is to examine the shape of the trend line.

If the trend line is completely linear (and thus can be closely fit with a single regression line), the use of this quasi-experimental design is not appropriate. But if the trend is better conceptualized as two lines (one before and one after the event) which are significantly different from each other, the rival hypothesis of no difference between the before and after segments is rendered less plausible. Figure 7.1 presents a number of possible patterns of behavior of a time-series variable, illustrating general trend (line A), a cyclic pattern (B), random fluctuation (C), and "possible" true changes (D-G). Various statistical models analyze these lines according to a number of criteria.

Other hypotheses should be explored; comparative research is particularly useful in reducing the plausibility of rival explanations.[32] Thus, a particular event may be

FIGURE 7.1

Possible Patterns of Behavior of a Time-Series Variable

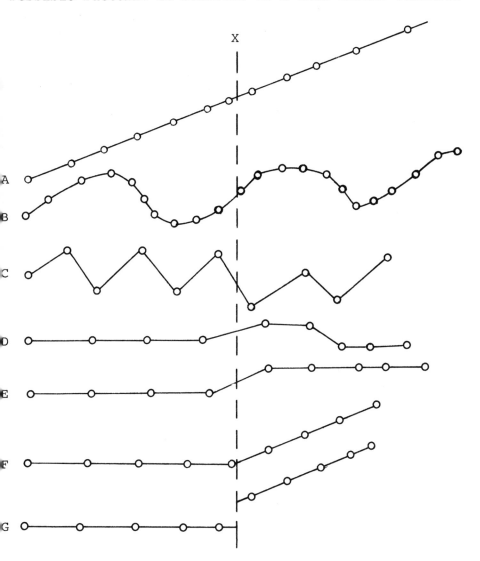

Source: J. Caporaso, "Quasi-Experimental Approaches
to Social Science: Perspectives and Problems," in
Quasi-Experimental Approaches: Testing Theory and
Evaluating Policy, ed. J. Caporaso and L. Roos (Evanston,
Ill.: Northwestern University Press, 1973), p. 20.

judged to have certain consequences (changes in one or more dependent variables) in a given site (river, organization, nation, or whatever). By a multiplicity of replications, by what Campbell has called a "control series," plausible rival hypotheses based on "history" and "maturation" may be down-graded.[33]

Up until now, the interrupted time-series design has been treated in accord with its general description in the literature. In this standard interpretation, an event is seen as affecting a variable; the presence or absence of such an effect is measured statistically.

The same longitudinal data used in the interrupted time-series design suggests another design, one where a shift in variable "causes" an event. Thus, two sorts of causal frame-works, both depending on the time-precedence of the independent variable, seem possible: (1) E (event) $\longrightarrow$ V (a change in intercept or slope of a variable); (2) V (some characteristic of a variable) $\longrightarrow$ E (event). Although a fair amount of systematic research has been done using the E $\longrightarrow$ V framework, the situation differs with regard to the V $\longrightarrow$ E framework. Although this latter model underlies much social science research, it has seldom been clearly articulated.

There are several logically distinct possibilities based upon the V $\longrightarrow$ E causal formulation: (1) the <u>level</u> of the variable led to the event, that is, the overall level of pollution led to the enactment of pollution control laws; (2) the <u>rising (or falling) value</u> of the variable led to the event, that is, the rising level of pollution led to legislation. The outline of possibilities clearly parallels the interrupted time-series design in terms of the treatment of level (intercept) or rising-falling value (slope) of a variable.*

Several points should be made here. First of all, the (independent) variable in the V $\longrightarrow$ E sequence might be at a macro-level, a level several steps removed from the direct cause of the event. Secondly, unmeasured intervening variables are often introduced into the analysis; in the above

---

*It has been suggested that the well-researched Connecticut crackdown on speeding was instigated by a <u>level</u> of traffic fatalities that was extraordinarily high in December 1955. Governor Ribicoff's action was taken on December 23, 1955 and instituted on January 1, 1956. "The December 1955 fatality rate which precipitated Ribicoff's action was higher than at any time in the preceding 60 months." A perusal of the 1955 data indicates that there may also have been a change in slope between 1955 and the previous years.[34]

example "public opinion" might be such a variable. Attempts to directly measure public opinion (favorable, unfavorable, or whatever) are desirable to buttress the analysis. Without direct measurement of an intervening variable, such an argument raises the possibility that (3) the <u>constant value</u> of the variable led to the event. This argument is weakened by the question: Why did the event not take place earlier? For example, the level of pollution might be constant, yet suddenly there might be a marked policy change. Answering this question leads one to refer to an unmeasured intervening variable, to some explanation such as "public opinion (unmeasured) was not yet vocal enough." In order to restrict such weak, ex post facto arguments, it is suggested that the "constant value" explanation not be accepted; measurement of intervening variables is particularly important in this case.

This discussion of the V ⟶ E formulation should consider some of the threats to validity of causal interpretations resulting from this design:

1. Inability to distinguish between <u>level</u> of a variable and <u>rising (or falling) value</u> of the variable as the predominant causal factor. Even cyclical phenomena might be important!

2. Several variables may have been involved in causing the event. Both might have to be present in order to trigger the event.

3. One variable may be able to substitute for another, perhaps in affecting an intermediate variable that is causally critical.

4. Another completely unrelated variable may have been responsible for the event. Its association with the variable being measured may have been fortuitous; except for its reversal of the E - V sequences this threat corresponds to what Campbell has called "history."[35]

5. "Maturity" might also be a threat. The passage of time might in due course have led to the event.

Questions of level and slope need to be treated more systematically than has been done thus far. If "slope"--the rising (or falling) rate of a variable--is proposed as causally important, the question of "why the event has not taken place earlier" remains relevant. If new data points are relatively close to the slope generated by older data, the "new" slope would not be greatly altered. The argument becomes one of a "slope of a particular magnitude extended over a given length of time." Obviously, level is affected by these "growth rate" considerations. One clue as to the importance of absolute level--beyond that expected from "growth rate"--comes from examining the residuals. If the

last data point is off the slope--markedly higher than a
rising slope, for example--then level would seem to be of
independent importance.

A multiple replication or "control series" strategy
would seem particularly appropriate, both substantively and
methodologically. This suggests replications across different sites or countries (or systems of other types) in order
to consider the possibility of other variables being operative. Only in this way can various competing hypotheses,
various threats to internal validity, be treated.

Some Conceptual Difficulties

A problem common to both the $E \longrightarrow V$ and the $V \longrightarrow E$
models is the level at which both events and variables are
often conceptualized. The strengths of the formulations are
their weaknesses: The "black box" approach to measurement
permits linking rather different phenomena, but does not allow the investigator to precisely specify causal linkages.
As noted earlier, this suggests the desirability of microanalysis to try to probe more deeply into possible causal
relationships. These event-variable approaches raise questions that will have to be discussed more extensively:

1. As noted elsewhere, variables can often be recon-
ceptualized in a way that has implications for both research
design and substantive findings.[36] Alternate reconceptuali-
zations need to be treated and explicitly compared.

2. Any research design has characteristic threats to
internal validity, characteristic plausible rival hypotheses
suggested by the approach. What additional types of data
may be necessary to help substantiate a particular causal
formulation?

A partial approach to the problems of feedback might be
gained by combining the $V \longrightarrow E$ and $E \longrightarrow V$ formulations.
For example, certain levels of pollution (V_1) might cause a
policy change (E) which then led to new pollution levels
(V_2). Each segment in this possibly causal linkage could be
studied according to the guidelines set out above.

Given the state of theory and measurement in social
science generally, a focus upon events seems most appropriate. The interrupted time-series design is particularly
suitable when longitudinal data on at least a single dependent variable--coupled with information on the timing of at
least one event--are available. Besides its relevance for
theory-building, the design seems especially useful for policy analysis, output evaluation, and so forth. As noted
earlier, various other sorts of information aid in dealing
with different plausible hypotheses threatening the $E \longrightarrow V$
causal interpretation.

Site Selection in Experimental Designs

Another set of issues concerns the choice of sites in which experimental and quasi-experimental research is done. The discussion is facilitated by a division of designs according to the presence or absence of random assignment to experimental and control situations. Two of the clearest designs will be presented first; then some less clear-cut designs will be treated.

The presentation might be clarified by an outline of the relevant types of variables:

1. Experimental variables that pertain to the experimental intervention. They are, of course, used as independent variables.
2. Dependent variables are affected (or not affected) by the experimental variables.
3. Background variables are characteristics of sites. The levels of such variables will vary across sites, but they cannot be manipulated in experimental fashion.

One clear-cut design is a true experiment with random assignment to treatment and control situations. There are many ways to elaborate on this basic design.[37] The advantages of randomization have been aptly summarized by Campbell:

> The magic of randomization is that it attenuates the causal threads of the past as they might codetermine both exposure to the treatment and gain scores. Randomization renders implausible innumerable rival explanations of the observed change by cutting the lawful relationships that in the natural setting would determine which person gets which treatment. This provides the persuasive "causal" interpretations made possible by experiments involving randomization.[38]

The researcher must select the criteria by which units are included in the pool from which experimental and control cases are drawn. Such random selection is, of course, performed before any experimental intervention is performed.

This most powerful type of design has been used in several areas of evaluation research other than environmental studies; a recent paper by Rivlin notes significant ongoing experiments in income maintenance, housing, health, and education.[39] Some of the reasons for such a lack of true experimental designs in environmental research are discussed later in this chapter.

Site Selection in Quasi-Experimental Designs

At the other end of a "randomness" continuum is the common situation in which quasi-experimental designs (often the interrupted time-series design) are used to structure the data analysis after an event has occurred. Data from a particular site(s) to which the event is presumed important are to be collected and the question of appropriate criteria for selecting control sites is relevant. Random assignment of cases to treatment and control conditions is obviously not possible. Instead, an effort should be made to obtain considerable similarity between the already chosen experimental site(s) and the control site(s). What characteristics of the control sites need to be specified in order to satisfy this criterion of "similarity"? A concern with background variables appearing to influence values of the dependent variables seems appropriate. A conservative approach is suitable; if possible, a number of sites that fall within a satisfactory range of values across the background variables should be chosen. The emphasis is upon finding several satisfactory control sites rather than the one that maximizes similarity between control and experimental sites. There are good reasons for this tactic:

1. Because of the retrospective nature of this research, the researcher may know some or all of the scores of dependent variables on possible control sites. Choice of the relevant background variables might be influenced by this knowledge, but the dangers inherent in trying to fairly select one control site given such information should be clear. The researcher's hypotheses about the influence (or lack thereof) of the event might bias his selection of the control site.

2. Selection of a single control site might well involve selection of the one physically closest to the "experimental" site. The possibility of diffusion of the effects of the event to contiguous sites could obviously hinder interpretation.

3. A single control site might be affected by idiosyncratic factors that could facilitate or dampen change in the dependent variables. The use of several control sites would thus provide additional increments of internal validity. If too large a number of sites met the criteria for control sites, random selection within this group might lessen this number in a satisfactory fashion.

Some examples of this quasi-experimental design are available. In addition to the previously mentioned research by the author,[40] the legal struggle against DDT has produced valuable summaries of experimental and quasi-experimental evidence on pesticide use.[41] But the quantity and quality of available research is hardly overwhelming.

Site Selection in "Intermediate" Designs

Random selection of sites for the testing of public policies seems relatively rare, even when the treatment is under the control of the individuals (or agency) empowered to experiment and evaluate. A number of political reasons underlie this "fact of life."[42] Policy makers feel under pressure to distribute experimental benefits widely. Moreover, administrators are often very concerned with generalizability and feel that systematic variation of background variables is called for. Government investment in waste treatment has often been criticized for helping to supply collective goods (clean water and waste disposal) in a way that does not provide appropriate incentives to users. Experimentation might be most useful here. For example, officials might want to know if a particular strategy for the construction and operation of waste treatment plants would be suitable for both highly urbanized and less urbanized areas. The background variable would in this case be "degree of urbanization." One intellectual problem with this tactic is the uncertainty as to what is changing when background variables are used; systems assumed to be similar along measured background variables probably differ along a number of dimensions. Sechrest has usefully expressed this design dilemma in terms of the "heterogeneity of irrelevancies," which is most important for generalizability, versus the "heterogeneity of relevant factors," which is often useless.[43] These concepts bear some resemblance to Przeworski and Teune's ideas of the most different and most similar systems design.[44]

Such variation in a background variable can be fitted within a framework utilizing randomization. Pairs of sites can be chosen according to their position on the background variable; then, one member of each pair can be randomly selected for the experimental treatment. This approach is illustrated in Figure 7.2. (Introducing as much randomization as possible into site selection is generally desirable. If sites are to be ranked along some variable, pairing sites with the closest scores and randomly selecting one site from each pair is preferred.) If an effort is to be made to evaluate the effect of a background variable, sites might be varied as much as possible along dimensions that informed opinion and previous research results suggest will not affect the relationship between the experimental (or quasi-experimental) variable and the dependent variables. Geographical location, a particularly sensitive political factor, may be such a dimension. But sites should be similar along almost all dimensions thought to affect the outcome. Only one dimension thought to affect the outcome should vary; obviously this is very difficult to achieve in

FIGURE 7.2

Pretest-Posttest Design with "Most
Similar Systems" Variation

Intervention
$\downarrow$

$\underline{T_1}$		$\underline{T_2}$	
A_1		A_2	Experimental Site
A_1^1		A_2^1	Control Site

Simple Pretest-Posttest Design with Control Group

Intervention
$\downarrow$

Low X

A_1	A_2	Experimental Site
A_1^1	A_2^1	Control Site

Intervention
$\downarrow$

B_1	B_2	Experimental Site
B_1^1	B_2^1	Control Site

Intervention
$\downarrow$

Nonexperimental
Attempt to Also
Study Effects
of Background
Variable X

C_1	C_2	Experimental Site
C_1^1	C_2^1	Control Site

Intervention
$\downarrow$

D_1	D_2	Experimental Site
D_1^1	D_2^1	Control Site

Intervention
$\downarrow$

High X

E_1	E_1	Experimental Site
E_1^1	E_1^1	Control Site

(Interventions take place only at the experimental sites)

practice. Inferences based on such nonexperimental variation will, of necessity, be weak. The main inferences will
concern the effects of the independent, experimental variable. (If the units are individuals, characteristics of
these individuals may partially determine whether or not a
treatment has an effect. The larger "N" in such research
may permit a statistical analysis, although causal inferences based on such background characteristics will not be
as strong as might be desired.)

Despite the potential utility of this strategy, it does
not seem to have been applied to any public policy studies.
Demonstration projects--perhaps run at several different
sites--are popular in environmental, health, and other issue
areas. But systematic evaluation taking advantage of explicit variation in site characteristics is almost nonexistent.

Discussion

This chapter has raised both theoretical and applied
questions relevant for future research. From a theoretical
perspective, new combinations of experimental and analytical
techniques to help structure different problems are most desirable. In particular, I would stress the need for a discussion of possibly appropriate designs and approaches that
emphasized the assumptions underlying each approach.

Questions of "design validity," of the extent to which
the underlying assumptions of a given approach are met by
the data, might profitably be discussed. Longitudinal designs that modify the powerful assumptions of experimental
research need to be treated from a design validity perspective. Design validity is important because the usual time
sequence of design⟶ data collection⟶ analysis is
often reversed in quasi-experimental research. Design assumptions may be changed on the basis of preliminary research results--an obviously dangerous procedure. Guidelines and trade-offs between different types of data collection and various threats to validity would be useful. By
addressing themselves to these questions, scholars will help
create sounder methodological underpinnings for policy research.

One of the reasons for this lack of evaluation research
may be the disciplinary backgrounds of researchers and funding agencies. Environmental research has been dominated by
engineering approaches, as compared with interdisciplinary
cooperation. Influences from the behavioral sciences have
generally been slight. A number of economists have done
valuable theoretical and applied work,[45] but little of it
has been directed toward program evaluation.

Some very useful work has been performed by Haveman who has tried to combine the ex ante thrust of economic analysis with an ex post concern for the actual results of Corps of Engineers' programs.[46] Haveman's work is most valuable; in another study he has systematically looked at some of the multiple objectives of water resource development.[47] At the same time, however, his research is subject to a number of criticisms from evaluation researchers with a "purist" bias:

1. Control sites are not studied. Thus, such threats to internal validity as history and maturation are not treated.
2. Much of the evaluation of projects is retrospective. Systematic long-term evaluation was not built into the project design. Because of this, there are gaps in the data and the data may be subject to a number of biases.
3. Wide variations in "events" and "treatments" make it difficult to equate one treatment with another.

Evaluation strategies need to be pitted against the feelings of administrators who must fund, read, and possibly implement research results. Deliberate suppression of results undoubtedly occurs,[48] but other administrative characteristics may be more important. Administrators may be neither "trapped" nor "experimental"; they are perhaps most likely to be "well meaning." Administrators are typically impressed, and often overwhelmed, by the richness and complexity of the environment with which they must deal. They tend to argue that every case is unique and are suspicious of efforts to generalize in the face of such variety. Such a perspective is compatible with the "social audit" approach discussed above.[49] A great deal of attention to measurement of treatments and events is undoubtedly necessary to overcome the argument that seemingly similar treatments may be administered differently.

Political difficulties make it unlikely that public works projects can ever be assigned on a random basis. Incentives for pollution control might be more susceptible to random or quasi-random manipulation. A compromise position might concentrate on the following themes:

1. Strategies for site selection and standardization of "events" and "treatments" should be developed by such relevant governmental agencies as the Environmental Protection Agency. Such strategies are necessary to improve the generalizability of research findings.

2. Time-series data collection should be built into programs requiring environmental impact statements. Envi-

ronmental impact statements might include detailed plans for collecting such data. Continuation of projects should be contingent upon such data collection.

3. The multiple objectives typical of large-scale projects should be spelled out and subject to monitoring.

4. This emphasis on over-time data collection suggests that preexisting time-series data should be used as fully as possible. Variations across sites in "treatment" and background variables may mean that each site be conceptualized as a more-or-less unique experiment. This is particularly likely until some overall strategies are developed. Such "N=1" situations require that each site serve as its own control and act to increase the importance of obtaining long time series.

5. The "no treatment" control site can be particularly useful in assessing the effects of history and maturation. Strategies for data collection in such sites might also be included in impact statements.

6. Implementation procedures involved in "treatments" of various sorts should be documented as fully as possible. Given the pressures for adapting administrative activities to local conditions, such documentation is especially necessary to help learn from ongoing programs. "Process" evaluation, the description of program implementation, may be useful here.

The goals of these proposals should be clear. They are directed toward realistically linking the concerns and constraints of administrators with those of social scientists interested in evaluation. The list of "dilemmas" forwarded elsewhere by Rivlin are very real.[50] Evaluation based on an experimental or quasi-experimental model is characterized by problems of design, implementation, timing, and so forth. Stragegies for dealing with these dilemmas are needed. Hopefully, this chapter represents a step toward developing such strategies.

NOTES

1. L. L. Roos, Jr. and N. P. Roos, "Pollution, Regulation, and Evaluation," Law and Society Review 6 (May 1972): 509-29; L. M. Wenner, "Enforcement of Water Pollution Control Laws," Law and Society Review 6 (May 1972): 481-507.

2. T. R. Dye, Understanding Public Policy (Englewood Cliffs, N.J.: Prentice-Hall, 1972).

3. M. A. Levin and H. D. Dornbush, "Pure and Policy Social Science: Evaluation of Policies in Criminal Justice and Education," Public Policy 21 (Summer 1973): 383-424.

4. J. L. Sullivan, "A Note on Redistributive Politics," American Political Science Review 66 (December 1972): 1301-05.

5. Q. McNemar, Psychological Statistics (New York: John Wiley, 1969).

6. Sullivan, op. cit.

7. Wenner, op. cit.

8. Council on Economic Priorities, Paper Profits: Pollution in the Pulp and Paper Industry (New York: CEP, 1970). Also published in a revised version (Cambridge, Mass.: M.I.T. Press, 1972).

9. Dye, op. cit.; I. Sharkansky and R. I. Hofferbert, "Dimensions of State Politics, Economics, and Public Policy," American Political Science Review 63 (September 1969): 867-79; J. L. Walker, "The Diffusion of Innovations Among the American States," American Political Science Review 63 (September 1969): 880-99.

10. Wenner, op. cit.

11. Dye, op. cit.

12. See, for example, ibid. and Sullivan, op. cit.

13. Roos and Roos, op. cit.

14. W. W. Cooley and P. R. Lohnes, Multivariate Data Analysis (New York: John Wiley, 1971), and P. Rao and R. L. Miller, Applied Econometrics (Belmont, Calif.: Wadsworth, 1971).

15. Roos and Roos, op. cit.

16. Sullivan, op. cit.

17. L. L. Roos, Jr., "Panels, Rotation, and Events: Some Uses of Quasi-Experimentation," in Quasi-Experimental Approaches: Testing Theory and Evaluating Policy, ed. J. Caporaso and L. Roos (Evanston, Ill.: Northwestern University Press, 1973).

18. D. T. Campbell, "The Social Scientist as Methodological Servant of the Experimenting Society," Policy Studies Journal 2 (Autumn 1973): 72-74.

19. Levin and Dornbush, op. cit.

20. D. T. Campbell and J. Stanley, "Experimental and Quasi-Experimental Designs for Research on Teaching," in Handbook of Research on Teaching, ed. N. L. Gage (Chicago: Rand McNally, 1963).

21. Ibid.; D. T. Campbell, "Reforms as Experiments," American Psychologist 24 (Summer 1969): 409-29. Reprinted in Caporaso and Roos, op. cit.

22. R. Duvall and M. Welfling, "Determinants of Political Institutionalization in Black Africa: A Quasi Experimental Analysis," in Caporaso and Roos, op. cit.

23. J. S. Coleman, "Problems of Conceptualization and Measurement in Studying Policy Impacts," a paper presented at the Conference on the Impacts of Public Policies, St. Thomas, U.S. Virgin Islands, 1971.

24. S. S. Nagel, "Incentives for Compliance with Environmental Law," a paper prepared for meetings of the International Political Science Association, Montreal, 1973.

25. M. I. Goldman, "The Convergence of Environmental Disruption," Science 170 (October 2, 1970): 37-42. Reprinted in Economics of the Environment, ed. R. Dorfman and N. S. Dorfman (New York: W. W. Norton, 1972).

26. G. E. P. Box and G. C. Tiao, "A Change in Level of a Non-Stationary Time Series," Biometrika 52 (1965): 181-92; G. E. P. Box and G. M. Jenkins, Time-Series Analysis: Forecasting and Control (San Francisco: Holden Day, 1970); G. V. Glass, V. L. Willson, and J. M. Gottman, Design and Analysis of Time-Series Experiments (Boulder: University of Colorado, Laboratory of Educational Research, 1973).

27. Campbell, "Reforms as Experiments," op. cit.

28. See the examples in Dorfman and Dorfman, op. cit.

29. See the ideas as expressed in such econometric texts as J. Johnston, Econometric Methods (New York: McGraw-Hill, 1963) and H. Thiel, Principles of Econometrics (New York: John Wiley, 1971).

30. T. W. Caldwell with L. L. Roos, Jr., "Voluntary Compliance and Pollution Abatement," in The Politics of Ecosuicide, ed. L. L. Roos, Jr. (New York: Holt, Rinehart and Winston, 1971); L. L. Roos, Jr. and H. J. Bohner, "Compliance, Pollution, and Evaluation--A Research Design," in Caporaso and Roos, op. cit.

31. J. Caporaso, "Quasi-Experimental Approaches to Social Science: Perspectives and Problems," in ibid. Also see valuable reviews of this design in H. L. Ross, "Law, Science, and Accidents: The British Road Safety Act of 1967," Journal of Legal Studies 2 (1973): 1-78, and Glass, Willson, and Gottman, op. cit.

32. Duvall and Welfling, op. cit.

33. Campbell, "Reforms as Experiments," op. cit.

34. Glass, Willson, and Gottman, op. cit., p. 56.

35. Campbell, "Reforms as Experiments," op. cit.

36. Roos, op. cit.

37. Campbell and Stanley, op. cit.

38. D. T. Campbell, "From Description to Experimentation," in Problems in Measuring Change, ed. C. W. Harris (Madison: University of Wisconsin Press, 1963), p. 213.

39. A. M. Rivlin, "Social Experiments: The Promise and the Problems," The Brookings Bulletin 10 (Summer 1973): 6-9.

40. Caldwell with Roos, op. cit.; Roos and Bohner, op. cit.

41. H. Henkin, M. Merta, and J. Staples, The Environment, the Establishment, and the Law (Boston: Houghton Mifflin, 1971).

42. D. T. Campbell, "Methods for the Experimenting Society," working paper, Northwestern University, Department of Psychology, 1972; N. P. Roos, "Evaluation, Quasi-Experimentation and Public Policy," in Caporaso and Roos, op. cit.

43. L. Sechrest, personal communication, 1973.

44. A. Przeworski and H. Teune, The Logic of Comparative Social Inquiry (New York: John Wiley, 1970).

45. Some of which is summarized in Dorfman and Dorfman, op. cit.

46. R. H. Haveman, The Economic Performance of Public Investments (Baltimore: Johns Hopkins University Press, 1972).

47. R. H. Haveman and J. V. Krutilla, Unemployment, Idle Capacity, and the Evaluation of Public Expenditures (Baltimore: Johns Hopkins University Press, 1968).

48. Campbell, "Reforms as Experiments," op. cit.

49. Coleman, op. cit.

50. Rivlin, op. cit.

Section

8

INTERNATIONAL RELATIONS
AND THE ENVIRONMENT
Robert Rienow

A trenchant picture of today's world is a bamboo juju hut in the forest lined with more than a hundred fetishes-- ugly little images clothed in many national costumes and presided over by the witch goddess Sovereignty. While the destroying hurricane approaches, the hut shakes, the trees bend and the sea roars, the members of the tribe prostrate themselves before their impotent juju gods, intoning their national anthems of worship, confident of being saved.

Unlike the dinosaurs and the flying reptiles, the woolly mammoths and prehistoric man himself, the brief so-journ of Homo sapiens has been no respecter of Earth's cosmic rhythms.[1] Indeed, we are told that man, as one species, has effected more changes in the evolution of the planet in the last 100 years than occurred in the past 3 billion.

THE FRAGILE GLOBE

That the world is sick needs little further diagnosis.[2] Whether its affliction is terminal and irreversible calls for more clinical analysis. But so far, politically, the institutional devices we have commandeered to confront this physical crisis of the biosphere are thoroughly outmoded. They are hoary relics of a bygone age that knew no need for haste or even expeditious action. The official international scene is marked by no sense of the crucial urgency it justifies.

We perpetuate an illusion of internationalism that culminates in placatory gestures and ponderous words. Meanwhile the world festers with its grievous wounds. There is a chance, therefore, that the crisis we are concealing may constitute in its very excesses a catalyst for institutional reform.

It is symbolic that the Parthenon, the Coliseum, St.
Paul's of London, and the Lincoln Memorial are all disinte-
grating because they cannot contend with the forces of modern technology: the acid-laden air and the pounding of the
trucks. The Western culture is being hammered to quick extinction by its own excesses.

But if the works of man are fragile, so more seriously
is the handiwork of nature. What is reputed to be the most
beautiful reef in the world on the shores of Israel is now
besmeared with oil, its intricate chains of life destroyed,
all because of the siting of a refinery as a part of the
world petroleum network. A new chemical plant on the French
island of Corsica is dumping its ugly wastes in the fast-
dying Ligurian Sea where Italian fishermen must now cut
bait.[3]

The port authorities at Ohammedia, near Casablanca,
have forbidden all fishing and eating of seafood as a result
of a spill of concentrated insecticide in the harbor. The
West German tanker, Papenburg, became disconnected from its
pipeline while unloading. The headlines announce that
"Chemical Debris is Fouling Vast Areas of the Atlantic."
The National Oceanic and Atmospheric Administration found
that an estimated 665,000 square miles from Cape Cod to the
Caribbean were covered with the debris of oil tankers and
chemical factories.[4]

All these are nagging reminders that the world commons,
the oceans, are in need of husbandry if we would, indeed,
conserve them as the breadbasket of the future. But it's
not only the oceans that are a common concern of mankind.
On all Earth there are, on the outside, some 4,500 tigers;
one subspecies is already extinct, five are virtually extinct (ten Javanese tigers are all that are left), one subspecies is doomed, and only one has a chance of being saved.
The extermination of a species is, in the view of intelligent men, a cosmic crime,[5] carrying as well some suicidal
implications. According to Dr. Lee Talbot of the Smithsonian Institution, man today is exterminating other species
of animals at a rate that is 5,500 percent that of 150 years
ago; if he keeps up this pace he will have eliminated all
the remaining 4,000 species of mammals over the next 30
years. That, of course, spells his own end. By any man's
measurement there is an unparalleled crisis of the biosphere.

ILLUSIONS OF INTERNATIONALISM

Admittedly these problems are universal in scope. If
all is collapsing, then, so the myth goes, surely world

leadership has set up agencies to try to contend with the crisis. Such is, indeed, a minimal expectation.

True, the world scene is speckled with institutions and agencies ostensibly equipped to grapple with issues such as the environmental crisis. Foremost among them is the United Nations itself with its galaxy of associated bodies. In the public mind there does exist the machinery for international government. Little is it appreciated that these assorted bodies are eunuched. The conclusion of a seminar on "Strengthening the United Nations" with a scintillating roster of attendants at the Rensselaerville Institute on Man and Science was reported by Professor Richard N. Gardner as follows:

> The public does not always appreciate that the
> United Nations is not a super-state but only
> an organization of sovereign states. Part of
> the problems of the UN could be solved by de-
> flating excessive expectations and promoting
> greater realism about the nature and capacity
> of the world organization.[6]

The presence of the United Nations and its agencies misleads the world public into believing that international decisions can be made to deal with the resources and the environment of the world. But the processes of the Security Council, for instance, revolve around confrontations of member and member. It would be unprecedented for the Security Council to debate and take action on the extermination of whales, the mercury contamination of the seas, or the dwindling rhinoceros.

A CLUMSY PROCESS OF LAWMAKING

As we continue to abuse the world with the crassest of brigandry there exists no expeditious lawmaking process whatever; nothing to reflect the critical nature of the crisis. In the first place, someone has to call a confer-ence; that is the ad hoc legislature convened to negotiate a single brand of agreements. Rules are agreed to through the bickering, tedious mode of treaty making except in very technical matters where the regulations might be promul-gated by an international organization such as the World Health Organization.[7] But in all cases the thesis is strict: No nation-state does anything it does not want to do. If it is going to affect tourism it is unlikely that a nation-state will accept even a quarantine for cholera.

Suppose the states manage, at long length, to get together in a conference. The delegates are in no sense popularly representative; they have been issued their credentials by the national executive, a fact that bears more resemblance to Sforza's Prospero in Louis XI's court than it does to modern democratic theory. Thus, a great welling up of public concern for the environment has no <u>direct</u> international outlet at all for its expression. The proceedings are standardized and formalized. But overshadowing the deliberations is the smug (and fatal) appreciation that no nation-state need abide by a treaty it did not sign, and that no nation-state need sign a treaty with which it is not in full accord![8] The premium is on obstruction. Each participant must be lured into avowed support of all proposals because of the fear that his government may refuse to ratify the treaty once it is made.

One is compelled by even the slightest scrutiny of the treaty-making process to underline its tragic unwieldiness in an age when so many people are milling so close to the edge of catastrophe. The premium is on delay, on procrastination, on sovereign irresponsibility, all deadly elements in our hair-trigger society of today. There is an anonymity in all that takes place; there are too many dark closets where knives can be plunged into the heart of a proposal without witnesses.

This incapacity of the system to respond to the environmental emergency was epitomized by the much-publicized United Nations Conference on the Human Environment at Stockholm in June 1972.[9] From the five-foot pile of preliminary reports came agreement on an Action Plan with little force, on the setting up of a functional organization to add to the illusion of internationalism, and on the pious adoption of the Declaration on the Human Environment, which gave more attention, indeed, to sovereign ambitions for development than to the world hazards of overpopulation.

Traditionally the substance of international relations deals with the elements of confrontation, nation against nation. So it is with issues of trade, of investment, of maritime competition, of exploitation of resources, of territorial claims, of security against one another.

ENVIRONMENTAL ISSUES AS A CATALYST

But the drama has changed. The adversary now is an outraged Earth, its natural cycles unable to absorb the wastes and poisons, its scalped surface bared to the pitiless sun, its water supplies shrinking, its oceans dying, its genetic heritage corrupted by mutagenic pollutants. This is the new international relations, not man against man, but mankind coming to terms with nature. If only this changed conception is grasped before irreversible damage has been done (and there are no signs of this), the environmental crisis may yet serve as the catalyst for launching a more meaningful international legal order.

In the interim what we need to grasp for is a lawmaking agency, a Survival Council, sustained by an intellectual constituency that still passionately loves Earth and its wonders, scientific and esthetic, and has at least a general understanding that Earth's wounds are indeed ours. This kind of crusading force has never in the history of the world been mobilized, but then, we have never had such a powerful communications network, nor such a threat of collapse. Wisdom in international relations must be urgently innovative.

Jujuism belongs to the dark ages.

NOTES

1. "Homo Sapiens . . . entertaining the illusion that he could manipulate, command and conquer it (the world) wholly for his own designs," Barbara Ward and Rene Dubos, Only One Earth (New York: W. W. Norton, 1972), pp. 36-41.
2. The eminent Paul B. Sears, professor emeritus at Yale, did a masterful diagnosis in a chapter of Michael Hamilton, ed., This Little Planet (New York: Scribners, 1970), pp. 11ff.
3. "Corsicans Still Seeing Red," Environmental Action, March 17, 1973, p. 7.
4. As reported by Richard D. Lyons in New York Times, February 13, 1973, p. 1.
5. For scientific substantiation see David W. Ehrenfeld, Conserving Life on Earth (New York: Oxford University Press, 1972), Chapter 9.
6. The Institute on Man and Science, The Journal 2 (1968): 3.
7. See "The Proper Law of International Organizations and the Future of Public International Law," C. Wilfred Jenks, The Proper Law of International Organization (New York: Oceana, 1962), Chapter 29.
8. Thus, the United States publishes the law as it has accepted it under such a title as "Treaties and other International Agreements on Oceanographic Resources, Fisheries and Wildlife TO WHICH THE UNITED STATES IS A PARTY" (capitals mine), Committee on Commerce, United States Senate,

91st Cong., 2d sess. (Washington: Government Printing Office, December 1970). See also Clive Parry, "The Law of Treaties," in Max Sorenson, ed., <u>Manual of Public International Law</u> (New York: St. Martin's Press, 1968), pp. 175ff.

    9. See Terri Aronson, "World Priorities," <u>Environment</u>, August 1972, p. 4.

9

ENVIRONMENTAL POLICY
AND INTERNATIONAL LAW
Clifton E. Wilson

"The basic issue posed by the environmental crisis is
how man is to manage the world's first technological civilization in which he has the power to shape his own future--
the power to create and the power to destroy."[1] These words
by Maurice F. Strong Head of the United Nations Environment
Program, would be challenged by few environmental experts.
But speculation on whether happy valley or doomsday lies
over the smoggy horizon would find these kindred souls in
sharp disagreement. The world may face population doom, environmental catastrophe, technological disaster, famine or
slow death by assorted land, water, and air poisons,[2] or
ecological collapse may be readily avoided if the world's
people would only buckle down and adopt problem-solving policies aimed at avoiding starvation or asphyxiation.[3]
While experts debate alternate futures, policy makers
--often feebly and futilely--attempt to cope with consequences of foul air and water. The ecological crunch is a
factual situation and this chapter starts on that assumption
in order to speculate on the role of international law in
environmental policy making.[4] Two other assumptions also
are relevant to the discussion that follows:
1. The environmental problem is truly global in nature and transcends political boundaries and stages of economic growth. Only if the biosphere is preserved can man
survive; national boundaries are no barriers to carbon mon-
oxide, sulfur dioxide, pesticides, and other noxious substances. International environmental policies must flow
both from international action related to the "common heritage of mankind" areas and within nations on ecological
problems that both directly or indirectly affect their
neighbors and the rest of the globe.

2. All people everywhere have the right to a quality
environment as is clearly stated in the Declaration of Principles from the Stockholm Conference in 1972 and in Human
Rights Conventions.[5] This right includes not only the en-
joyment of reasonably clean soil, air, and water but the
right to survive without the life-choking burdens of starvation, disease, and poverty.

The following propositions will be considered within
the context of these general assumptions:

1. International law is an integral part of the international system and should not be considered in isolation,
   especially from political forces.
2. Development of effective environmental norms is hampered
   by national adherence to the concept of sovereignty and
   a failure to recognize the critical nature of the ecological crisis.
3. Development of effective environmental norms is hampered
   by two basic political problems: (a) national adherence
   to the concept of sovereignty and a failure to recognize
   the critical nature of the ecological crisis, and (b)
   national failure to squarely face and attempt to resolve
   the conflict between ecological and developmental interests.

LAW AND POLITICS

The study of environmental policy has been complicated
and perhaps to an extent obscured by the proliferation of
diverse taxonomies, and for the social scientist, analysis
might best be undertaken within categories based upon political feasibility in achieving environmental policy goals.

Too often it is assumed that in environmental and other
policy considerations, law is separated from politics. Law
relates to treaties, customs, judicial decisions; politics
relates to diplomatic maneuvering, the exercise of power,
the realities of foreign policy. Such a presumption is not
surprising since the traditional emphasis has been on international law as a set of binding rules that invoke some
type of sanctions. Although this chapter deals essentially
with "rules"--or preferably norms--the multipurpose functions of international law also should be recognized. It
provides the basis for communication. Actually, national
decision makers would stand mute most of the time and diplomatic intercourse would be enfeebled without utilizing
the concepts of international law. Law also establishes
the parameters of state interaction; law is integrally

involved in procedure, process, and policy selection. But
its most familiar role is that of "rules."

The thrust of this argument is not that international
legal norms are inadequate, but that they are more effective
and extensive than might be presumed if analysis is based
upon the assumption that one international system exists,
that law, politics, economics, etc., are elements of that
system, and that it is difficult to distinguish law from
politics. A state response to a political action could be
more important in ascertaining existing "rules" than would
be a treaty that remains partially ratified, or a national
court case that might or might not reflect international
practice. Unfortunately, little study has been done on this
aspect of global rules.

The legal rule definition prevails because too often
international law is equated with domestic law even though
the neater legal-political lines of the domestic system are
obscured or eliminated in the decentralized somewhat anar-
chic international system. National laws are clearly defined and understood; international practices are often uncertain in acceptance; international treaties range from
weak guidelines to "strong legislation"; General Assembly
resolutions may range from pious pleadings to "quasi-
legislative" acts. For pure analytical purposes, a distinction might be made between legal, or law-oriented rules,
and political, or power-oriented rules. In this context,
the former usually are based on custom or convention, are
commonly observed or are considered binding, and are found
in the traditional sources of international law and thus
have some stamp of legitimation. The latter flow from state
interaction, are closely related to the national interest,
may or may not be widely accepted, and do not always meet
law-acceptance legitimation criteria. Within this context,
diplomatic immunities would be an example of the former and
spheres of influence an example of the latter.

However, a strict separation of what are known as legal
rules from political rules is artificial and unproductive.
Norms vary in content, validity, specificity, and function
as they are related to problems and issues. All international norms incorporate elements that are usually labeled
legal or political. The major difference arises directly
from the function they are intended to perform. This functional test helps to explain the variance between specific
rules such as international trading regulations and what
are often viewed as political understandings such as the
"cold war ground rules," some of which still apply to U.S.-
Soviet relations.[6]

In essence, it is difficult to distinguish law from politics. For example, Karl Deutsch has defined politics as "more or less incomplete control of human behavior through voluntary habits of compliance in combination with threats of probable enforcement,"[7] while Richard A. Falk notes that "politics is concerned with the management of human affairs."[8] It could be argued that Deutsch is defining international law and that Falk is explaining the concerns of the international legal system. It would be wrong to conclude from this observation that a course in international law would be the same as one in international politics. The latter deals with forces affecting the system such as nationalism, deterrence, etc., which is outside the direct purview of international law. The essential argument is that the narrow perception of rules, by restricting study to treaties, U.S. official statements, cases, etc., should be avoided in assessing the role of international law.

For analytical purposes, it is preferable to avoid political and legal labels and devise categories that can accommodate both law and politics as they are known, and that are based on norm similarity and predictability. This would involve both the function of the norm and the political feasibility of its creation and implementation.

NATIONAL SOVEREIGNTY

Political feasibility hinges upon the political limitations inherent in sovereign attitudes. Sovereign in this context refers to adoption of policies that are basically compatible with perceived national interests with international spillover, incidental or accidental, or at least of secondary importance. Ideally, the world should usher in a new ecological age, in the words of Maurice Strong, by adopting "new concepts of sovereignty" with "a greater sense of responsibility for the common good," which would preserve "the oceans and atmosphere beyond national jurisdiction for the benefit of all mankind."[9] Or people should endorse (as this writer does) the efforts of the world-order advocates to scrap the present system in favor of a new order that would be capable of heading off the global disaster[10] or replace the balance of power with "world power to balance the ecological crisis."[11]

However, national sovereignty is a fact of political life in the 1970s and people must retain their visions while recognizing that more limited action must be taken within the confines of the present nation-state system. The concept of sovereignty becomes more meaningful when applied to

specific problem areas. Nations bend their sovereign pre-
rogatives when concerned with such areas as the high seas
because the actual political price is often of little consequence and may, indeed, improve the national position. At
this level, "what distinguishes the law of environmental
protection from many other areas of international law is the
overriding extent to which it remains dominated by these two
laissez-faire principles [national sovereignty and freedom
of the seas]."[12] But when internal actions require sacrifices for the international good, only national sovereignty
remains as the distinguishing factor.

The problem of developing international environmental
norms is more than coping with national or individual selfishness. It also rests in part upon the failure of man to
alter his attitudes and remove the blinders that hide his
view of the cancerous environmental morass. Ironically, nations do recognize the potential tragic consequences of nuclear war while, at the same time, they discount the dangers
of ecological collapse. It is somewhat like the homeowner
reacting forcefully to fire while ignoring expanding hordes
of termites in his attic.

Both nuclear war and ecological collapse pose a threat
of global catastrophic breakdown, but the policy outlook
differs for each. Possible nuclear annihilitation has been
visibly and ably demonstrated by the United States at Hiro-
shima and Nagasaki and by major power testing. Human skele-
tons on a nuclear wasteland are easy to visualize. The
threat is readily perceived and national and international
preventive action taken. Also, nations could--although the
odds might not be high--maintain the nuclear balance, or a
modified version, under the present system.

In contrast, the threat to the life cycle from technological developments, population growth, environmental decay, and resource depletion is incremental and not easily
perceived. To the starving millions, the increasing pollution makes little direct impact. Much of the action is post-
crisis, such as the oil pollution conventions that followed
the Torrey Canyon disaster, or are adjuncts to other concerns.[13] People don their rose-colored glasses and conclude
that new scientific developments and blind faith, coupled
with a strong dose of optimistic fervor, will somehow head
off environmental disaster.

Again, as in the case of the sovereign state system,
an alternative is posed. Man must transfer his allegiance
from narrow national interests to collective needs.[14]
States must accept an obligation within their territories
to stop deterioration of the environment, restore the environment where it has already been sadly damaged, and

cooperate to avoid future pollution damage. Perhaps this
lesson was partially learned at Stockholm.[15] It may be that
man will awake to the fact that his self-interest is best
served by international environmental cooperation, just as
it may be that nuclear weapons never will be used. But in
the meantime, greater efforts should be made to ascertain
what small incremental steps might be taken that, at a minimum, would peck away at the edges of the ecological crisis.

Even if policy makers (and the public at large) recognize the seriousness of the problem, fully effective environmental law will never be achieved unless policy makers
honestly face and resolve the major environmental political
issue--the conflict between rich, ecologically oriented nations and the poor, development-oriented nations. Just as
international law arose and still is partly the captive of
the Western state system, international environmental law
arose from and still is partly the captive of the developed
nations. Antipollution treaties are commonplace; global
food guarantee treaties are visionary dreams. Both are essential to a viable environmental law.

The major dispute at the Stockholm Conference was this
conflict between rich nations and poor nations. (This is
not to imply that the poor nations are not able and ener-
getic polluters.) The dispute was exposed, analyzed, dis-
sected, and debated but not resolved because of the crucial
gap in national interests. Basically, the poor nations view
industrial growth as often incompatible with a clean environment and poverty as a more important issue than pollution. The poor nations view development, industrialization,
expanded trade, full employment, and better living conditions as prime imperatives. They fear that growth will be
hampered by the cost of pollution control, that trade will
be restricted by environmental controls, that Western political dominance will be perpetuated by population control
measures. And "some poor-world leaders fear that the Western countries will improve the quality of their life and
environment while leaving the poor nations polluted with
poverty, economic dependency, and quasi-colonialism."[16]

Furthermore, the developed nations' sometime grandiose
schemes for new international machinery and broader international agreements have little appeal for the poor nations
that lack institutions and trained people to carry out the
programs. The implementation of environmental programs in
the poor nations is a major obstacle to an effective global
environmental policy.[17]

The need is to identify the problems of the poor nations and adopt policies and codes of conduct that will improve the lives of their people. "Environmental considera-

tions cannot be made effective unless they are built into, and thus modify, men's so-called developmental activities.'"[18] It is not strange that many in the poor nations find environment irrelevant, if they are even aware of the issue, but also find much of the network of environmental agreements, which the Western world points to with pride as being at least the strong start of an international environmental code, as immaterial and irrelevant to their needs.

However, at least within the context of Western values, there is a mushrooming body of treaties, custom, and practices that deal directly with environmental issues. (However, we should entertain no illusions that the present system in any way--legally, politically, economically--is ready to cope with the ecological crisis.) A shift in focus from the substantive political issue to problems of analysis spotlights another problem: the need to develop a framework suited for the social scientist. Diverse taxonomies used by experts and observers in recent years often make it difficult to ascertain and understand the problem from a political and policy perspective.

Most observers would agree that the main components of the complex ecological problems affecting man's survival may be identified as overcrowding, food shortages, natural resource depletion, and pollution. However, while a majority of texts on international law are remarkably similar in legal categories, the analysis of environmental law is marked by varied approaches. In part, this reflects the lack of agreement or divergent emphasis on environment as an object of analysis.

CLASSIFICATION DILEMMA

The conceptual framework dilemma is illustrated by changing categories as proposed for the Stockholm Conference of 1972. The planners started with problems of human settlement, territorial problems, and global problems. These were revised to cover environmental aspects of human settlements, rational management of natural resources, and environmental degradation from pollution and nuisance. Finally the topics emerged as economic, financial, and social aspects, educational aspects of environmental issues, and international institutional implications of action proposals.[19] The final Stockholm Recommendations for Action are clustered under the following topics: human settlements management, natural resources, management, general pollution, marine pollution, educational, informational social and cultural aspects, and development and environment.[20]

The classification dilemma also is reflected in the varied approaches in the environmental literature. For purposes of illustration, some of these can be grouped under three broad categories: (1) the pollutant itself: by type of pollutant[21] or extended to include data on where those particular pollutants are found and how they are transmissed;[22] (2) characteristics of the physical world: by resources such as air and water;[23] by geographic divisions such as airspace and maritime areas;[24] or by the level of decision-making activity, usually international, continental, regional, and national; and (3) activities and impact: by the nature and scope of the international linkages involved[25] or by the arena that is affected most directly by environmental policies.[26]

The first category is of limited value for the social scientist since its divisions overlap in pertinent analytical areas and also since it is restricted to only one of the four major ecological concerns. The second category lends itself to legal and institutional analysis but is more limited for political analysis. The third category includes approaches with which the social scientist can be most comfortable. The environmental policy section of this chapter will utilize the activity-impact orientation.

Political feasibility for achieving environmental policy that leads to acceptable international norms will serve as the basic criteria in adapting an analytical scheme. The categories will progress from one within which national sovereignty and freedom of the commons permits the greatest political activity toward achieving common international environmental goals to one within which national sovereignty and national interest allows the least activity toward achieving these global objectives. The three categories are:

1. International: activities that occur on and affect the international commons (high seas and outer space).
2. National-International (Direct Effect): activities that occur within national borders but that directly affect other nations or the international commons.
3. National-International (Indirect Effect): internal activities that occur within national borders but that indirectly affect other nations.

Since political feasibility and functional possibilities for environmental action are key reasons for following such a scheme, it is hoped that it will provide a useful perspective within which to study international law and politics. Some brief generalizations, including illustrations

of recent _legal_ activities, will be made for each of the
categories, to be followed by observations on the state of
and prospects for further development of global environmental policies.

International Activities

Most of the existing international treaty law on the
environment applies to the commons, primarily because the
policy area lies outside of national jurisdictions and the
payoff is greater than any political price nations might
have to pay. There have been a remarkable number of treaties adopted since World War II that deal with the environment. However, most of this effort applies only to one of
the key ecological problems--pollution--while largely ignoring the other three: overcrowding, food shortages, and
resource depletion. Most of the international environmental
agreements are on an international basis, although some
dealing with oil pollution and dumping, for example, are of
regional character.[27] Several of these are concerned with
air and outer space. The Outer Space Treaty contains an
anticontamination article;[28] a major objective of the Nuclear Test Ban Treaty is to avoid contamination of the atmosphere, outer space, and underwater; and the proposed moon
treaty is designed to protect the lunar environment and
guard against contamination.
A growing network of conventions is designed to protect
the marine environment from oil and other pollutants. The
stage for this conventional approach was set by the Geneva
High Seas Convention, which requires states to take steps
toward preventing pollution from oil discharges and from
sea-bed exploitation,[29] and the Continental Shelf Convention, which requires states to install safety zones and protect the sea from harmful agents.[30] The London Oil Pollution Convention of 1954, as amended, bans discharge of oil
in prohibited zones--normally extending 50 miles from land,
a principle that hopefully will be extended to other areas
under a 1969 proposed amendment, not yet in effect. Two
companion conventions, adopted in Brussels in 1969 as a result of the _Torrey Canyon_ oil-spill disaster, permit coastal
states to act in the case of maritime casualties and guarantee compensation in case of pollution damage from oil-laden
vessels.[31] In 1972, the commons-oriented ecological campaign was extended by the London Convention, which is designed to prevent pollution caused by dumping of poisonous
waste at sea and supplements the earlier regional Oslo Convention. A companion London convention (1973) on the pre-

vention of pollution from ships covers all aspects of international and accidental pollution by oil, noxious substances
carried in bulk, sewage, and garbage. Both conventions were
sponsored by the Intergovernmental Maritime Consultative Organization.

An exception to the international approach is Canada's
antipollution regulations covering oil transport through the
Northwest Passage. But even in this case, Canada claims
that its action was taken to prevent damage to the environment during the interim period until international agreement
is achieved, although the United States objected to what it
viewed as unilateral extension of jurisdiction into the international commons.[32]

National International (Direct Effect)

In contrast with the first category where both the
arena and instrument of action were international, efforts
in this more restricted policy area tend to be bilateral and
regional. Pollution remains the major policy topic.

The bilateral agreements deal with specific problems
where national interests coincide. A pioneering effort was
the International Joint Commission established by the U.S.-
Canadian Boundary Waters Treaty of 1909 that provides that
waters on either side of the boundary should not be polluted.[33] The commission has a modest record in dealing with
pollution but did participate in the planning and conclusion
of a water quality agreement between the two states. The
Soviet-U.S. Environmental Protection Agreement of 1972 calls
for studies and possible future action on a wide range of
environmental and technological issues. Both the U.S.-
Soviet agreement and the later clear-water pact between the
United States and Canada appear to be of the showcase variety. The Soviet agreement was one of a number of agreements
signed during President Nixon's visit to Moscow in 1972.
Its intent may have been more political than legal, but both
it and the Canadian pact do catch the environmental spirit
of the times.

Two-state conflicts also have given the international
community what appears to be about its only case law on pollution. The International Court of Justice, in a dispute
between Great Britain and Albania, held that a state is
obligated not to allow knowingly the use of its territory
for acts contrary to rights of other states. This general
rule also emerges in two other decisions. The Trail Smelter
Arbitration, a permanent fixture for all articles on global
pollution, establishes a national responsibility for wayward

smoke wafting across a border and damaging crops in a neigh-
boring state. By analogy, the principle could be applied to
brackish river water and other water- and air-borne pollutants. And in the Lake Lanoux Arbitration, it was held that
French river alterations should not have adverse effects on
water quality and quantity in Spain.[34]
    Nations also have entered into regional agreements to
curb pollutants, but virtually all of these pacts involve
European nations. Perhaps the best known is the International Commission for the Protection of the Rhine Against
Pollution, which has played a role in construction of
sewage-treatment and purifying plants, has agreed on procedures to cope with waste salts from potassium mines, and
has considered without action questions of thermal pollution.
Other European cooperative efforts are concerned with detergents and air pollution (in both Western and Eastern
Europe). Both the Council of Europe and the European Economic Community have been active in promotion, conferences,
and studies.[35]
    In addition, numerous nations have entered into bilat-
eral agreements on air pollution and protection of inland
multinational waters that call for activities ranging from
consultation to action programs. These arrangements, when
coupled with basic environmental laws that are in force
within nations, add considerably to an environmental code.[36]
Obviously, any actions within a nation such as those curbing industrial smoke or automobile fumes will enhance the
quality of the biosphere to the advantage of all. However,
these policy steps are limited largely to pollution, fall
far short of reversing the trend toward environmental damage, and do little to cope with the remaining three ecological crises--overcrowding, food shortages, and resource depletion.

National-International (Indirect Effect) Activities

    Here again, national action has been limited largely to
coping with pollution and, in most cases, appears to be motivated directly by national needs with far less emphasis on
international interests. In reality, international politics
and law may face the greatest challenge in nonpollution
areas where one nation has an impact on another by way of
foreign trade, foreign investment, foreign aid, or any social or economic policy that normally transcends national
frontiers.[37] But if attention is limited to the pollution
area, even the most casual observer would find development
at a primitive level.

Control of chlorinated hydrocarbon pesticides (including DDT, dieldrin, and endrin) is an example. Some nations (Hungary, Sweden, Denmark) have banned the use of DDT, but the pesticides still enter the atmosphere, usually as pest control sprays, and in waters from agricultural area runoffs into the marine environment. Control depends upon discontinuing their use. The issue is not legal per se but partly economic and partly political. Most of the pesticides are manufactured in industrial countries, but the use is widespread in tropical areas where the claimed need still exists for malaria control.

Another pollution example is the discharge of domestic and industrial wastes that spawn destructive red tides, poison marine life, and contaminate coastal and deep-sea areas. The discharge of these wastes is likely to continue as populations cluster more and more along coastal areas, as industrialization spirals, and as nuclear power plants are built to meet energy requirements.[38] The task of controlling these wastes is complex and diverse. Sane international environmental policies clash with national political and economic goals and globally effective measures have been largely nonexistent.

ENVIRONMENTAL POLICY

Again, as noted in the previous section on direct effect, national actions can indirectly affect the general environment. Also the United Nations, operating within the rigid financial limits imposed by its national benefactors, has been impressive. Efforts of the United Nations and specialized agencies dealing with population, food, health, economic development--and now the environment--have made inroads into the problem. But only the most optimistic would maintain that nations themselves have taken significant environmental action to curb human expansion, redress economic inequities, and guarantee the good life for the world's majority who cling to poverty existence. Effective measures require political action and individual sacrifices that place global above personal or national interests.

This may not come about until nations adopt a social policy anticipating and avoiding injury in place of the present policy favoring freedom of action. An example given by one writer is the pollution of the atmosphere by exhausts of SSTs. Potential victims are not aware of the dangers or the consequences even though "the possible environmental damage is of such magnitude as to possibly endanger life on earth." However, under the freedom of action social policy

114

found in the United States and other countries, principles of law do not permit action unless a victim or potential victim appears to prove injury or threatened injury.[39]

Effective measures will depend both upon anticipating and avoiding--under treaty arrangements--harmful effects of products and technologies and upon recognition of the grim environmental implications of the facts that 10,000 people in the world die every day from malnutrition and 200,000 are added daily to the global population--a growth rate of 70 million a year. In considering the special problem of weather modification, one writer has observed that the classical form of law through claims, negotiation, and evolution of custom is too slow, too limited, and too uncertain.[40] The need is for a better understanding of existing state policy and global agreements on substantial changes in internal policies.[41]

Hopefully, the spirit of the Stockholm Conference and the calls of the new environmental agency from its African headquarters will nudge nations toward a more complete ecological code of conduct. In his most recent report, Maurice Strong has again pleaded for a change in man's economic and social attitudes if he is to manage successfully "the critical relationships with the natural environment."[42] Evidence of this change is difficult to detect. Nations have made some progress in recent years toward creating an international environmental code but with varied results in the three arenas.

The most productive arena of policy making has been regulation of activities in the international commons where there is the least threat to national sovereignty. Most nations support, to varying degrees, the modest number of formal agreements that deal with oil, radioactive fallout, and other pollutants. Advance in this area has been limited primary to antipollution measures, and the future agenda appears to be restricted.

The second most productive policy-making arena is the national-international (direct effect). Pollution again is the principal target; policy making is at the bilateral and regional level with Europe the major action area for multilateral arrangements. Individual national environmental policy also has been a contributing factor. Future efforts probably will extend along similar lines but with some continued attempts, as have already been made under European Community programs, to resolve population, food, and resource issues.

The least productive policy-making arena is the national-international (indirect effect). Only minor gains have been made in promoting an international environmental code, especially outside (but including) the pollution issue. In this arena the threat to national sovereignty is greatest, but in this arena lies the hope (whatever it might be) for policies that will permit global assaults on overcrowding, food shortages, and resource depletion. Unfortunately, threat to human environment is closely linked and remains secondary to policies flowing from the concept of state sovereignty.[43]

The need is not for greater technical research but for social-science analysis that might facilitate matching of proper policy with functional requirements. These policies should be based in an environmental world as a physio-economic-social unit unhampered by political frontiers. The function of law is to balance the exclusive demands of states (national interests) with the inclusive demands of the world community (international interests).[44] Even a myopic vision of world order might suffice as a start.

It also is imperative that legalists not lose touch with political reality. Hopefully that has been a major message of this chapter. This is not an isolated plea.[45] A colleague has warned: "We should not lose touch with the political realities (some with new dimensions) of the milieu upon which international agreement must rest [and] not have any illusions about the adequacy of current international law to control environmental abuse (especially in light of the tremendous international implications)."[46]

Further, despite all of the bilateral, regional, and international agreements that have been extensively analyzed by the most proficient observers, the degree of normal development and acceptance and the dimensions of the environmental problem are not fully known. "At the beginning of 1971," one environmentalist noted, "very little was known in a systematic way about the specific reactions of governments around the world to the emergent crisis of the environment."[47] The same statement holds true at the beginning of 1974.

For example, the customary rule of nonallowance of state territory to cause injury in another state may be "pseudointernational law of environment" since the stated doctrine relates "only to particular situations" and upholds "national, rather than international, rights and interests."[48] This judgment may be overly harsh but certainly customary rules now existent do not protect against long-range global deterioration in most of the major ecological crisis areas. In fact the nature and extent of these norms really are not known.

Further, current conventional law is extensive, but adherence to the law and effectiveness of its application falls within a patchwork pattern. Some conventions are not

in force; others carry the endorsement of only a few nations. Realistically, ratification is not always the major
indicator; but state adherence, formal or informal, is. For
example, the United States has a sorry record in ratifying
human rights conventions but its policies are far more important than its formal legal procedures in ascertaining its
support of such international principles as free speech,
genocide, and racial discrimination. The need is not to
downgrade the existing conventional arrangements but to attempt to determine what state policies and practices actually are followed. An analogy might be drawn with the Cuban
missile crisis. Probably no crisis in modern times has been
subjected to such careful, extensive, and detailed legal
analysis to determine if U.S. action was within the limits
of international law, and if the quarantine was legal. All
the basic legal notions--self defense, collective defense,
intervention, etc.--have been argued at great length. But
what is not known is general state response to the U.S. re-
visionist policy: conversion of the legal doctrine of pacific blockade into a new doctrine of quarantine. This
knowledge is crucial in assessing the state of this norm of
sea law. So it is for environmental law. It should not become isolated within the framework of assorted conventions.

International law, within the context of international
politics, is a vital key in developing an international environmental code of conduct. And understanding of political
realities, and new approaches within a framework of policy
possibilities, might enhance this development.

                            NOTES

    1. Maurice F. Strong, "The United Nations and the En-
vironment," in World Eco-Crisis, ed. David A. Kay and Eu-
gene B. Skolnikoff (Madison: University of Wisconsin Press,
1972), p. 4.
    2. See, for example, Rachel Carson, Silent Spring
(Boston: Houghton Mifflin, 1962); Barry Commoner, The Closing Circle (New York: Alfred A. Knopf, 1971); Paul R.
Ehrlich, The Population Bomb (New York: Ballantine, 1968);
William and Paul Paddock, Famine 1975 (Boston: Little,
Brown, 1967); and Donella H. Meadows et al., The Limits to
Growth (New York: Universe Books, 1972).
    3. This more optimistic view probably is best ex-
pressed by John Maddox, The Doomsday Syndrome (New York:
McGraw-Hill, 1972).
    4. This chapter deals with some general issues in-
volving international law and environmental policy and is
not intended either as a review of the literature or as an

analysis in depth of existing international environmental law. For a helpful study on law and the environment see John Lawrence Hargrove, ed., Law, Institutions and the Global Environment (Dobbs Ferry, N.Y.: Oceana, 1972). More general international environmental problems are covered in a large body of recent literature. Among the more useful are Peter Albertson and Margery Barnett, eds., Managing the Planet (Englewood Cliffs, N.J.: Prentice-Hall, 1972); Lynton K. Caldwell, In Defense of Earth: International Protection of the Biosphere (Bloomington: Indiana University Press, 1972); Richard A. Falk, This Endangered Planet: Prospects and Proposals for Human Survival (New York: Random House, 1971); Kay and Skolnikoff, op. cit.; Meadows et al., op. cit.; Harold and Margaret Sprout, Toward a Politics of the Planet Earth (New York: Van Nostrand Reinhold, 1971); Eugene B. Skolnikoff, The International Imperatives of Technology (Berkeley: University of California Press, 1972); Albert E. Utton and David H. Henning, Environmental Policy: Concepts and International Implications (New York: W. W. Norton, 1972); and Thomas W. Wilson, Jr., International Environmental Action: A Global Survey (New York: Dunellen, 1971).

The "explosion" of pollution articles has not left lawyers or political scientists in its wake. The existing literature is far too vast to cite. Perhaps representative is the considerable number of journal issues devoted to environmental law, many of them the results of environmental conferences. Among those found by this writer to be very useful were "A Conference on International Law and Pollution," Oregon Law Review 50 (Spring 1971): 223-598; "Human Environment: Toward an International Solution: Symposium," Natural Resources Journal 12 (April 1972): 131-285; "The International Legal Aspects of Pollution [Symposium]," University of Toronto Law Journal 21 (1971): 173-251; "(Symposium on International Environmental Law)," Natural Resources Journal 13 (April 1973): 177-390; and "Symposium on International Protection of the Environment," Texas International Law Journal 7 (Summer 1971); 1-118. The American Society of International Law also has included the topic on its annual meeting agenda: "The United Nations and the Environment," American Journal of International Law 64 (September 1970): 211-38; and "Post-Stockholm: Influencing National Environmental Law and Practice Through International Law and Policy," American Journal of International Law 66 (September 1972): 1-14.

5. Principle 1 of the United Nations Conference on the Human Environment held in Stockholm in 1972 reads in part: "Man has the fundamental right to freedom, equality and adequate conditions of life, in an environment of a

quality that permits the life of dignity and well-being, and
he bears a solemn responsibility to protect and improve the
environment for present and future generations." United Nations, Center for Economic and Social Information at U.N.
European Headquarters, Environment: Stockholm (Geneva,
1972), p. 11. The pledge for this basic human right also
is found in the Universal Declaration on Human Rights, Art.
25 (1), and in the Covenant on Economic, Social and Cultural
Rights, Art. 11(1).

   6. This "rules of the game" concept of law has been
developed rather extensively by Edward J. McWhinney. See,
for example, his "Peaceful Coexistence" and Soviet-Western
International Law (Leyden: Sythoff, 1964). For an excellent discussion of the "law-in-action" approach taken by
McWhinney and others, see Chapter 1 in Irvin L. White,
Decision-Making for Space (West Lafayette, Ind.: Purdue
University Press, 1970). This writer has discussed the
law-politics "rule" dilemma at some length with Professor
White of the University of Oklahoma, and his contribution
certainly is reflected in this analysis.

   7. "On the Concepts of Politics and Power," Journal
of International Affairs 21, no. 2 (1967): 232 (his emphasis). Cited from Anthony D. D'Amato, "Classical Theories of Jurisprudence and Their Relevance to World Politics," a paper delivered before the American Political
Science Association, 1967, p. 10. D'Amato called attention
to the fact that this description of politics came close to
a definition of international law.

   8. Falk, op. cit., p. 93.

   9. Environment: Stockholm, op. cit., p. 11.

   10. Plans for a new world order have been extensively
promoted in publications in recent years by the Institute
of World Order (formerly the World Law Fund). For more
specific application to world order and the environment,
see Falk's Endangered Planet, op. cit. He has reiterated
the same theme in numerous articles. See his "Toward
Equilibrium in the World Order System," American Journal
of International Law 64 (September 1970): 217-24, "Environmental Policy as a World Order Problem," Natural Resources Journal 12 (April 1972): 161-71, and "Toward a
World Order Respectful of the Global Environment," Environmental Affairs 1 (January 1971): 251-65.

   11. E. Thomas Sullivan, "The Stockholm Conference: A
Step Toward Global Environmental Cooperation and Involvement," Indiana Law Review 6, No. 2 (1972): 282.

   12. Hargrove, op. cit., p. 93.

   13. Oil pollution and ocean dumping of radioactive
wastes are regulated by the Geneva Convention on the High
Seas; scientific research is dealt with in the Convention

on the Continental Shelf; and nuclear explosions, dumping of nuclear wastes, and preservation and conservation of living resources are included in the Antarctic Treaty of 1959. These points are made by Samuel A. Bleicher, "An Overview of International Environmental Regulation," Ecology Law Quar-terly 2 (Winter 1972): 2. His article (pp. 1-90) is one of the best detailed discussions of this question within a structured conceptual framework.

14. Ward and Dubos, op. cit., p. 218.

15. See John B. Yates, "Unilateral and Multilateral Approaches to Environmental Problems," University of Toronto Law Journal 21 (1971): 189. The blueprint for the world's ecological future was designed in some detail in the United Nations Conference on the Human Environment held in Stock-holm, June 5-16, 1972. For a summary of resolutions and other activities, see Environment: Stockholm, op. cit. The U.S. approach is detailed in a report of the Secretary of State Advisory Committee on the Stockholm Conference, U.S. Department of State, Stockholm and Beyond (Washington, D.C., 1972).

16. Quotation and essence in this paragraph from Sullivan, op. cit., pp. 271-72.

17. Alan R. Kasdan, "Third World War-Environment ver-sus Development?," Record of the Association of the Bar of the City of New York 26 (June 1971): 461.

18. Lynton K. Caldwell, "The Changing Structure of International Policy: Needs and Alternatives," Natural Re-sources Journal 12 (April 1972): 155.

19. Bleicher, op. cit., p. 3.

20. Environment: Stockholm, op. cit., pp. 4-11. See also Louis B. Sohn, "The Stockholm Declaration on the Human Environment," Harvard International Law Journal 14 (Summer 1973): 423-515. Sohn traces the main steps of the intri-cate legislative process through which agreement was reached on the Declaration and also analyzes the text of the Declaration in detail.

21. Liquid or solid waste disposed in the marine en-vironment or on land; air pollution (sulfur dioxide, nitro-gen oxides, hydrocarbons, particulates), thermal pollution, radiation hazards, the oxygen-carbon dioxide balance and the nitrogen cycle, and pesticides, defoliants, and other chemicals found unacceptably harmful to man or his environ-ment. Gerald L. Morris, "The Dimensions of the Environmen-tal Problem," University of Toronto Law Journal 21 (1971): 177.

22. Particular pollutants (radioactive materials, oil, other toxic substances); the medium of transmission (rivers, oceans, airspace), and the source of pollution. See Bleicher, op. cit., p. 2.

23. Renewable (air, water), nonrenewable (coal and most other minerals), and combination of resources (ecological systems). See Dante A. Caponera, "Towards a New Methodological Approach in Environmental Law," Natural Resources Journal 12 (April 1972): 134-36.

24. Territorial environment, including rivers and internal waters but excluding national airspace and marine "territory," airspace environment, outer space environment, and marine environment. E. D. Brown, "The Conventional Law of the Environment," Natural Resources Journal 13 (April 1973): 210-34. A modification of this scheme includes a category to accommodate the important economic and trade problem that is largely ignored by most environmentalists: pollution through the atmosphere; pollution through water bodies--rivers, lakes, and oceans; and, finally, pollution that arises through international transfer of goods, especially through trade. C. I. Jackson, "The Dimensions of International Pollution," Oregon Law Review 50 (Spring 1971): 223-43.

25. Physical-linkage effects, including global and regional; and social-linkage effects, including pecuniary and nonpecuiniary. Clifford S. Russell and Hans H. Landsberg, "International Environmental Problems--A Taxonomy," Science 172 (June 25, 1971): 1308-11.

26. Those activities physically affecting other states, those affecting shared resources, and national environmental legislation affecting global economic activities. This classification is used by Bleicher in a detailed analysis of the environmental problem. Bleicher, op. cit., pp. 1-90.

27. See, for example, the Bonn Agreement for the Cooperation in Dealing with Pollution of the North Sea by Oil (1969). Entered into force August 9, 1969 (1970), International Legal Materials 9 (March 1970): 359.

28. Art. 9: ". . . State Parties to this Treaty shall pursue studies of outer space, including the moon and other celestial bodies, and conduct exploration of them so as to avoid their harmful contamination and also adverse changes in the environment of the Earth resulting from the introduction of extra terrestrial matter and, where necessary, shall adopt appropriate measures for this purpose. . . ." Treaty on Principles Governing the Activities of States in the Exploration and Use of Outer Space, including the Moon and other Celestial Bodies (1967), 18 U.S. Treaties and Other International Agreements (UST) No. 2410; Treaties and Other International Acts Series (TIAS) 6347.

29. Art. 24: "Every State shall draw up regulations to prevent pollution of the seas by the discharge of oil from ships or pipelines or resulting from the exploitation

and exploration of the sea-bed and its subsoil, taking account of existing treaty provisions on the subject." Geneva Convention on the High Seas, April 28, 1958, 13 UST 2312; TIAS 5200; 450 U.N. Treaty Series 82.

30. Art. 5(7): "The coastal State is obliged to undertake in the safety zone all appropriate measures for the protection of the living resources of the sea from harmful agents." (These zones are established for installations and devices on the Continental Shelf.) Geneva Convention on the Continental Shelf, April 29, 1958, 15 UST 471; TIAS 5578; 499 U.N. Treaty Series 311.

31. For a discussion of these conventions, see Brown, op. cit., pp. 222-24.

32. The Canadian legislation is reproduced in International Legal Materials 9 (May 1970): 543-54. The same issue contains statements by the U.S. and Canadian governments.

33. Art. (4(2): "It is further agreed that the waters herein defined as boundary waters and waters flowing across the boundary shall not be polluted on either side to the injury of health or property on the other." Boundary Waters Treaty of 1909, UST No. 548. The 1973 U.S.-Mexican arrangement, under which the United States agreed to build a desalinization plant to improve the quality of Colorado River water, indicates an assumption of water quality responsibility by the upper riparian state, although the treaty between the two nations does not deal specifically with the issue. See New York Times, August 31, 1973, p. 23, and Mexico-United States: Agreement on the Permanent and Definitive Solution to the International Problem of the Salinity of the Colorado River (August 30, 1973), International Legal Materials 12 (September 1973): 1105-07.

34. Corfu Channel Case (United Kingdom-Albania), [1949] International Court of Justice Rep. 4; Trail Smelter Arbitration (United States-Canada), 3 U.N. Rep. Intl. Arb. Awards 1905 (1941); Lake Lanoux Arbitration (Spain-France), 12 U.N. Rep. Intl. Arb. Awards 281 (1963).

35. See Brown, op. cit., passim, for a concise but extensive review of these and other conventional laws relating to the environment.

36. See Caponera, op. cit., pp. 146-48.

37. See Russell and Landsberg, op. cit., pp. 1309-11.

38. Oscar Schachter and Daniel Serwer, "Marine Pollution Problems and Remedies," American Journal of International Law 65 (January 1971): 95-105. This article deals with specific pollutants, where they originate, the extent found in the marine environment, the present controls, and future possibilities. It is an excellent survey.

39. Gray C. Dorsey, "Proposed International Agreement and Aerial Environmental Damage," <u>Indiana Law Review</u> 6, no. 2 (1972): 190-201. Quotation at p. 201.

40. Charles M. Hassett, "Weather Modification and Control: International Organizational Prospects," <u>Texas International Law Journal</u> 7 (Summer 1971): 105.

41. Dorsey suggests that "the United States should propose immediately a treaty that would obligate all industrially advanced nations to test, or require their nationals to test, proposed new products and technologies in mathematical or physical model ecosystems and to avoid harm to substantial environmental interests of other states, if necessary by abandonment." Dorsey, op. cit., p. 201. C. Wilfred Jenks has proposed a sonic boom treaty, an ocean depth treaty, a cybernetics treaty, a weather modification treaty, etc. "New Science and the Law of Nations," <u>International and Comparative Law Quarterly</u> 17 (1971): 367, quoted in Hassett, op. cit., p. 105.

42. United Nations, Office of Public Information, Press Section, <u>Weekly News Summary,</u> November 23, 1973, p. 8.

43. See Carl August Fleischer, "An International Convention on Environmental Cooperation Among Nations: Proposed Draft, Policies and Goals," <u>Texas International Law Journal</u> 7 (Summer 1971): 75.

44. E. G. Lee, "International Legal Aspects of Pollution of the Atmosphere," <u>University of Toronto Law Journal</u> 21 (1971): 203-04; 207.

45. The need for greater interaction between academic political and legal approaches to international law has been carefully interpreted, explained, and documented by Larman C. Wilson in <u>The Teaching of International Law: An Assessment and Bibliography,</u> Institute Series No. 15 (Tucson: University of Arizona, Institute of Government Research, 1973).

46. Forest Grieves, "International Law and the Environmental Issue," <u>Environmental Affairs</u> 1 (March 1972): 833.

47. Thomas W. Wilson, op. cit., p. 45.

48. Brendan F. Brown, "International Environmental Law and the Natural Law," <u>Loyola Law Review</u> 18, no. 3 (1971-72): 682-83.

10

THE COMPARATIVE STUDY
OF ENVIRONMENTAL POLICY
Lennart J. Lundqvist

A PROMISING FIELD

Within a few years, "environment" has become a top-priority issue in a number of countries around the world. Japan presents us with a most instructive example of this development. In 1955, Japanese dictionaries did not mention the word kogai, meaning environmental deterioration. But less than 15 years later, kogai was indeed a painful reality in the daily life of the Japanese people. And in most other industrialized countries, the deterioration of man's physical environment has turned dramatically into an issue of public concern. Between 1965 and 1973, the environmental "challenge" or "crisis" produced a continually increasing number and variety of policies, programs, laws, institutional changes, and other responses in the politics of the industrialized countries.

These countries have many similarities with regard to socioeconomic conditions while, at the same time, they possess ideological, constitutional, and political conditions that exhibit considerable variation. There is thus a rich potential for comparative research. Yet social science interests in environmental policy questions have not developed to the degree warranted by the importance of the subject or by its intrinsic social interest.

The rich potential is suggested in the proposals made recently by a group of American and European scholars, known as the Council for European Studies. They identify six problem areas particularly suitable for comparative study: (1) contextual analysis of environmental policies, (2) institutional adaptation to environmental problems, (3) decision making and environmental planning, (4) environmental ideologies and social movements, (5) transnational impacts of national policies, and (6) learning from the developing countries: man-nature relations and alternative technologies. Certain comparative studies are already underway concerning at least five of these problem areas, with only the sixth still left out.

PROBLEMS AND NEEDS: THE QUESTIONS
OF WHAT AND WHERE

But as was pointed out in Dean Mann's essay on "Environmental Policy Studies" in the first issue of Policy Studies Journal (PSJ; see Chapter 2 of this book), the very term "environmental policy" suggests the difficulty of defining this field of policy analysis. The scholar inevitably confronts the problem of defining exactly what he intends to study. Such difficulty is multiplied when a comparative approach is attempted. The comparative scholar will soon find that the concept of "environmental policy" has different connotations in different countries, with the concomitant result that the policy area differs widely between political systems. Furthermore, these problems of defining the subject are bound to increase as "environmental" concerns more and more penetrate other policy areas, such as energy, transportation, and foreign policies.

If such difficulty is mitigated by the fact that so few political science studies of national environmental policies have been made, this is even more so with respect to comparative studies, where almost nothing has been done as yet. However, this presents comparative scholars with the need to define the subject of environmental policy in such a way that we improve our conceptual understanding of environmental problems and strengthen the comparative approach to environmental policy analysis.

In his essay in the first issue of PSJ, Mann seems to look at environmental policy as one chiefly concerned with matters of ecological balance and the quality of life. To Lynton Caldwell, the environmental problem is essentially concerning the set of relationships existing both between man and his physical environment and between the various parts of this environment. Since many countries add environmental policies to the existing web of social and economic policies, actual decisions affecting the environment might be made on the basis of other than environmental considerations. In order not to get lost in the contextual analysis, comparative scholars might find it profitable to approach environmental policy as "governmental actions concerning those activities which societies will undertake, permit, or prohibit in order to solve environmental problems," where solutions mean enhancement of the quality of the relationships just mentioned.

There is, however, the risk that the great number of alternatives of <u>where</u> to make comparisons might serve as a "pollutant" to a successful comparative effort. Potentially, there are as many answers to this problem as there are students of environmental policy. Besides, as Mann points out, the criteria for any lasting agreement on the solutions of environmental policy research problems do not seem to be at hand. This is even more the case since the answers to <u>where</u> are so intimately connected with the solutions of the problems of <u>how</u> and <u>why</u> we should attempt a comparative environmental policy analysis.

Maybe an answer could be obtained by looking at some of the fundamental principles of the environmental master science, that is, ecology. One of its principles is diversity, and another is the organic wholeness of ecosystems. When the principle of diversity is broken, like in the case of mono-crop cultures, the environment will utlimately suffer from decay. On the other hand, diversity cannot be pushed too far (rabbits in Australia being a good example), because that might jeopardize the principle of organic wholeness. The lesson for the kind of comparative research we are interested in here would be that such research would thrive from a diversity of approaches and answers to the question of where to make comparisons, provided that there is a commonly accepted framework of analysis--or an "organic wholeness"--into which we can fit different comparative research efforts.

PROBLEMS, NEEDS, AND PRIORITIES:
THE QUESTIONS OF HOW AND WHY

When designing frameworks for their studies, most political scientists are heavily influenced by their ideas, answers, and justifications of the purposes of their research. There is thus always the possibility that the number of analytical frameworks might run into the extreme. But as I pointed out above, environmental problems facing the modern societies are quite similar in character. For example, irrespective of whether it appears in Tokyo, London, or Los Angeles, the incidence of smog causes the same or similar problems. Likewise, the problems caused by the pollution of water and soil are much the same in many countries. Therefore, on the basis of the similarity of environmental problems and issues, it should be possible to develop a framework of analysis that could be commonly accepted. The problem appears to be one of assessing the compatibility of the principles of diversity and wholeness with the overall purposes of our comparative enterprise.

It appears to this author to be evident that the environmental problem poses new and fundamental challenges to all political systems. These challenges raise some very basic questions about which goals societies should try to--or even will be able to--achieve. If the conjectural futurist studies have at least some credibility, the answers and solutions to these questions are likely to be in the form of some fundamental changes in societal values and in their structural expressions. To me, the question of why has a very simple answer. We must do comparative environmental policy research in order to find out which factors in different societies promote or prevent necessary change, which would thus enable us to provide more valid recommendations for improvement in society policy making. By applying a common framework to our comparative research, we might be able to build a common pool of cumulated knowledge that could be applied to the early stages of emerging problems. Thus, as Eugene Skolnikoff points out, we could "contribute to the design of alternative policies for the future."

Such answers to the question of why do not exclude intrascientific purposes of comparative environmental policy studies. There is in fact a convergence of increasing social and political change caused by the environmental problem and of renewed scientific interest in the concept of political change. This points to the conclusion that a comparative endeavor in this policy field could make substantial contribution to the elucidation of intrascientific theories of political change and could clarify the role of policy in such change.

In view of these answers, and in view of the premature state of comparative environmental policy research, the project "Environmental Policy and Political Change" (Bloomington, Indiana, and Uppsala, Sweden) has given priority to the development of an analytical framework. The aim has been to put together unambiguous categories, exhaustive but limited in number and rich enough in theoretical potential to allow a diversity of approaches and research strategies within the framework.

The main concepts within the framework are political change and policy. The context of change can be studied in four dimensions: (1) in the character and distribution of values, (2) in the control of governments, (3) in the institutional structure, and (4) in the performance levels of the

different actors of the system. As a process, change begins
with some state of equilibrium. Then, changes in the physical environment cause changes in political demands and in
the distribution of political resources. Soon these political factors become independent variables and must be manipulated by the political elites in order to produce new coalitions and policies. In the next phase, these new coalitions
and policies produce changes in the political systems of the
content just indicated above. There might be a possible
fifth stage, in which once again some kind of equilibrium is
established.

Central in this process of change is policy, which is
seen as both a dependent and an independent variable. The
content of policy can be studied in at least three dimensions: (1) statements of goals to be achieved, (2) recommendations concerning the ways and means of implementation,
and (3) the actual performance and actions of those implementing the policy. The last element is very important, for
the framework must be broad enough to provide possibilities
for impact studies. As a process, policy ranges from the
first vague formulations to the stages of implementation and
evaluation.

In order to enhance the "comparativeness" of the framework, factors have been identified that would explain--in a
general fashion--the variations found among the processes of
political change in different countries. Environmental policies will differ as agents of change depending on the intensity and character of (1) issue-relevant knowledge in the
policy process, (2) ideologies, values, and constitutions,
(3) historical development, habit, and routine in decision
making, (4) existing power relations among policy-affected
groups, and (5) considerations of utility.

Admittedly, these answers to the questions of why and
how are very broad and tentative. However, this broad
framework, while providing opportunities for a beneficial
diversity of approaches and studies, will lead to a greater
comparability of the results from different environmental
policy studies. It will thereby allow political scientists
to make more valid recommendations concerning the elements
favorable to such political change that is necessary because of the environmental problem.

ONGOING RESEARCH EFFORTS

According to the Policy Studies Organization list of
"Political Scientists Interested in Environmental Policy
Studies" of November 1972, very few of the scholars listed

have a direct interest in comparative environmental policy studies. However, two of the centers for such research are not listed--the comparative research efforts now being built up by and around Lynton Caldwell at Indiana University and Eugene Skolnikoff at MIT and the Council for European Studies. The first center consists mostly of political scientists and is mainly concerned with problems of contextual analysis, institutional adaptation, environmental management, and transnational impacts. The Council for European Studies aims at comprising scholars from most social sciences for a cooperative program of research and training in the six problem areas mentioned above. Common to both centers is the intention to improve conceptual understanding of environmental problems, throw light on concrete policy problems, and contribute to the design of alternative future policies.

Researchers from participating universities will be in contact through conferences, workshops, student and faculty exchanges, joint publications, and circulation of research results. The Council for European Studies will give special care to the building of international and interdisciplinary research teams. Representatives of six universities met in January 1973 to discuss the further development of an integrated research effort. A similar meeting of European scholars was held in Paris in March 1973. Readers of PSJ will receive continuous information on the progress of these efforts.

There were a number of specialist meetings on environmental policy during the Ninth World Congress of the International Political Science Association (IPSA) in Montreal in August 1973. Apart from a general session on "Environment as a Political Problem," there were five smaller meetings. A look at the topics for these meetings suggests that they will have a considerable impact on the future of comparative environmental policy research. Thus the IPSA is forming a special committee for environmental politics.

REFERENCES

Caldwell, L. K., ed., Organization and Administration of Environmental Programmes: With Special Reference to the Recommendations of the United Nations Conference on the Human Environment, Stockholm, 5-16 June, 1972. Prepared for the Public Administration Division, Department of Social and Economic Affairs, United Nations, by the International Union for the Conservation of Nature and Natural Resources (New York: United Nations, 1974).

Lundqvist, L. J. "Crisis, Change and Public Policy: Considerations for a Comparative Analysis of Environmental Policies," _European Journal of Political Research_ 1 (June 1973).

_____. "Do Political Structures Matter in Environmental Politics? The Case of Air Pollution Control in Canada, Sweden, and the United States," _Canadian Public Administration_ 20 (Spring 1974). An abridged, revised version is published in the _American Behavioral Scientist_ 17 (May-June 1974).

_____. "Environmental Policies in Canada, Sweden, and the United States: A Comparative Overview," _Sage Professional Papers in Administrative and Policy Studies,_ No. 03-014 (Beverly Hills: Sage Publications, 1974).

Skolnikoff, E. B. et al. "Social Sciences and Environmental Problems: A Program for Comparative Research," working paper for a Conference on Comparative Environmental Research at MIT, Cambridge, Mass., January 15-16, 1973 (mimeo).

Mann, Dean. "Environmental Policy," _Policy Studies Journal_ 1, no. 17 (Autumn 1972).

11

COMPARATIVE GOVERNMENT
AND ENVIRONMENTAL POLICY
Eugene E. Dais

Any discussion of environmental policy should begin with what it is. As usual it is easier to say what it is not. An environmental policy is not a doctrinaire posture for protecting values associated with "environment" against all other values at all costs. It is rather the product of hard choices often made by necessity on incomplete information. These choices would include inaction when deliberately adopted as the more acceptable option for a given time. The better choice among competing options in any instant context, we may posit, depends on criteria of adequacy.*

POLICY ADEQUACY

As any policy, environmental policy is the product of necessarily implicated decisional functions, whether

---

*This chapter emphasizes "policy" in its prescriptive sense and defines that sense of it as objectively limited to criteria of adequacy. "Policy" can also be used in the pure descriptive sense of recording what certain actors do in fact in positing goals, devising means, and making differences in who gets what, when, and how much. The limited prescriptive sense cannot be sharply separated from the descriptive sense. But it can be usefully distinguished as trying to understand policy actions as achievements or failures of varying degrees. To what extent this focus confuses the fact-value dichotomy unscientifically is a matter for separate discussion.

performed avowedly or not. The quality of the policy prod-
uct--barring accident--depends on the adequacy in explicitly
performing the decisional functions. Differing conceptual
spaces likely foreclose any general agreement on distinguishing and defining those functions. But the need for
them seems reasonable in principle. Without the analytical
identification of the logically implicated choices in the
making and implementing of policy, it would be impractical
to discuss intelligently whether differing policy options
are better or worse in terms of reasoning and evidence.

By way of illustration, an environmental policy in the
analytic sense would be better than others depending on the
adequacy in performing in differing contexts the following
decisional functions:

1. Identification Function: What harms will likely
be inflicted on the environment by various activities? What
harms have been inflicted, and what activities have caused
them?

2. Disvaluation Function: What is the gravity of the
various harms as discounted by their improbability? Do they
present a sufficient deprivation or danger to support the
mobilization of consensus for collective action?

3. Revaluation Function: What is the cost of avoiding the environmental harms? What benefits are foregone,
or collateral harms inflicted? Who pays the price? Is the
cure worse than the disease, especially for those who
highly value social justice for the deprived? How many
jobs, for example, should be a trade-off for how much environmental protection?

4. Judgmental Function: What is the acceptable balance in varying situations between environmental protection
and other values? Who decides? How are they made publicly
accountable?

5. Rationality Function: What means are more econom-
ical and effective in implementing the balance in a given
situation? What means are less costly in foregone benefits
or collateral harms? Again, who decides, and how are they
made publicly accountable?

6. Self-Correcting Function: In what ways does experience with the impact of carrying out the means require
rethinking and redoing the other functions? Who, if anyone, has the responsibility for insuring that this is done?

These decisional functions, or their equivalents,
would be applicable to any policy area. The distinctive
feature in environmental policy, compared, say, to foreign
policy or educational policy, is the specific concern with
values associated with the "ecological balance and the
quality of life."[1] The aim of the decisional functions

would be to correct imbalances, if any, in prevailing policies that may have slighted or neglected environmental values in pursuit of other such values as economic growth and
individual liberty.

One task in satisfying the analytic requisites in answering the evidentiary demands. An adequate environmental
policy needs reliable information on existing circumstances,
the efficacy of optional remedies or programs in changing or
preserving the existing situation, and the alternative consequences of competing courses of action. For such descriptive and causal knowledge, it has to draw on the technical
data of the physical and biological sciences, as well as on
supportive data from the social and behavioral sciences.

But in addition to the factual tasks, the performance
of the decisional functions has to cope with the legal-
political task of allocating values authoritatively. In the
final result, successful policies presuppose mobilizing and
allocating on their behalf the needed resources of time,
materials, energy, and expertise that are in constant competition with other demands. Not only does environmental
policy, however technically adequate, need sanctioning by
governmental systems to be legitimate and effective, but
also, assuming the danger to the environment is a potential
crisis in the ecosystem on which life on earth depends,
there would have to be a viable consensus on environmental
policy among all nations. This poses enormous difficulties
in gaining legal and political unity. It may be that a
technically adequate environmental policy is unworkable unless effective transnational institutions are devised, or
unless all nations cooperate in foreign policy in ways his-
torically unprecedented.

NEEDS FOR COMPARATIVE GOVERNMENT RESEARCH

The contribution of the comparative government perspective to this problem can be a valuable one. It can identify
the difficulties or successes of formal or informal structures (interlocking roles for performing the six decisional
functions) and ideologies (probable bases for choosing policy options and mobilizing political and legal resources)
of various governmental systems as they relate to the adequate performance of the decisional functions. It can do
this on two levels.

First, comparison is essential to recognition. We better understand structures and processes of one governmental
system by inspecting apparently corresponding activities in
other systems. Elections in some nations like the United

States, for example, serve to facilitate the influence of
public opinion--rightly or wrongly--on official policy making.   In other nations, as the Soviet Union, for example,
elections serve an expressive function as if they were pa-
triotic celebrations for publicly demonstrating political
loyalty.   Thus elections, as an effective mechanism for
identifying environmental harms and performing other decisional functions, can be expected to vary among nations in
ways that relate to the adequacy of environmental policy
outcomes.   The same may be true of other structures and
processes.

Besides disclosing the real functions of structures
and processes, such others as judicial processes, written
constitutions, party systems, leadership roles, interest
groups, and bureaucratic arrangements would have to be
dealt with comparatively on the recognition level for defining the problem.   To what extent are they a part of the
solution in enhancing the adequacy of environmental policy?
Or to what extent are they a part of the problem in that
their reform or removal would enhance the adequacy sought?
For this purpose, comparative analysis would have to become
interdisciplinary without losing the coherency of its methodology.[2]   In some fashion yet to be developed, it would
have to include, along with the legal and political, relevant aspects of religious, economic, and social institutions.   It would have to deal with the social system, not
unlike Talcott Parsons' conception of it, as an interdependent whole.[3]

Comparison for recognition can also usefully be applied to ideologies.   The consequences of liberalism, democracy, authoritarianism, totalitarianism, colonialism,
and nationalism, to name some conventional "isms," may be
relevant to evolving more adequacy in environmental policy.
One example should suffice.   Surely comparative analysis
of ideologies on the recognition level could have anticipated the position of the developing nations in favor of
economic growth over environmental protection at the
United Nations Stockholm Conference in June 1972.   Such a
recognition would likely have led to a better definition
of the problem and thus better use of the conference's resources.

A third task in comparison as recognition is reliable
description of the existing policy posture of a government.
Whether intended or not, every government with the power
to change the existing situation for the better will have
an environmental policy in the rudimentary, descriptive
sense at least.   It may be the negative one of refusing,
consciously or otherwise, to use available legal, political,

economic, and other resources to prevent harms to the environment. Or it may be a positive one that despite best efforts falls short of adequacy in varying degrees. In any event, before analytical and institutional analysis and evaluation can take place, there is need for the information. This can be accomplished by no casual effort. What is needed is not only the formal legal statutes, regulations, precedents, and the like, together with official understandings of political policies and actual practices, but also the informal practices and understandings that often become decisive in bureaucratic decision making. Not only "law-in-books" but "law-in-action" must be reliably known.

As difficult as the above tasks may be, the key one remains. Comparison for recognition is not an end in itself. It should serve to define better the problem of policy adequacy. A clear, realistic perception of need dissatisfaction or deprivation is as necessary for sensible choices in allocating scarce legal and political resources of authority and legitimacy in environmental policy as elsewhere.[4] To what extent are there analytical and evidentiary--not to mention conceptual--difficulties in evolving an adequate environmental policy for all nations, or at least the critical number of them? What is the "political" price that has to be paid in decisional costs (in research, education, personnel, for example) to overcome them in time enough for the policy to be effective? Who should pay this price? Can they be expected to do so?

Comparative government study cannot be expected to yield the solution to the problem of policy adequacy. But, given the global dimensions of an adequate environmental policy, it is less likely one will be forthcoming without the comparative contribution on the recognition level of analysis.

Second, comparison is essential beyond recognition of difficulties for clarifying and resolving the problem of policy adequacy. It can also contribute to the cumulative body of scientific knowledge that enables control of the factors affecting the adequacy of performing the necessary decisional functions. Such a task may be expecting too much. It is one thing to describe, explain, and predict for recognizing how much of a problem of policy inadequacy exists, or for providing conceptual, analytical, and evidentiary support for remedying the inadequacy. It is something far different to describe, explain, and predict for manipulating the behavior of official actors and other participants in the processes of governmental systems.

For one thing, the shift in approach from (1) policy-relevant knowledge for defining, choosing, and implementing goals and values internal to the participants within the system to (2) manipulative knowledge for controlling official behavior for the sake of goals and values externally imposed on system participants raises all the risks attendant on a "Project Camelot." In the second place, one has to be skeptical whether valid manipulative knowledge is obtainable at all, and if so in time for a matter such as environmental policy. In the third place, even if such manipulative knowledge were available, how and who could employ it when, as in the case of environmental policy, it is likely the behavior of officials that most needs manipulation? Are we back to Plato's "philosopher-king" not for the "Republic" but for the "Laws?"

Aside from such a parade of research horrors, it is nonetheless true that comparative analysis is, in theory, relevant for increasing manipulative knowledge. Comparison is probably the more reliable laboratory for political scientists. But the record so far is not an encouraging one for the theory. The literature in political development is most cognate.[5] But the effort in this field-- which has attained a commendable level of sophistication-- to describe, explain, and predict the factors in need of manipulation, such as modernizing traditional ideologies, developing industrial economies and democratizing political participation, has fallen short of confirmed hypotheses for successfully controlling the societal change needed to make democracies stable.

Perhaps the outlook is more promising in the environmental field. Lennart Lundqvist optimistically states that

> we must do comparative environmental policy
> research in order to find out which factors
> in different societies promote or prevent
> necessary change, which would thus enable us
> to provide more valid recommendations for
> improvement in society policy making. . . .
> a comparative endeavor in [the environmental]
> policy field could make substantial contribu-
> tion to the elucidation of intrascientific
> theories of political change, and clarify
> the role of policy in such change.[6]

It is noteworthy that Lundqvist openly admits that such an endeavor is still in the early stage of reconciling conceptual spaces, agreeing on a common analytical framework, and specifying a coordinated division of research tasks.[7]

THE INQUIRY-POLICY DILEMMA

A basic problem still remains even if the optimistic outlook on research in environmental policy proves warranted. This problem has to do with the gap between inquiry (knowledge) and policy (action). The analysis of Max F. Milliken 14 years ago remains remarkably apt. Those responsible for making hard choices that visibly affect human lives view research as

> useless or irrelevant to the problems they are struggling with. The work is obviously painstaking and thorough, a great deal of material has been surveyed, elaborate classifications have been developed, and a great many facts have been assembled. . . . All this is complicated by the [decision maker's] impression that the research is playing with complex intellectual machinery for its own sake. . . . The whole process appears to be a peculiarly complicated way of saying the obvious. . . . [Or] there is a frustrated and irritated feeling that, when one has waded through [the] fat research . . . one is no nearer to the answers he is seeking than when he began. . . .
> [Moreover, the] scientist is apt to have a strong conviction that applied research cannot be "fundamental," that there is something inherently contradictory in the advance of knowledge and the service of practical ends, and that to work for a policy maker is therefore somehow to prejudice one's professional standing. Allied with this . . . is a set of moral qualms concerning the ethics of placing scientific analysis in the service of persons who wish, for whatever purposes, to manipulate human beings.[8]

The result invariably is to leave the policy maker with the belief that the researcher has stubbornly avoided real problems "for some relatively unimportant or narrow aspect of a general issue, one which happens to interest him or to which his disciplinary tools happen to apply, leaving the central problem posed but unresolved."[9]

A cursory survey of the literature reveals little effort to come to grips with the inquiry-policy dilemma.[10] Much, nay, just about everything, remains to be done in making comparative analysis or other approaches in policy

studies more than tangentially relevant to those who have
to make the hard choices in policy action. More dismaying
is the paucity of preliminary efforts to develop a focus
specifically on environmental policy within comparative government studies, and further to develop research strategies[11] for productively making the needed contribution that
takes due account of the inquiry-policy dilemma. Perhaps
the reflections presented here may stimulate such efforts.

NOTES

1. L. J. Lundqvist, "The Comparative Study of Environmental Policy," Policy Studies Journal 1 (Spring 1973):
138, 139-40.
2. Ibid., p. 140.
3. Talcott Parsons, The Social System (1951).
4. For an elaboration of this theme, see L. L. Jaffe,
"Ecological Goals and the Ways and Means of Achieving Them,"
West Virginia Law Review 75 (1972): 1.
5. Notably Gabriel A. Almond and James S. Coleman,
The Politics of the Developing Areas (Princeton, N.J.:
Princeton University Press, 1960); David E. Apter, Some
Conceptual Approaches to the Study of Modernization (Englewood Cliffs, N.J.: Prentice-Hall, 1968); Louis Hartz, The
Founding of New Societies (New York: Harcourt, Brace,
1964); Samuel P. Huntington, Political Order in Changing
Societies (New Haven, Conn.: Yale University Press, 1968);
Lucian Pye and Stanley Verba, Political Culture and Political Development (Princeton, N.J.: Princeton University
Press, 1965); as well as the well-known texts in the field.
6. Lundqvist, op. cit., p. 141.
7. Cf. the conceptual and analytical approach of
Richard Rose, "Concepts for Comparison," Policy Studies
Journal 1 (Spring 1973): 122, for a useful variation.
8. Max F. Milliken, "Inquiry and Policy: The Relation of Knowledge to Action," in Max Lerner, The Human
Meaning of the Social Sciences (Cleveland: World, 1959),
pp. 160-61.
9. Ibid.
10. A respectable attempt in the general policy field
is the Eighth Annual Review, Economic Council of Canada,
Design for Decision Making: An Application to Human Resources Policies (Ottawa, September 1971).
11. Cf. Harold Lasswell, "Strategies of Inquiry: The
Rational Use of Observation," in Lerner, op. cit., p. 89.

12

ECOLOGICAL POLITICS
AND AMERICAN GOVERNMENT:
A REVIEW ESSAY
Michael E. Kraft

Although this chapter was originally envisioned as a commentary on the politics of environmental policy at the American national government level, the symposium on which the present volume is based was also concerned with surveying and assessing the efforts of political scientists and other social scientists in studying the subject of politics, policy, and the environment. More precisely, we are interested in the kinds of issues and questions that ought to be examined in the future if we are to make a substantial contribution to understanding and resolving our ecological predicament. Since I believe our achievements on the whole to be rather modest and the direction of many current efforts to be lamentable, much of this discussion will focus on this state of affairs and some suggestions for improvement. Thus the reader will have to look elsewhere for a detailed summary of governmental policy making as such. Fortunately, other chapters in this volume deal with the subsystems of American politics--public administration; the judicial process and constitutional law; the legislative process; parties, groups, and public opinion; and state and local government--and, I presume, more with the substance of recent politics. The criticisms offered here hopefully complement the other chapters.

_____

Some of the ideas expressed in this chapter derive from conversations and collaboration with the author's colleague, Peter G. Stillman. The author thanks him for his many perceptive comments, but of course absolves him of any responsibility for the essay or particular notions expressed therein.

The present literature on environmental politics defies easy categorization. It is an enormously diverse assortment of popular polemics, investigative journalism, and scholarly inquiry of varying purpose, scope, and quality. The substantive focus varies from the politics of conservation or resource use to contemporary air and water pollution control politics to a broad collection of concerns including the politics of population growth and distribution; energy development and use; land use; pesticide, radiation, and noise control; transportation; urban development; and the quality of life in general in highly developed technological societies. Within such diverse subject areas, analysis varies in focus from the social, cultural, political, and economic causes of ecological problems to various aspects of governmental policy formation to the substance of current and proposed public policy (and environmental law). For these reasons, the labels "environmental policy studies" or "environmental politics" appear ambiguous, slightly inaccurate, and even seriously misleading in some important respects. We are not dealing only with "policy" nor only with "the environment" in a narrow meaning of the word. The term ecological politics (or even the politics of ecology) might better capture the range of concerns shared by political scientists actively involved with these matters.

More than semantic games is involved in making these kinds of distinctions. The way this emerging aggregation in the political science literature is defined--assuming that we can refer to it as a reasonably cohesive subfield-- might very well affect how we come to think about ecological problems and the kind of research in which we engage. Ecological politics is a convenient holistic term that suggests the interrelationship of all of these public problems much as the study of ecology reveals, as Barry Commoner puts it, that "everything [in an ecosystem] is connected to everything else."[1] The term also hints at the connections between the isolated parts of a political system that we artificially separate for analysis but that are, of course, intimately related (for example, the political culture and mass attitudes; the institutional arrangements of government; elite values, beliefs, and attitudes; the processes of policy making and the distribution of power in society; and public policy outputs and outcomes). Furthermore, it suggests the ideal of a politics based upon ecological principles or an ecological ethos, presumably a long-range goal on which substantial agreement can be reached, the normal conflicts of value notwithstanding--and one worth frequent repetition lest it be forgotten.[2] There are still problems with this term--including some ambiguity--and conceptualizing a subject is only a preliminary, though important, exercise; but perhaps its use can help foster sorely needed innovation, boldness, and experiment in studies of ecological problems and politics while at the same time giving us a useful frame of reference intellectually tied to the widely used systems model of political life.[3]

THE LITERATURE: INTRODUCTION

Whatever the definition or terms used, the aggregate literature on ecological politics has obviously expanded tremendously in the past three or four years. In many respects it is still quite underdeveloped, especially as regards the contributions of political scientists. As Dean Mann and Geoffrey Wandesford-Smith have noted, one looks in vain for significant coverage in the major journals of the discipline.[4] And there are few book-length treatments compared to virtually any other area of political science, no doubt largely for similar reasons.[5] Yet, this situation is changing rapidly and the literature is likely to grow considerably both in volume and in professional stature. The large number of doctoral dissertations in political science completed or being completed on ecological topics (over 20 finished in 1973) is one good indicator of this growth potential.[6] Others include the ongoing research listed in the directory compiled by Wandesforde-Smith and Mann[7] and the number of papers presented at recent professional meetings.[8] In the area of population and politics alone (which I would call an integral part of ecological politics, though it is often excluded from discussions of "environmental" politics), the past two years have seen the publication of six major books or collected works by political scientists, much of the material of a surprisingly sophisticated nature.[9] Other social scientists have responded in a similar fashion to judge from recent bibliographical compilations.[10]

This rather surprising productivity--and the promise of much more to come--of course guarantees neither excellence nor political or disciplinary significance. To date the work of social scientists on matters ecological has been several notches below excellent by contemporary standards and, although this is more a matter of personal values and judgment, on the whole the output has simply not been terribly significant. There is very little we could not just as well have managed without and very little that has even modestly altered either the climate of opinion in the country or the political process surrounding ecological issues. One should add that important spin-offs for the

discipline have been extremely limited as well, although I
think this a rather minor concern.[11] It seems sensible at
this time, then, to encourage rather extensive examination
of the assumptions and goals, implicit as well as explicit,
that characterize the developing literature. As research
agendas are built, courses at both the undergraduate and
graduate levels developed, sizable amounts of money allocated to ecological research, and various personal and institutional commitments made, critical evaluation can be a
vitally important antidote for the premature dogmatism and
ossification that frequently attend the maturation stage of
a new field.

The kind of questions we ought to be asking easily
come to mind. Is the purpose of research on ecological
politics more or less the same as that of social science or
political science in general? Should it be? What do we
hope to accomplish in research endeavors? Why this? To
whom do we address ourselves primarily? To other political
scientists? To governmental officials? To a concerned
public? What have we learned that stands out as particularly valuable and worth the effort invested? What difference does political research seem to make? What obligations, if any, do students of politics have in directing
themselves to the enormously complex and enormously important task of adapting social, economic, and political
institutions and practices to the requirements of an ecological sound social order? Do we really have anything of
importance to contribute to a dialogue on ecology and politics? Or do we rationalize present accomplishments and
future intentions out of habitual professional immodesty?
If we do have something to say, what most needs saying?
What do we need to know for what purpose? And what research is of the highest priority; where should we concentrate our limited collective resources? And how shall we
determine that; what are reasonable and proper criteria
for evaluating the adequacy of political research or recommended research strategies? Students in the classroom
frequently wonder about the utility or intellectual importance of the literature to which they are exposed and
are admirably perceptive about our failure to address the
most difficult and interesting questions. Perhaps we have
been so profligate in allocating research energy in part
because we traditionally have so few guides to what is
really worth knowing and so little understanding of how
best to use knowledge.[12] Serious consideration of these
questions may help fill in some of those gaps. At a minimum it should decrease the likelihood of producing narrowly trivial research and increase the probability of
creating interesting and significant work.

BASIC ISSUES

What are the basic issues in ecological politics? Indeed, what _are_ they? There really isn't much agreement among analysts here as the above discussion indicates. And certainly various factions or partisans in the environmental movement define the issues in strikingly different ways to defend their prejudices and advance their causes.

Determining what issues are "basic" normally involves some fancy theoretical footwork. A statement of the issues usually specifies the nature of the public problem (what it is), its scope (how extensive it is and how widespread its potential impact), the objectives of public policy (what is expected or asked of the government), the points of contention or conflict between relevant publics over these objectives (who disagrees about what), and the major characteristics of the political process of conflict resolution (for example, who gets what when, and how).[13] The purist concerned with an accurate empirical description of the agenda of politics would add "nonissues," which are at times equally if not more important than more obvious and visible issues, but which suffer the misfortune of being ignored altogether or--as the term is more often used-- are intentionally kept off the agenda (through "nondecisions") out of fear for their potentially divisive or disruptive nature.[14] However, for present purposes, these theoretical complexities can mostly be dispensed with.

In general terms, Harold and Margaret Sprout put the major issues well enough: "How, and how well, does the political system respond, or can it be made to respond, to the accelerative spoliation, depletion and pollution of our physical habitat? Is the response vigorous, informed, imaginative and courageous? Or is it negative, or timid, or ambiguous, or simply niggardly and trivial? And if the latter, what should be done about it?"[15] I would put the same concerns (more likely to impress environmentalists as the "basic issues" than others, of course) somewhat more comprehensively and more explicitly. The list could serve as a general inventory of major issues and as a point of departure for specific research questions (about which more will be said shortly). What is the nature of our ecological problems as defined by relevant experts and in what ways, singularly and collectively, do they threaten us with what consequences--social, economic, political, ecological? To what extent is there agreement among these experts on the causes of these problems and on the severity of the threats? What are the long-range as well as the short-range consequences of major developments as far as we are able to determine them?[16]

Toward what general and specific goals should we be aiming--and how much agreement is there on those goals? What are the major conflicts between ecological values implied in such goals and other values, for example, human freedom and self-fulfillment, democratic processes, equality, justice, community, social, and political stability, and economic well-being? What solutions are proposed for reaching the goals? What are the political options (especially policy options) both for the short range and for the long range? Their ethical acceptability? Economic and political feasibility? What are the likely effects on ecological problems of adopting those proposals?

What significant governmental (and private) actions have been taken to date, how can we best explain those actions, and, most importantly, how adequate do they appear to be? In particular, what public policies have been adopted and what have been their effects, measuring policy impact after a suitable lapse of time and in a moderately systematic fashion? How can we judge the adequacy of these actions? Against what standards or using what criteria shall such evaluations be made?

If governmental and private efforts are deemed inadequate and change is considered possible, what kinds of changes and of what magnitude are, or appear to be, necessary or desirable in public policies; in processes of decision making; in the values, attitudes, and motivations of key political actors; and in political institutions and political culture? In short, if change is possible, what precisely do we need or want and how do we go about getting it? What is presently being suggested or tried with what degree of success or failure? Under what conditions are necessary or desirable changes most likely to occur and what strategies seem likely to make a difference?

ISSUES IN CONTEMPORARY POLITICS AND ANALYSIS

The issues as they are defined in contemporary ecological dialogues and as they come to constitute the empirical and "legitimate" agenda of political organizations fall far short of such a comprehensive list of possibilities; they are instead remarkably narrow and relatively noncontroversial. Perhaps this is to be expected in a nation whose politics are generally characterized by moderation, a lack of consistent ideological conflict, and a high degree of consensus among influential elites on the fundamental rules of the game (the net effect of which is bargaining and compromise as the prevailing style of interaction).[17] Never-

theless, one never ceases to be amazed by the chasm sepa-
rating the more radical ecological enthusiasts with their
"subversive" arguments for major changes in our government,
politics, and life style and the more sober and "realistic"
assessments and proposals of establishment elites. For example, nearly all major environmental conflicts are over the
extent of involvement of the federal government ("states'
rights," federalism), the stringency of regulatory standards
and enforcement processes (the heart of pollution-control
programs and frequently taking the shape of business regulation issues), the extent of financial commitment (especially in the water pollution control area where Republicans
and the Nixon administration have fought endlessly with
Democrats and congressional "big spenders"), and the general balancing of environmentalist and other values in setting national priorities in various policy areas (for example, land use, energy development, transportation). These
kinds of conflicts are not at all unique to the environmental area; they have characterized mainstream politics in
this country since the New Deal days of Franklin Roosevelt.
And, although we have witnessed some major and well-
publicized battles over the past few years (for example,
the SST, the Alaska pipeline, key provisions in the most
recent air and water pollution-control laws), on the whole
the politics of environmental issues have been rather ordinary and routine.[18]

Furthermore, there has not yet been a serious challenge to the dominant or core values of American politics
(for example, private property and capitalism, individualism
and the unrestrained right to pursue one's self-interest,
limited government, and, perhaps above all, material abundance and economic growth). Congressmen differ over the
desirability of having an SST or over how much money to
spend on pollution control or how sympathetic to be toward
the troubles of the automobile or oil industries--and these
are certainly important disputes; there is no question about
that. Yet, one seldom hears fundamental criticism of the
core values in the halls of Capitol Hill or serious concrete proposals that would radically alter the status quo.
Even with the degree of public shock and outrage over the
cost and availability of gasoline and other energy supplies
in this period of extraordinary preoccupation with the entire energy situation, who among key political elites
speaks of, for example, nationalizing the oil industry? Or
a complete discontinuation of oil tax subsidies? Instead,
we have the rather familiar spectacles of the president assuring us that our troubles are strictly "temporary," proposing that we launch a crash program to develop new energy

145

sources, and assuring us that we will achieve self-suffi-
ciency in energy by 1980, and of the Senate being unwilling
to disallow "windfall profits" of the oil industry. All in
all, 1973 was an extraordinarily instructive year in American politics.

The complex nature of ecological politics makes a capsule statement of prevailing characteristics difficult.
One would like to make endless qualifications and refine-
ments if space allowed. However, it seems reasonably fair
to suggest that in spite of very substantial--and often un-
expected--progress since, say, 1969 (for example, the effects of the National Environmental Policy Act, the adoption
of the Clean Air Amendments of 1970), the dominant political response to the ecological crisis has been characterized
by marginal and superficial attention to, understanding of,
and concern for ecological problems; a weak and uncertain
commitment to new environmental priorities both on the part
of the American public and on the part of political leaders;
timidity and moderation at best in public policy developments adversely affecting the basic economic system and the
values of our central (though possibly outmoded) political
philosophies; the frequent use by politicians of rhetorical
and symbolic gestures as a substitute for material, real
accomplishments; dedication to palliative measures and
technological fixes aimed at relieving highly visible symptoms rather than treating underlying social and economic
causes of environmental problems; and, of course, devotion
in the customary fashion to incrementalism--that is, to
"muddling through," to business as usual, to satisfying
behavior as a way of life, to preoccupation primarily with
short-range goals that are immediately "feasible" or "realistic," to dealing with problems in a piecemeal and frag-
mented rather than comprehensive and coordinated manner.
In short, the political response has favored inertia and
old priorities rather than vigorous and imaginative progress and new priorities. Our goals have seemingly been
more the achievement of short-term comforts and sociopolitical stability with a minimum sacrifice of customary
conveniences and a minimum irritation of traditional political sensibilities than the heralding of a new environmental ethic.[19]

There are some very good reasons for these characteristics and for expecting a similar response in the future.
They have to do with the basic nature of American politics
that has not thus far been greatly affected by the environmental movement. Observers of environmental politics
more optimistic or conservative than I (most of whom would
not likely agree with the thrust of the previous paragraph)

might retort that to ask any more than has already been delivered is unreasonable, excessively costly, and, in any
case, not politically feasible. As always, that is, of
course, a matter of judgment. We can differ over what is
reasonable or too costly, even with substantial agreement
on the extent of the problem (which is generally lacking).
I find particularly regrettable, though, the reliance on
the crutch of political feasibility, especially by those
who purport to favor more extensive environmental change.
What is feasible depends upon what kind of changes take
place in the political system, which is at least in part
conditioned by whether we attempt to encourage such changes
through persuasive criticism and personal involvement (for
example, encouraging the American public to lend more support to environmental initiatives). I sometimes wonder if
we do not condemn ourselves needlessly to a very narrow
range of alternatives, none of which would lead to a state
of affairs markedly different from the status quo. We
ought to be asking whether the kind of political response
we have seen in the past three or four years and that might
reasonably be projected for the near future is really sufficient for adequately coping with the ecological challenge.
And whether it will be adequate in the more distant future
as environmental conditions presumably deteriorate further.
To the ecological reformer policy objectives of comprehensive and coordinated ecological planning and management, a
highly regulated and eventually probably steady-state economy, some form of population limitation, and the fostering
of a new public environmental ehtos--all in the not so distant future (say in 30-100 years) and all eventually on a
global scale as well as in the United States--quite clearly
call for more than marginal adjustments in present policies
and behavior. Yet, they have obviously not been forthcoming and there are innumerable political obstacles to frustrate their achievement.[20]
    Are present institutional structures and political
processes inherently incapable of producing a satisfactory
response to the accelerating deterioration of the environment and the quality of life in this country? This is an
exceedingly difficult question to address, but I suspect
the answer is yes. If it is, do we have any alternatives?
What are they? To the confirmed cynical observer of American politics it seems logical that we should balance our
research interests by focusing much more of our attention
and energy on such formidable questions as these and per-
haps--assuming a corresponding sacrifice is called for--
somewhat less on the more immediately practical searching
for temporary "solutions" to pressing public problems

(which might better be left to economists and policy makers). One of the major weaknesses of the social science literature on ecological matters, in fact, is a notable failure to come to grips with such questions. This seems largely derived from an unwillingness or incapacity to face the full challenge so clearly posed by ecological imperatives, especially the long-range implications of adapting to an ecologically sound social order. While deficient in attending to these tough and subversive questions, we have by comparison absolutely lavished attention on trivial descriptions of routine issues in contemporary environmental politics and administration, on microanalysis of largely inconsequential environmental behavior,[21] and on the development of methodological sophistication in policy analysis that seems greatly to exceed the marginal payoffs of the final product. I even detect the beginnings of an invidious conspiracy to convert the study of ecological politics into--God forbid--a hard-core social science in an ill-advised and hasty attempt to imitate the often bland and shallow product for which contemporary social science is so well noted. Let us at least approach that kind of development with more concern for its consequences. There is nothing at all undesirable about _careful_ analysis that draws on the tools and theories of social science. Quite the contrary. But we need to exercise the greatest care that truly significant work--even if far more speculative than empirical--is not overwhelmed by a flood of analyses of essentially petty concerns.

The "basic issues" in ecological politics, and therefore the questions to which research might be directed, should by no means be formulated to mandate an _exclusive_ focus on contemporary political conflicts and attendant social and political behavior. That notion should provoke little opposition. Yet, while a very good case can be made for studying the longer-range and more controversial issues, one suspects that the dominant norms and reward structures of contemporary political science (the same could be said for other social sciences) will tend to inhibit challenges to political and disciplinary orthodoxies inherent in such studies and therefore to inhibit the studies themselves. For example, consider the monumental effect of current paradigms within the discipline, especially as reflected in the orientation of major scholarly journals and in the expectations of academic employers; the continued aspirations of political scientists to that fundamental goal of scientific and professional respectability; individual ambition toward successful careers and personal profit; the ubiquitous reliance on universities, governments, and foundations for vital but highly uncertain research funds; the audience most researchers seem to have in mind for their work (chiefly other political scientists and governmental personnel, though the latter may not find the work exceptionally useful);[22] and the understandable bias of a good many scholars who _are_ concerned with environmental problems toward practical and "realistic" analysis, preferably with an immediate and highly visible payoff. Would these conditions and motivations provide much incentive to study nebulous, unwieldy, and frustrating questions of large-scale social adaptation? It would not seem so. Still, some individuals _are_ now so motivated, and with all the hoopla given the emergence of the so-called postbehavioral movement, one might expect the gradual propagation of a different breed of analyst for whom ecological politics will be a more attractive field of study. That makes the discussion of research needs and strategies a worthwhile activity.

RESEARCH NEEDS

Since I have perhaps inflated the potential contribution of social scientists to enlarging our understanding of the ecological predicament and our ability to shape man's future intelligently, I should immediately preface these few concluding remarks by acknowledging the limits to what we can or should expect to materialize. The field is an extremely promising one and there are many varied avenues of potentially profitable research, particularly, I should like to think, if some of the failures and shortsightedness to which I have called attention can be overcome. But of course there are substantial limits to our talents, and our actions constitute a rather small segment of ecologically relevant human activity.

The task of compiling a research agenda to guide future efforts is not particularly difficult. However, it _is_ difficult to perform that task with firm conviction that one knows precisely what is most important. The sage advice of letting a thousand flowers bloom is apt for a still-developing field. We need to foster more experiment, more imagination, and more diversity and rather consciously avoid the insufferable confinement that seems coincident with the arrival of new academic orthodoxies. One never knows for certain what may prove to be important or useful in the future. That fact forms the basis for a common justification for the pursuit of basic science; it also provides a rationale for diversity in general. Within those limits, some sort of direction is useful to ward off the growth of utter chaos and a debilitating lack of a sense of purpose.

I have argued that we need to foster more critical inquiry: to ask what really needs study, what the important questions in fact are, to ask what political science does have to offer and what approaches or methodologies are appropriate to the tasks. There still isn't enough of this kind of critical self-analysis. As part of this effort, we could begin by attempting to assess the work to date, to try to tie together disparate findings and insights, perhaps in the form of a catalogue of propositions: a guide to what we do and do not know and how reliable that knowledge is. Since much of the work on resource use and environmental politics has been historical, descriptive, and nontheoretical and since few studies of the newer foci of inquiry exist yet, this kind of sorting out and evaluation of the literature should not be an elaborate undertaking; it can, however, help clarify profitable directions of research and hasten the advancement of knowledge. Presumably, this volume constitutes a beginning. Eventually, we might aim toward building more complete descriptive and explanatory theories of ecological politics and ecological change, allowing valid generalization beyond the conclusions of case studies and other limited treatments. In addition, the development of normative and evaluative analysis would fill a need to be able to state more clearly exactly what goals are desirable and how close we are to achieving them. An added benefit of such exercises would be some degree of deterrence against the excessively narrow or insubstantial inquiry that seems to flow from a clouded vision of one's purpose.

As far as specific research agendas go, there have been several attempts recently to compile some logical and comprehensive suggestions. Lester Milbrath and Frederick Inscho cast their net particularly widely and offer a sketch of innumerable possibilities.[23] I would add only a few additional comments here. Four lines of research of special importance come to mind, all of which may be pursued in theoretical (basic or pure) or applied modes of analysis: explorations in normative political theory and corollary innovative developments in institutional arrangements of government; elite values, attitudes, and behavior, and especially political leadership; the nature and role of, and possible change in, public values and attitudes; and public policy studies in general.

There is much truth to the proposition that the ecological crisis arises fundamentally from man's world-view and the political and social arrangements that he has

developed over time. Consequently, we need to inquire into
the confrontation between ecological imperatives and the
philosophical foundations of modern industrial political
systems. And nothing less than a full reevaluation of those
philosophies and institutional arrangements will suffice.
Political scientists can play an important role in this
monumental intellectual effort by attempting to answer the
question of what an ecologically sound future society will,
or should, look alike; what kinds of problems, conflicts,
and choices are likely; and perhaps most significantly, how
we can move through the uncertain period of transitional
politics to whatever lies beyond with minimal cost and maximum gain in human values. Whether through excursions in
utopian thought and the construction of scenarios of possible ecological futures, through practical discussion of
immediate innovation in and reform of U.S. governmental
institutions, or through any of the possibilities between
those extremes, this kind of dialogue should be a key element of future research.[24]

Most environmentalists seem to believe--accurately in
my mind--that our failure to deal adequately with the ecological crisis stems more from a lack of concern and a lack
of political will than from the absence of requisite technological knowledge or the intractability of the problems
per se. For example, part of the solution to the "energy
crisis" is not technological at all; we can permanently reduce our consumption of energy and avoid unnecessary waste
rather than put major emphasis on attempts to locate new
oil fields or develop nuclear power plants. The choice between such alternatives is a matter of public values and
political leadership. So far there has not been much public interest in the conservationist approach nor much
leadership from above to encourage it. Whatever one's
appraisal of the need for environmental policy change,
clearly elite attitudes and public opinion are high-
priority research questions.

Initiation and shaping of ecological policy lies with
political elites for the most part, though certainly their
policy preferences and behavior are conditioned by the
American public, and even more by various politically active and influential citizens and groups. Logically, then,
we ought especially to inquire into elite values, attitudes, ideologies perceptions, motivations, and behavior.
Why do political elites or decision makers hold the values
and attitudes they do? What are their perceptions and definitions of ecological problems? How well informed are
they on the problems themselves (for example, on their
causes and especially on social and economic origins)? How

do they respond to policy advice (from ecological scientists and from relevant social scientists)? Why are they motivated or not to devote scarce time, energy, and attention to ecological problems at all or to adopt particular policy preferences? What personal and political rewards attend commitment to, and action on, ecological issues? We can hardly expect the normal laws of political behavior to be suspended in this area, although environmentalists often act as if they do expect this. Under what kinds of limitations or constraints must political elites operate (institutional, political, and behavioral)? What kinds of policy leadership are provided by whom and with what effects. What major interest groups are active and what strategies and tactics do they use with what effects? What seems most significantly to shape beliefs and decision making? The answers to such questions may tell us something about the causes of present attitudes and behavior, and thus possibly tell us something about the prospects for, and paths to, ecological change of one kind or another.

Analogous questions might frame research on public values and public opinion. There is good reason to suspect that no matter how extensive the governmental change or what kind of political leaders come to power, without the strong support and willing cooperation of the American public major efforts at ecological change will amount to little. Fundamental social and political change in a democracy does not occur without support of broad segments of the population, including the mass public. Ecological change cannot be forced down the throat of an unwilling or hostile public, nor will democratically elected leaders attempt to do so. Much of the maneuvering of President Nixon and Congress over energy initiatives in the winter of 1973-74 provides a good illustration of that. Thus, we need to know much more about public attitudes and the processes of attitude formation and change (for example, through early socialization, later personal experience, formal education, exposure to religious and cultural institutions, the mass media, and political leadership). There have been innumerable public opinion polls on environmental matters over the past few years, most of which, however, tell us precious little about public feelings and perceptions beyond the superficial indication of what percent of the public respond positively or negatively to highly structured policy alternatives or the percent declaring their "concern" for the environment, whatever that means.[25] We have few good measures of public values and commitment; knowing the simple facts of opinion direction is insufficient to draw significant conclusions. It would be useful to know a great deal more about the role public opinion actually plays in influencing political decisions, how much support or opposition can be expected from various segments of the public for policy initiatives (always a matter of concern for ambitious but insecure politicians and one on which they are normally forced to seek out often unreliable data), and, broadly speaking, what values and beliefs various publics now have: How aware are people of environmental problems? How do they perceive their seriousness? How salient are the problems? What are they willing to pay for corrective actions? How intensely do they feel about such matters? How resistant to change are these attitudes?

Finally, public policy analysis in its many and varied forms obviously constitutes an integral part of any research agenda. We touched on this earlier and there is no need for redundancy. This area is likely to receive the lion's share of efforts in the near future: evaluations of previously adopted environmental policies, critical analysis of alternative policies (including assessments of costs and consequences), etc. Perhaps we ought especially to guard against the weaknesses of policy analysis, however, precisely because it will become so popular. As Charles Lindblom has observed in another context, policy analysis is often conservative "because it does not ask radical questions about fundamental features of the social structure." And it is often superficial "because it considers only those ways of dealing with policy that are close cousins to existing practices."[26] If there is a need to ask some radical and nonsuperficial questions, these kinds of biases should be recognized.

The next few years offer an exceptional opportunity to study ecological politics. This new area of study can still move off in any one of many directions and nearly all the basic research and defining of the interesting questions remain to take place. Given this fact, major conflicts over proper goals, theories, and methods are certain to emerge and will likely occupy a not insignificant portion of our time. The productive development of the field can be aided considerably at this time through the encouragement of eclecticism, interdisciplinary research, diversity in approaches and methodologies, creative ventures, sensitivity to long-range as well as short-range goals, and a willingness to engage in specific empirical, normative, and prescriptive analysis as the occasion fits. There is simply no good reason to settle for a casual imitation of other political science fields or for premature rigidity. It is currently fashionable in some circles to despair of man's intelligence, ingenuity, and his future on this small planet and to assess our willingness to confront ecological challenges in highly skeptical terms. Perhaps intelligent political analysis can make a small contribution to the demise of such pessimistic visions, or at least it would be comforting to think so.

NOTES

1. Barry Commoner, The Closing Circle (New York: Alfred A. Knopf, 1971), p. 33.

2. Lynton Caldwell has provided a well-reasoned case for this in Environment: A Challenge to Modern Society (Garden City, N.Y.: Doubleday, 1971).

3. David Easton, A Systems Analysis of Political Life (New York: John Wiley, 1965).

4. Dean E. Mann and Geoffrey Wandesforde-Smith, "Environmental Policy," Policy Studies Journal 1 (Winter 1972): 78.

5. One list can be found in Charles O. Jones, "From Gold to Garbage: A Bibliographical Essay on Politics and the Environment," American Political Science Review 66 (June 1972): 588-95.

6. See "Doctoral Dissertations in Political Science," P.S. 6 (Fall 1973): 506-34.

7. Geoffrey Wandesforde-Smith and Dean Mann, eds., "Political Scientists and Environmental Studies: A Preliminary Directory" (mimeo from University of California, Davis, Department of Political Science, February 1973).

8. Especially notable for the abundance of environmental politics papers (approximately 18) was the Ninth World Congress of the International Political Science Association at Montreal, Canada, August 1973. Many of the papers, I understand, are to be published in the May-June 1974 issue of the American Behavioral Scientist.

9. Richard L. Clinton, William S. Flash, and R. Kenneth Godwin, eds., Political Science in Population Studies (Lexington, Mass.: D. C. Heath, 1972); Richard L. Clinton and R. Kenneth Godwin, Research in the Politics of Population (Lexington, Mass.: D. C. Heath, 1972); Richard L. Clinton, Population and Politics: New Directions in Political Science Research (Lexington, Mass.: D. C. Heath, 1973); Phyllis Tilson Piotrow, World Population Crisis: The United States Response (New York: Praeger, 1973); Peter Bachrach and Elihu Bergman, Power and Choice: Formulation of American Population Policy (Lexington, Mass.: D. C. Heath, 1973); and A. E. Keir Nash, ed., Governance and Population: The Governmental Implications of Popula-

tion Change (Washington, D.C.: Government Printing Office, 1972).

10. See U.S. Environmental Protection Agency, Office of Research and Development, Environment: A Bibliography of Social Science and Related Literature, compiled by Denton E. Morrison, Kenneth E. Hornback, and W. Keith Warner, Socio-economic Environmental Studies Series 600/5-74-011 (Washington, D.C.: Government Printing Office, February 1974); and Michael L. Fox, "An Air Pollution Bibliography for the Social Sciences," in Air Pollution and the Social Sciences: Formulating and Implementing Control Programs, ed. Paul B. Downing (New York: Praeger, 1971), which is of broader importance than its title suggests. See also Nedjelko D. Suljak, ed., Public Policymaking and Environmental Quality: An Annotated Interdisciplinary Bibliography (Davis: University of California, Institute of Governmental Affairs, July 1971); and Dr. Lyle Sumek, Environmental Management and Politics: A Selected Bibliography (DeKalb: Northern Illinois University, Center for Governmental Studies, January 1973).

11. For a contrary perspective on the importance of disciplinary concerns see Terry L. McCoy, "Political Scientists as Problem-Solvers: The Case of Population," Polity 5 (Winter 1972): 250-59.

12. Robert Lynd's discussion of these questions is still very instructive. See Knowledge for What? The Place of Social Science in American Culture (Princeton, N.J.: Princeton University Press, 1959). The more recent debate over postbehavioralism raises similar issues still insufficiently considered by many practitioners it would seem. See, for example, Kenneth Dolbeare, "Public Policy Analysis and the Coming Struggle for the Soul of the Postbehavioral Revolution," in Power and Community: Dissenting Essays in Political Science, ed. Philip Green and Sanford Levinson (New York: Vintage Books, 1970); and David Easton, "The New Revolution in Political Science," American Political Science Review 63 (December 1969): 1051-61.

13. See Roger W. Cobb and Charles D. Elder, Participation in American Politics: The Dynamics of Agenda-Building (Boston: Allyn and Bacon, 1972), esp. Chapters 5 and 6; and Charles O. Jones, An Introduction to the Study of Public Policy (Belmont, Calif.: Wadsworth, 1970).

14. See Peter Bachrach and Morton Baratz, Power and Poverty: Theory and Practice (New York: Oxford University Press, 1970), pp. 3-63; Bachrach and Bergman, Power and Choice, op. cit.; and Matthew A. Crenson, The Un-Politics of Air Pollution: A Study of Non-Decisionmaking in the Cities (Baltimore: Johns Hopkins University Press, 1971).

15. Harold and Margaret Sprout, "Public Policy and Environmental Crisis: What Role for Political Scientists?" Policy Studies Journal 1 (Summer 1973): 194.

16. It should be noted that I base the comments in this chapter reflecting a particular vision of our ecological problems, their causes, and the degree of change mandated by their existence on a reading of the major general works of the last few years, for example, Commoner, The Closing Circle, op. cit.; Paul R. Ehrlich and Anne H. Ehrlich, Population, Resources, Environment: Issues in Human Ecology, 2d ed. (San Francisco: W. H. Freeman, 1972); Barbara Ward and Rene Dubos, Only One Earth: The Care and Maintenance of a Small Planet (New York: W. W. Norton, 1972); Donella H. Meadows et al., The Limits to Growth (New York: Universe Books, 1972); and Herman E. Daly, ed., Toward a Steady State Economy (San Francisco: W. H. Freeman, 1973). Readers under the impression that only alarmists speak in such terms are encouraged to examine the very sober and reasonable essays by Robert L. Heilbroner, "Growth and Survival," Foreign Affairs 51 (October 1972): 139-53, and "The Human Prospect," The New York Review of Books 20 (January 24, 1974): 21-34; the works of Lynton Caldwell, Environment, op. cit., and In Defense of Earth: International Protection of the Biosphere (Bloomington: Indiana University Press, 1972); or even the annual reports of the Council on Environmental Quality.

17. See Thomas R. Dye and L. Harmon Zeigler, The Irony of Democracy: An Uncommon Introduction to American Politics, 2d ed. (Belmont, Calif.: Wadsworth, 1972) for a comprehensive treatment of American politics supporting this rather common view.

18. Since I will not be discussing national politics in any detail, I might note here some of the key sources and research materials. For overviews of environmental politics see J. Clarence Davies III, The Politics of Pollution (Indianapolis: Bobbs-Merrill, 1970); Walter A. Rosenbaum, The Politics of Environmental Concern (New York: Praeger, 1973); and the more polemical James Rathlesberger, ed., Nixon and the Environment: The Politics of Devastation (New York: Village Voice Books, 1972). The key sources of data on national politics and contemporary issues are National Journal, Congressional Quarterly Weekly Report (and the annual Almanacs), the annual reports of the Council on Environmental Quality (the latest being Environmental Quality: The Fourth Annual Report of the Council on Environmental Quality (Washington, D.C.: Government Printing Office, 1973), the National Wildlife Foundation's Conservation Report (and of course the publications of any

number of other environmental groups), and assorted congressional and other governmental documents. Congressional
hearings in particular can be gold mines of information on
public policy and the workings of various environmental programs. And the Congressional Research Service's Environmental Policy Division's surveys of congressional action in
the 91st and 92nd Congresses (Congress and the Nation's Environment: Environmental Affairs of the 91st Congress and
Congress and the Nation's Environment: Environmental and
Natural Resources Affairs of the 92nd Congress, both prepared for Senator Jackson's Committee on Interior and Insular Affairs), along with the exceptionally useful Congressional Information Service's Index, greatly facilitate location of items of importance.

    19. Obviously it is still early to assess the full
"political response" to the ecological crisis in any systematic fashion, but the following works contain sufficient
evidence to support the summary description, I think:
Caldwell, Environment, op. cit.; Davies, The Politics of
Pollution, op. cit.; Rosenbaum, The Politics of Environmen-
tal Concern, op. cit.; Ronald O. Loveridge, "Political
Science and Air Pollution: A Review and Assessment of the
Literature," in Downing, Air Pollution and the Social Sci-
ences, op. cit.; and "The Environment: New Priorities and
Old Politics," in People and Politics in Urban Society, ed.
Harlan Hahn (Beverly Hills: Sage Publications, 1972);
Richard A. Cooley and Geoffrey Wandesforde-Smith, eds.,
Congress and the Environment (Seattle: University of Wash-
ington Press, 1970); Roy L. Meek and John A. Straayer, eds.,
The Politics of Neglect: The Environmental Crisis (Boston:
Houghton Mifflin, 1971); Leslie L. Roos, Jr., ed., The Politics of Ecosuicide (New York: Holt Rinehart and Winston,
1971); Michael E. Kraft, "Congressional Attitudes Toward
the Environment," Alternatives 1 (Summer 1972): 27-37, and
"Congressional Attitudes Toward the Environment: Attention
and Issue-Orientation in Ecological Politics" (Ph.D. dissertation, Yale University, 1973); Henry Steck, "Nixon and
the Environment: A Critique," Alternatives 1 (Winter 1972):
12-19; John C. Esposito, Vanishing Air (New York: Grossman, 1970); David Zwick and Marcy Benstock, Water Wasteland
(New York: Grossman, 1971); Rathlesberger, Nixon and the
Environment, op. cit.; and William Ophuls, "Locke's Paradigm Lost: The Environmental Crisis and the Collapse of
Laissez-Faire Politics," a paper delivered at the 1973
Annual Meeting of the American Political Science Association, New Orleans.

    20. For one inventory of such obstacles see Loveridge,
"Political Science and Air Pollution," op. cit. For a much

longer inquiry of that sort see William Ophuls, "Prologue to a Political Theory of the Steady State: An Investigation of the Political and Philosophical Implications of the Environmental Crisis" (Ph.D. dissertation, Yale University, 1973).

21. There are many examples, but I would particularly call attention to many of the essays in two volumes: William R. Burch, Jr., Neil H. Cheek, Jr., and Lee Taylor, eds., Social Behavior, Natural Resources, and the Environment (New York: Harper and Row, 1972), and Joachim F. Wohlwill and Daniel H. Carson, eds., Environment and the Social Sciences: Perspectives and Applications (Washington, D.C.: American Psychological Association, 1972).

22. Geoffrey Wandesforde-Smith, "Environmental Administration: Sources of Aid and Comfort?" Public Administration Review 32 (November/December, 1972): 881-88.

23. Lester W. Milbraith and Frederick R. Inscho, "The Environmental Problem as a Political Problem: An Agenda of Environmental Concerns for Political Scientists," a paper delivered at the Ninth World Congress of the International Political Science Association, Montreal, Canada, August 1973. See also Environmental Quality and Social Behavior: Strategies for Research (Washington, D.C.: National Academy of Sciences, 1973); Lennart J. Lundqvist, "Environmental Quality and Politics: Some Notes on Political Development in 'Developed' Countries," Social Science Information 12 (April 1973): 43-65; and Michael E. Kraft, "Ecological Politics: Research Needs and Strategies," a paper delivered at the 1972 Annual Conference of the New York State Political Science Association.

24. Such inquiry is beginning. See "The No-Growth Society," Daedalus 102 (Fall 1973), entire issue; the Environmental Protection Agency's Alternative Futures and Environmental Quality (Washington, D.C.: Government Printing Office, 1973); Daly, ed., Toward a Steady State Economy, op. cit.; Peter A. Corning, "Comparative Survival Strategies: An Approach to Social and Political Analysis," a paper delivered at the 1973 Annual Meeting of the American Political Science Association, New Orleans; Michael E. Kraft and Peter G. Stillman, "Toward a Political Theory of Ecological Survival," a paper delivered at the 1973 Annual Meeting of the American Political Science Association, New Orleans; and Ophuls, "Prologue to a Political Theory," op. cit.

25. See, for example, Hazel Erskine, "The Polls: Pollution and Its Costs," Public Opinion Quarterly 36 (Spring 1972): 120-35. A number of surveys are examined in Allan Langowski and Jeanne Sigler, "Citizen Attitudes Toward the Environment: An Appraisal of the Research"

(Chicago: Illinois Institute for Environmental Quality, November 1971, distributed by the National Technical Information Service, U.S. Department of Commerce). The best discussion I have seen of public opinion and the environment, though limited by the data available, is by Donald Munton and Linda Brady, "American Public Opinion and Environmental Pollution" (Columbus: Ohio State University, Behavioral Sciences Laboratory, November 1970, mimeo).

    26. Charles E. Lindblom, "Integration of Economics and Other Social Sciences through Policy Analysis," in Integration of the Social Sciences through Policy Analysis, ed. James C. Charlesworth (Philadelphia: American Academy of Political and Social Science, 1972), p. 1.

13

STATE AND LOCAL
ENVIRONMENTAL POLICY:
A MODEST REVIEW
OF PAST EFFORTS
AND FUTURE TOPICS
Paul A. Sabatier

State and local environmental policy is of interest to the political scientist for at least two reasons: (1) It provides a testing ground for the study of federalism and, more generally, of policy formulation and implementation in what Morton Grodzins has termed "the American system." In his view, policy making in the United States often involves all three levels of government in a more or less integrated fashion: the American system is not a three-layered cake but rather a marble cake.[1] Air and water pollution policy is, as we shall see, of particular interest in this respect because of the changing roles of the various levels of government over the past two decades. (2) In addition, the very multiplicity of state and local governments makes them ideal instruments for comparative studies of either the implementation of federally initiated programs or of programs initiated within some states and localities but not others. Analysis of variations in policies should provide important insights into the respective roles of political culture, socioeconomic variables, governmental structure, the strength of competing interest groups, etc.

Those few political scientists concerned with environmental policy making have focused their attention primarily on the federal government.[2] By indicating some of the promising areas of inquiry and some of the work that has already been done, perhaps this brief chapter can help to stimulate efforts by the vast majority of the profession

The author would like to thank Geoffrey Wandesforde-Smith, Matthew Holden, Charles Jones, and John Sacco for comments on earlier drafts of this chapter.

whose access to Washington is limited either by geography or by the lack of substantial research funds.

ENVIRONMENTAL POLICY WITHIN THE AMERICAN SYSTEM

The history of air and water pollution policy since World War II provides an excellent case study of the dynamics of policy making within the federal system.

Concern with air and water pollution was first manifested in the latter decades of the nineteenth century. For many years it was almost exclusively the concern of local governments as part of their police powers. Local control proved inadequate, however, in part because the rivers and air refused to confine the transport of pollutants within the originating jurisdictions. The state governments thus gradually became involved, first with water (in the 1930s and 1940s) and then with air (in the 1950s and 1960s).[3] But the states, too, have proven inadequate to the task, and the years since World War II have witnessed a steadily expanding federal role, first in providing monetary assistance and then in assuming regulatory authority.

While federal efforts in water pollution control date from the Refuse Act of 1899, the first major legislation was not passed until 1948. It was an exceedingly weak statute, however, as funds were never allocated and enforcement was subject to state veto. The first grants for the construction of treatment plants were provided by the 1956 Act, which also established a very cumbersome enforcement procedure via interstate conferences. (Only one court action was brought under the 1956 Act and that was not filed until 1960.) The federal role in enforcement was increased under the 1965 Water Quality Act, which provided for federal review of the water quality standards and subsequent implementation plans that the states were required to prepare. Progress under the act was slow and punctuated by periodic conflicts between the secretary of the Interior and state officials over the adequacy of state-proposed standards. The situation was more or less resolved in 1972 when, after two years of effort, the Congress assumed primary enforcement authority in the form of establishing zero discharge standards for 1985. But until that date the states will continue to establish and enforce their own water quality standards; they will, moreover, play a key role in the implementation of any federally sponsored efforts simply because of inadequate federal manpower.

Air pollution policy has followed a similar pattern, although the concentration of the problem in urban areas has meant that the states have played a much less significant role than in water pollution control (with the exception of California's pioneering efforts in the control of automotive emissions). By the late 1950s there were at least minimal programs in 85 cities, including fairly major ones in Chicago, Pittsburgh, St. Louis, Los Angeles, and New York. Most states did not become involved until the 1950s, and even as late as 1966 only 18 states had any programs at all.[4]

Because of inadequate information about the health effects and deference to local police powers, the federal government did not become involved until passage of the 1963 Clean Air Act.[5] While the statute provided for enforcement via a cumbersome conference procedure (resulting in only one court suit), it was mainly designed to provide grants to local agencies and to subsidize research into the effects of sulfur oxides. That research provided the rationale for an expanded federal role in the form of the 1967 Air Quality Act. It established a complicated and time-consuming procedure whereby the Secretary of Health, Education, and Welfare would first publish compilations of scientific findings about the effects of various pollutants; the states were then required to develop air quality standards and plans for implementing those standards--both of which were subject to federal review.

While the standards proposed by the states proved to be quite adequate--in large part due to the efforts of the National Air Pollution Control Administration in stimulating the formation of local air pollution groups[6]--the delays involved and increasing concern over the health effects convinced Congress to pass the Clean Air Amendments of 1970. This statute gave the Environmental Protection Agency the authority to establish national air quality standards and, in some cases, even national emission standards. Moreover, it provided for a 90 percent reduction in automotive emissions by 1975 (compared with the 1970 emission levels). States and localities are permitted, however, to require more stringent standards from stationary (non-automotive) sources; moreover, they will--because of inadequate federal manpower--continue to have primary responsibility for implementation of federal standards.

This brief review of the dynamics of air and water pollution control policy has at least two theoretical implications of interest to political scientists. Pollution control policy since the mid-1960s illustrates a significant departure in policy formulation within the American system as it conforms to neither the framework of grants-in-aid nor to the basically informal collaboration between the traditional federal and state regulatory commissions.[7] Instead, the federal role has evolved from the informal review of state and local programs via grants-in-aid to active review (in the 1965 Water Quality Act and the 1967 Air Quality Act) to the point where there is now a rather distinct division of labor. The federal government has primary responsibility for the establishment of (at least minimum) standards, while the states and localities retain primary responsibility for implementation, subject to as much oversight as federal manpower can provide. This pattern is not entirely dissimilar from that provided by the 1964 Civil Rights Act and the 1965 Voting Rights Act. As suggested by Daniel Elazar's 1966 study of the implementation of civil rights legislation, one would expect considerable variance in implementation of federal standards from state to state.[8] But, the the best of my knowledge, such a comparative study--despite its theoretical significance --has not yet been attempted.

While obviously a multitude of factors are involved in the shifting locus of responsibility for pollution control policy, the dynamics of policy formulation and implementation within this area of the American system illustrates the utility of E. E. Shattschneider's notion of "the scope of the conflict."[9] Beginning from the premise that "organization is the mobilization of bias," he argues that every governmental institution has a bias toward certain policies and against others. The presidency, for example, is generally less attuned to local concerns than is the House of Representatives; labor unions are better represented in Washington than in many state capitals. In such a system, actors generally seek to restrict the scope of the conflict to those loci of governmental authority whose policy bias most approximates their own.

The concern of most local and state governments with their tax base and with economic development renders them susceptible to industry pressure for "reasonable" pollution control regulations.[10] For example, the slogan of the industry-dominated Midwestern Air Pollution Control Association was "Air Pollution Control is a LOCAL Concern," and the 1963 Illinois Air Pollution Control Act was chiefly the result of industry efforts to forestall federal intervention.[11] It was in part to circumvent those pressures that the Conference of Mayors, and Chicago's Mayor Daley in particular, strongly supported the 1963 Clean Air Act.[12] Finally, while industry continued to oppose national emission standards at the time of the 1967 Air Quality Act, by 1970 the market inequities resulting from wide variations in state pollution control regulations had more or less neutralized industry opposition to national ambient air quality standards.[13]

The strategy of environmental groups has not, however, been nearly so clear-cut. While supporting the expansion of the scope of the conflict to the federal government, they have continued to focus considerable attention on pollution control programs at the state and local level. In part, of course, this is a recognition of the crucial role of these "lower" levels of government in implementing federal standards. At the same time, they have pressed for more stringent regulations by state and local authorities, thereby indicating an implicit awareness of what might be termed "the principle of beneficient overlap": The more governmental units involved concurrently in regulatory activity, the greater the probability that one of them will adopt and agressively enforce stringent regulations. By the same token, they have generally opposed--and industry has supported--efforts at federal preemption in, for example, automotive emission standards and radioactive air pollution.[14]

While the locus of governmental authority for pollution control can at any given point in time be partly explained by the efforts of various actors to control the scope of the conflict, the interstate nature of many pollution problems is another factor of considerable importance. The 1967 Air Quality Act, for example, established interstate air quality regions. Moreover, many river basins comprise more than one state and the formation of interstate basin commissions was the principle focus of federal efforts under the Water Pollution Control Amendments of 1956.[15] Perhaps the most intensive analysis by political scientists of the problems of a regional resource with a multistate clientele is represented by the numerous studies by Geoffrey Wandesforde-Smith, Edmond Costantini, and Kenneth Hanf on the Lake Tahoe Basin straddling the Nevada-California border.[16]

In sum, this brief review of air and water pollution control policy confirms Grodzins' hypothesis that the structure of policy formulation and implementation within the American system resembles a marble cake. At the same time, it suggests the dynamic nature of the system, that is, that the roles of various levels of government are constantly changing, in part as a response to the efforts of competing groups to manipulate the scope of the conflict, in part because pollution problems do not respect political boundaries.

THE STATES AND LOCALITIES AS SEMIAUTONOMOUS
POLITICAL SYSTEMS

While the previous section focused on states and localities as components of the federal system, they do, of
course, also have a considerable degree of autonomy and can
thus be employed to increase our understanding of political
processes in general and environmental policy making in particular.

The case study is a research device long employed by
political scientists and other investigators wishing to obtain detailed knowledge of a particular phenomenon. While
the explanatory utility of this strategy is limited by the
problem of generalizability, this can be minimized by carefully framing studies to answer questions posed by the relevant literature[17] and by the gradual accumulation of case
studies on related topics using similar research strategies.
The studies of water policy in Arizona by Dean Mann and
salmon fisheries in Alaska by Richard Cooley generally follow the former approach.[18] Unfortunately, there have not
been (to the best of my knowledge) any case studies testing
Matthew Holden's conception of pollution control regulation
as a bargaining process;[19] a particularly illuminating example would be Illinois, where the bargaining strategy was
followed for many years, only to be rejected in 1970 in
favor of an approach placing far greater emphasis on legal
coercion and formal legal proceedings. There have also
been numerous case studies--generally by lawyers--describ-
ing the pioneering and experimental efforts of a state or
locality to solve a particular environmental problem;[20]
while extremely limited in explanatory import, they can
provide part of the descriptive base for more theoretically
sophisticated interpretations of the same events or related
efforts in other political systems.

In addition to individual case studies of environmental
problems, a number of comparative case studies of varying
explanatory import are beginning to appear. These include
George Hagevik's study of air pollution policy in Los Angeles and New York City, Elizabeth Haskell and Victoria
Price's description of the legislative responses of nine
states to the increased environmental concern manifested in
1970, and my own analysis of the role of conservation and
environmental groups in policy formulation in the states of
Illinois, Indiana, and Michigan between 1969 and 1972.[21]
Additional possibilities for comparative case studies include the efforts of various states to pass coastal pro-

tection statutes and to establish wild and scenic river systems.[22]

The above studies all focus on the political response to environmental problems or environmental concern. A number of political scientists have, however, used environmental problems to illustrate and illuminate a theoretical issue of long standing within the profession. Recent studies have, for example, exploited the recent emergence of air pollution control as a major issue to analyze the dynamics of agenda-setting, a topic intimately related to the literature on both community power studies and policy formulation within a systemic perspective.[23]

In part due to the expense and methodological limitations of case studies, a number of political scientists have over the past decade begun to do comparative studies of all 50 states using sophisticated quantitative techniques. Indeed, one of the most theoretically significant and methodologically rigorous debates currently within the profession concerns the respective roles of socioeconomic variables (for example, urbanization, industrialization, aggregate personal income) and political variables (for example, interparty competition, malapportionment, level of voter participation) on policy outputs, particularly program expenditures.[24] While the initial studies dealt almost exclusively with largely distributive policies such as highways and education, this approach has recently been applied to regulatory programs in air and water pollution control.[25] John Sacco and Edgar Leduc's study of state expenditures for air pollution control programs in 1963 and 1967 concluded that political variables--with the exception of malapportionment--were insignificant, while industrialization, urbanization, and (to a lesser extent) median income accounted for some of the variance.[26]

The limitations of using expenditures as an indicator of policy output[27] have led at least two investigators to attempt a more systematic analysis of the nature of policy outputs in air and water pollution control, as well as the variables affecting them. An as yet uncompleted study by Peter Nelson of the University of Arizona hypothesizes that air pollution abatement expenditures will be most responsive to system resources at the extremes of socioeconomic development and most responsive to political variables at the middle range of development.[28] In addition, he attempts to relate a host of independent variables involving system resources, policy resources and constraints, and sociopolitical culture to the nature of air pollution statutes and administrative regulations.

Much of his model is based upon an earlier one employed by Lettie Wenner in her analysis of state water

pollution control efforts.[29] Using factor analysis techniques to explore the relationships among the strictness of
state statutes, the resources devoted by states to water
pollution control work, the nature of state administrative
agencies, the water quality standards promulgated by the
agencies, the agencies' enforcement efforts, the strength
of polluting and antipollution interests, and changes in
water quality, she reached the following conclusions: (1)
there is a modest relationship between the enforcement effort made by the state agency and both the strictness of
the law and resources expended; (2) the ratio of polluters
to nonpolluters on the governing boards--but neither the
strictness of the law nor the resources expended--is related to the strictness of water quality standards; (3) degradation of water quality increases legislative interest and
causes enforcement agencies to increase their efforts; (4)
legislative interest is more strongly correlated with the
efforts of administrative agencies than with the strictness
of the law itself; (5) the presence of polluting interests
on the boards is negatively correlated with water quality
standards but positively correlated with enforcement efforts; and (6) the strength of antipolluting interests
seems to affect only the strictness of water quality standards.[30] While one can question the means by which she
operationalized some of the variables,[31] her findings suggest that the factors affecting state air and water pollution control policies may be considerably more complicated
than have heretofore been assumed.

SUMMARY

This brief chapter has attempted to review some of the
research that has already been done on state and local environmental policy formulation and implementation. Much of
the work, however, is of little explanatory import, being
either largely descriptive in nature or failing to depart
from and build upon the knowledge--albeit limited--of the
American political system accumulated by the profession
over the last few decades.

Efforts directed at the following topics would be particularly valuable: (1) What have been the variables affecting the gradually increasing federal role in air and
water pollution control? For example, we still do not
have good legislative histories of the 1967 Air Quality
Act and the 1970 Clean Air Amendments.) In particular,
just how significant have been the efforts of various actors to manipulate the scope of the conflict? (2) What are
the variables affecting interstate variation in the imple-

mentation of the (minimum) regulations promulgated by EPA
with respect to air and water pollution, pesticides, etc.?
In air pollution, for example, one could determine EPA's
evaluation of the adequacy of various state programs through
an analysis of its review of state implementation plans (42
C.F.R. 420) and the number of enforcement actions instituted
by the federal agency in various states. These policy variations (the dependent variable) could then be correlated
with a variety of independent variables, for example, urbanization, industrialization, pollution levels, agency structure, political culture. (3) What is the nature of, and
the factors affecting, regulatory decision making? Specifically, Holden's characterization of pollution control as a
bargaining process needs to be carefully tested. (4) We
need theoretically sophisticated case studies of the experimental efforts of various states and localities in solving environmental problems. Why, for example, was Oregon--
but not Illinois--able to pass legislation regulating the
sale of nonreturnable bottles? How did a normally conservative state like Indiana come to prohibit the sale of
phosphate detergents? Why have Michigan and California--
but not Illinois--passed wild and scenic river legislation?
In short, we need individual and comparative case studies
that will explore in some detail the sources of variation
in state and local policies. (5) These comparative case
studies hopefully will suggest variables that can then be
tested statistically for a large number of political systems. In the meantime, we need to further explore the respective roles of socioeconomic and political variables in
explaining interstate variation in different types (for
example, distributive and regulatory) environmental policies. (6) Conversely, some of the relationships suggested
by rather gross statistical methods (for example, Wenner's
findings concerning the effect of the representation of
polluting interests on policy boards on standard-setting
and enforcement) need to be tested by a series of case
studies.

These are but some of the areas in which a study of
state and local environmental policy can both be based upon
and contribute to our understanding of policy formulation
and implementation within the American political system.

NOTES

1. Morton Grodzins, in The American System, ed. Daniel Elazar (Chicago: Rand-McNally, 1966).

2. Cf. Walter Rosenbaum, The Politics of Environmental Concern (New York: Praeger, 1973); J. Clarence Davies III, The Politics of Pollution (New York: Pegasus, 1970); Richard Cooley and Geoffrey Wandesforde-Smith, Congress and the Environment (Seattle: University of Washington Press, 1970); Michael Kraft, "Congressional Attitudes Toward the Environment," Alternatives: Perspectives on Society and Environment 1 (Summer 1972); Henry Steck, "Power and the Policy Process: Advisory Committees in the Federal Government," a paper presented at the 1972 Annual Meeting of the American Political Science Association, Washington, D.C. Most major work by lawyers has also dealt with federal policy. Cf. John Esposito, Vanishing Air (New York: Grossman, 1970); David Zwick and Marcy Benstock, Water Wasteland (New York: Bantam, 1971); James Rathlesberger, ed., Nixon and the Environment: The Politics of Devastation (New York: Village Voice Books, 1972).

3. Lettie Wenner, "Enforcement of Water Pollution Control Laws," a paper presented at the 1971 Annual Meeting of the American Political Science Association, Chicago, p. 34. The best general history of state and federal pollution policy is found in Frank Grad, George Rathgens, and Albert Rosenthal, Environmental Control: Priorities, Policies and Law (New York: Columbia University Press, 1971), pp. 47-183. See also Davies, The Politics of Pollution, op. cit.; Frank Barry, "The Evolution of the Enforcement Provisions of the Federal Water Pollution Control Act," Michigan Law Review 68 (May 1970): 1103-30.

4. In 1961 only 17 state and 85 local agencies were spending as much as $5,000 on air pollution-control programs. California alone spent about 56 percent of the state and local funds. Cf. U.S. Senate, Committee on Public Works, A Study of Air Pollution--Air, 88th Cong., 1st sess., 1963, pp. 32-4. Davies, The Politics of Pollution, op. cit., pp. 126-27.

5. Randall Ripley, "Congress and Clean Air," in Congress and Urban Problems, ed. Frederic Cleaveland (Washington, D.C.: Brookings Institution, 1969), pp. 224-78.

6. Paul Sabatier, "A Note of Optimism in Agency-Constituency Relations; the NAPCA-EPA Citizen Participation Program," manuscript in progress.

7. Grodzins, in The American System, op. cit., Chapter 3. For a discussion of intergovernmental relations in other environmental policy areas, see Philip Foss, The Politics of Grass (New York: Greenwood, 1960); Grant McConnell, Private Power and American Democracy (New York: Alfred A. Knopf, 1966), Chapter 7; Morton Grodzins, "The

Many America Governments and Outdoor Recreation," in Politics, Policy and Natural Resources, ed. Dennis Thompson (New
York: The Free Press, 1972), pp. 131-45.

8. Daniel Elazar, American Federalism: A View from
the States (New York: Crowell, 1966, pp. 8-11.

9. E. E. Schattschneider, The Semi-Sovereign People
(New York: Holt, Rinehart and Winston, 1960). The concept
has also been extensively used by Grant McConnell, Political
Power and American Democracy (New York: Praeger, 1966).

10. Ira Sharkansky, The Politics of Taxing and Spend-
ing (Indianapolis: Bobbs Merrill, 1969), Chapter IV;
Walter Heller "Financing the Federal System," in Governing
the States and Localities, ed. Duane Lockard (New York:
Macmillan, 1969), pp. 10-30; Hubert Marshall and Betty Zisk,
The Federal-State Struggle for Offshore Oil, ICP No. 98
(Indianapolis: Bobbs Merrill, 1966); Frank Smith, The Pol-
itics of Conservation (New York: Random House, 1966).

11. Paul Sabatier, "The Development of the Issue of
Air Pollution in Chicago" (unpublished Master's thesis,
University of Chicago, 1970).

12. Ripley, "Congress and Clean Air," op. cit., pp.
237-42.

13. Esposito, Vanishing Air, op. cit., Chapters 10-12.
U.S. Senate, Committee on Public Works, Subcommittee on Air
and Water Pollution Control, Hearings on S. 780, 90th Cong.,
1st sess. (Washington, D.C.: Government Printing Office,
1967), pp. 1783-1826, 2016-2103. By 1970, the National
Chamber of Commerce continued to oppose national emission
standards but was willing to live with national ambient air
quality standards. Cf. U.S. Senate Subcommittee on Air and
Water Pollution, Hearings on S. 3229, S. 3466, S. 3546,
91st Cong., 2d sess. (Washington, D.C.: Government Printing Office, 1970), pp. 473-78.

14. Cf. David Currie, "Motor Vehicle Air Pollution:
State Authority and Federal Pre-emption," Michigan Law Re-
view 68 (May 1970): 1083-1102, "Federal Pre-emption and
State Regulation of Radioactive Air Pollution," in ibid.,
pp. 1294-1313; Ann Morgenstern, "The Relationship Between
Federal and State Laws to Control and Prevent Pollution,"
Environmental Law 1 (Spring 1971): 238-57.

15. Marc Roberts, "Organizing Water Pollution Control: The Scope and Structure of River Basin Authorities,"
Public Policy 19 (Winter 1971): 75-142.

16. Kenneth Hanf and Geoffrey Wandesforde-Smith,
"Institutional Design and Environmental Management: The
Tahoe Regional Planning Agency," Research Report No. 24
(Davis: University of California, Institute of Governmen-
tal Affairs, August 1972); Edmond Constantini and Kenneth

Hanf, "Environmental Concern and Lake Tahoe," Environment and Behavior 4 (July 1972): 209-42.

17. For a discussion of "theoretical case studies," see Harry Eckstein, Division and Cohesion in Democracy (Princeton, N.J.: Princeton University Press, 1966).

18. Dean Mann, The Politics of Water in Arizona (Tucson: University of Arizona Press, 1963); Richard Cooley, Politics and Conservation (New York: Harper & Row, 1963).

19. Matthew Holden, Pollution Control as a Bargaining Process (Ithaca, N.Y.: Cornell University Water Resources Center, 1966).

20. (1) Citizens' suits: Joseph Sax, Defending the Environment (New York: Alfred A. Knopf, 1971); Joseph Sax and Roger Conner, "Michigan's Environmental Protection Act of 1970," Michigan Law Review 70 (May 1972): 1004-1106; Gregor McGregor, "Private Enforcement of Environmental Law: An Analysis of Massachusetts's Citizen Suit Statute," Environmental Affairs 1 (November 1971): 606-24. (2) Air Pollution: Austin Heller, "Low Sulfur Fuels for New York City," Patient Earth, ed. John Harte and Robert Socolow (New York: Holt, Rinehart and Winston, 1971), pp. 42-57; Ted Thackery, "Pittsburgh: How One City Did It," Ecology and Economics, ed. Marshall Goldman (Englewood Cliffs, N.J.: Prentice-Hall, 1972), pp. 199-202; Harold Kennedy and Martin Weekes, "Control of Auto Emissions--California Experience and Federal Legislation," Law and Contemporary Problems 33 (Spring 1968): 297-314. (3) Water Pollution: David Seckler, California Water (Berkeley: University of California Press, 1971); Nicholas Moros, "Effluent Fees in Water Quality Management: The Vermont Water Pollution Control Act," Environmental Affairs 1 (November 1971): 631-53; Janine Dalezel and Bruce Warren, "Saving San Francisco Bay," Stanford Law Review 23 (1971): 23; N. William Hines, "Decade of Experience under Iowa Water Permit System, Part I," Natural Resource Journal 7 (1967); "Part II," Natural Resource Journal 8 (1968): 23; Thomas Vituollo-Martin, "Pollution Control Laws: The Politics of Radical Change," in The Politics of Ecosuicide, ed. Leslie L. Roos, Jr. (New York: Holt, Rinehart and Winston, 1971), pp. 346-69. (4) Land: Richard Cooley, "State Land Policy in Alaska," Natural Resource Journal 4 (1964): 455; Fred Bosselman and David Callies, The Quiet Revolution in Land Use Control (Washington, D.C.: Government Printing Office, 1971). In addition, readers on environmental politics contain numerous case studies. Cf. Harte and Socolow, Patient Earth, op. cit.; Thompson, Politics, Policy, and Natural Resources, op. cit.; Roy Meek and John Straayer, The Politics of Neglect (Boston: Houghton Mifflin, 1971).

21. George Hagevik, <u>Decision-Making in Air Pollution Control</u> (New York: Praeger, 1970); Elizabeth Haskell and Victoria Price, <u>State Environmental Management: Case Studies of Nine States</u> (New York: Praeger, 1973).

22. Cf. Donald Wood, "Wisconsin's Statewide Requirements for Shoreland and Flood Plain Zoning," <u>Natural Resource Journal</u> 10 (1970): 327; Fred Doolittle, "Land Use Planning and Regulation of the California Coast," <u>Environmental Quality Series</u>, No. 9 (Davis: University of California, Institute of Governmental Affairs, May 1972).

23. Charles Jones, <u>An Introduction to the Study of Public Policy</u> (Belmont, Calif.: Wadsworth, 1970), Chapter 3; Roger Cobb and Charles Elder, <u>Participation in American Politics: The Dynamics of Agenda-Building</u> (Boston: Allyn and Bacon, 1972); Matthew Crenson, <u>The Un-Politics of Air Pollution</u> (Baltimore: Johns Hopkins University Press, 1971); Paul Sabatier, "Toward a Conceptual Reformulation of the 'Other' Face of Power: The Development of the Issue of Air Pollution in Chicago," unpublished paper, University of Chicago, February 1972. In addition, Harold Sims of the University of California, Riverside, is completing a dissertation on the role of the mass media in the development of air pollution policy in Los Angeles.

24. Thomas Dye, "Income Inequality and American State Politics," <u>American Political Science Review</u> 63 (March 1969): 157-62; Richard Dawson and James Robinson, "Interparty Competition, Economic Variables, and Welfare Policies in the American States," <u>Journal of Politics</u> 25 (May 1963): 265-89. Richard Hofferbert, "The Relationship Between Public Policy and Some Structural and Environmental Variables in the American States," <u>American Political Science Review</u> 9 (March 1966): 73-82; Ira Sharkansky, "Economic and Political Correlates of State-Governmental Expenditures," <u>Midwest Journal of Political Science</u> 11 (May 1967): 173-92, and "Regionalism, Economic Status, and the Public Policies of American States," <u>Social Science Quarterly</u>, June 1968, pp. 9-26.

25. This typology of policies is based upon the work of Lowi and Salisbury. Cf. Theodore Lowi, "American Business, Public Policy, Case Studies, and Political Theory," <u>World Politics</u> 16 (July 1964): 677-715; Robert Salisbury, "The Analysis of Public Policy," in <u>Political Science and Public Policy</u>, ed. Austin Ranney (Chicago: Markham, 1968).

26. John Sacco and Edgar Leduc, "An Analysis of State Air Pollution Expenditures," <u>Journal of the Air Pollution Control Association</u> 19 (June 1969): 416-19.

27. Ira Sharkansky, "Governmental Expenditures and Public Services in the American States," <u>American Political</u>

Science Review, December 1967, pp. 1066-77; John Fenton and Donald Chamberlayn, "The Literature Dealing with the Relationship Between Political Processes, Socioeconomic Conditions, and Public Policies in the American States," Policy 1 (Spring 1969): 388-404; Richard Hofferbert, "Socioeconomic Dimensions of the American States: 1890-1960," Midwest Journal of Political Science 12 (August 1968): 401-18.

28. Peter Nelson, "Dimensions of Air Pollution Policies Among the American States," a paper presented at the 1972 Annual Meeting of the American Political Science Association, Washington, D.C., p. 19.

29. Lettie Wenner, "Enforcement of Water Pollution Control Laws," op. cit.

30. Ibid., pp. 23, 25, 27, 36, 37, 38, 39, and 40.

31. To cite only two examples: (1) In composing her variable of "antipolluting forces," she included the Audubon Society, the Izaak Walton League, and the Sierra Club (p. 30), but left out the largest and (on water pollution matters) probably the most important conservation organization, that is, the state affiliates of the National Wildlife Federation. (2) The data used for measuring water quality are--as she acknowledges (p. 42)--based upon monitoring systems that are often neither reliable nor comprehensive.

PART

POLITICAL INSTITUTIONS WITHIN GOVERNMENTS

14

OBSERVATIONS ON
ENVIRONMENTAL POLITICS
Charles M. Hardin

THE PROBLEM OF FORMULATING A POLITICAL APPROACH
TO THE CONCEPT OF THE ENVIRONMENT

Great perplexities arise from the inclusiveness of basic ecological concepts such as the environment together with the sense of doom if a sweeping and detailed program of changes in human, group, and societal behavior is not designed, adopted, and enforced at once. The California Environmental Protection Act of 1969 defines the environment as "the aggregate of all factors that influence the conditions of life in or about the state or within any portions thereof. . . ." The Environmental Protection Act of the United States achieves the same olympian perspective by simply proposing that "man and nature live in productive harmony. . . ."

First written in late 1972, this chapter has not been revised to take into account the effects of the energy crises on the American polity. Predictably, the needs for energy will force major changes in policy at the expense of environmental objectives: building the Alaska pipeline, opening up off-shore oil exploration, reducing restrictions on burning coal with high sulfur content, easing restrictions on strip mining, and expediting the development of nuclear power plants are examples, some of which have already come to pass. On the other hand, reduced fuel consumption will significantly decrease air pollution and probably water pollution as well as the accumulation of solid waste. Nevertheless, environmental issues, while changing, will not disappear. The analysis in this chapter remains fundamentally relevant.

What is implied can be seen better in the expansive
"crisis of survival, through which the present generations
of man are fated to struggle," presented by the editorial in
National Parks and Conservation for November 1972. The crisis has

> many facets: air and water pollution, the ex-
> tinction of plants and animals, the destruction
> of soils and forests, of historical sites and
> artistic treasures, of natural beauty and sce-
> nery, the exhaustion of metal ores and mineral
> fuels, the impact of senseless urbanization,
> the constant threat of famine and nuclear war,
> the violence of the population and technologi-
> cal explosions, the complexity, instability,
> acceleration, expansion, and impersonality of
> governmental and economic institutions, the
> persistence of brutal tyranny in many countries,
> and seemingly a deep-seated death-wish, lying
> like a dark tide under the minds of too many
> people in too many places.
>   Each facet of the Crisis must be met for
> the dangers it presents in itself, and yet as
> part of the syndrome. The crisis commands
> obedience to the ecological imperative: men
> must live as part of the Community of Life or
> they shall not live at all. The attitude to-
> ward Nature as a thing to be dominated which
> has prevailed since the Renaissance, must
> yield to the purposes of care, concern, pro-
> tectivity toward all living things, from soil
> to fellow men. Else we shall not survive.

Where Paul Ehrlich discerned the original ecological
sin in the first hunters who turned to farming, and Lynton
Caldwell discovered it in Genesis (be fruitful, multiply,
replenish the earth, subdue it, have dominion), the editors
of National Parks and Conservation found it in the men of
the Renaissance.
    What commands our attention is the effort to create a
new political myth, with social and political implications
and a deeply religious dimension. A new myth, or a redefi-
nition of old myths, may be one of the time's profoundest
needs. President Nixon's instinct is to revive the protestant ethic; but he is handicapped by the loss of belief in
hell and damnation. The power of the protestant ethic lies
in its direct appeal to self-interest and its clear injunctions that men should devote themselves to hard work and

frugal living (not altogether manifest in San Clemente). It was similar with Plato's noble lie designed to get all men to accept their proper roles and functions in the political community--the injunctions were clear and understandable: to govern, to defend, or to produce the goods and services the community needed to live. Likewise with Marx plus Sorel. Marx's myth of historical materialism, economic determinism, and the classless society explained the inexorable laws of development; and Sorel's myth of the general strike told men exactly what to do to help history complete itself: Down tools!

Each of these myths appealed directly to self-interest; and each provided clear, simple, and practicable instructions. Contrast the myth implicit in the ecological literature. Rather than an appeal to self-interest, the appeal is to sacrifice--and for the diffuse benefits of all mankind, if not, indeed, of all living things, now and in the future. Rather than the simple injunctions of the great historical myths, the obligation is to attack every conceivable natural, psychological, national, and communal disorder simultaneously.

CAN ENVIRONMENTAL CONCERN BE DEFINED AND FOCUSED SUFFICIENTLY TO BECOME POLITICALLY VIABLE?

Phillip Foss argues that "policy changes ordinarily take place as a result of highly organized interest group activity."[1] A "small, tightly organized group with a direct personal interest" will usually defeat a large, inchoate, unorganized mass. The problem of environmental groups, he says, is the diffusion of objectives--some think of vanishing wildlife, some of air quality, or water quality, or population control, or noise, or stench, or open spaces, or access to beaches, or the aesthetics of urban structures, or the preservation of wilderness areas.

Generally, if one looks for prime movers or, at least, the most obvious agents of political change, he finds individuals or groups. Rachel Carson has been formidably influential in the general cause of ecology as well as in such specific matters as the ban on DDT. Silent Spring is full of descriptions of the activities of particular groups or agencies, typically with well-defined interests--personal gain or the enlargement of the bureau, for example--at stake. The role of the U.S. Department of Agriculture Plant Pest Control Division in the Fire Ant eradication program is an example.[2] So is the enforcement of California's laws on pesticides in the San Joaquin Valley. The extension of the permit system to proscribe DDT if it would drift to alfalfa came from dairy groups that were faced with enforced rules on zero tolerance in milk, and the ban on 2,4-D on grain that might drift to grapes or cotton was enforced by grape and cotton producers. Neither was enforced by environmentalist groups.[3] Where environmentalist groups have acted, they have typically been well organized and politically experienced; and they have worked for concrete ends, such as the collaboration of the National Audubon Society, Izaak Walton League, and the Sierra Club (with others) to get a national ban of DDT.

And yet one has to explain the rapid escalation in environmental legislation in recent years. Activity began in the states in the middle 1960s and greatly accelerated in 1970 and 1971. In 1972 more than half the states passed legislation dealing with environmental problems--examples were the consolidation of agencies into departments of environmental protection; the provision of land use planning; and the replacement of boards heavily representative of business or agriculture with advisory boards composed of representatives of the "public." I suspect that examination of any of these state changes would disclose the effective work and influence of one or a few leaders plus one or two organized groups. But the legislators must also have sensed a wider public interest.

THE ROLE OF PUBLIC OPINION

In Chapter 8 of _Environment_, Lynton Caldwell says that in the late 1960s the people were more responsive to environmental interests than Congress, which was more responsive than the president.[4] Responsive is a good word--the people had something and someone to _respond_ to, on the one hand, the aggravation of smog or water pollution and, on the other, militant groups and leaders. In Chapter 1, however, Caldwell, a political scientist, questioned whether environmental quality could be more than a vaguely defined social issue, supported by inchoate groups, differentially concerned. His language is similar to that of Phillip Foss, also a political scientist, who depreciated the political effectiveness of the large, inchoate, unorganized mass.

What groups are active and what kind of leverage do they have? Prestigious organizations like the Audubon Society (200,000 members) and the Sierra Club (140,000 members) clearly have access to government, an established reputation for the analytical and forensic ability of their spokesmen, and some resonance with larger publics. They can go to administrators, to lawmakers, or to the courts. But they cannot go into the hustings without jeopardizing their tax-free status. For the latter, which seems essential if public opinion is to be translated into votes, other organizations are required, such as Environmental Action (a descendant of Earth Day), the League of Conservation Voters, or Student Vote, which claims to be able to call out 11 million voters under 21 on environmental issues. Environmental Action (EA) has a handful of young people in its Washington office and publishes a monthly, Environmental Action. EA selected a congressional "dirty dozen" in 1970 and again in 1972. In 1970, seven of the "dirty dozen" were defeated, and EA claimed that 16 of the 22 it supported won their congressional races.

In 1972 EA supported Democratic Congressman Ken Hechler's successful bid for renomination in West Virginia where he had angered strip mining interests. It helped defeat the renomination of a ten-term veteran in Nevada, Democratic Congressman Walter S. Baring. In the Colorado primary, EA helped defeat the very senior Wayne Aspinall who, as chairman of the House Committee on Interior and Insular Affairs, had long responded to the demands of ranchers, irrigation farmers, lumbermen, and miners. The Republican legislature had redrawn Aspinall's constituency, earlier confined to the western slope, to include Greeley and Fort Collins, both with state universities, and Denver suburbs. He was defeated by Alan Merson, a Denver law professor, who subsequently lost the election.

Two elements were apparently important in Aspinall's defeat. One was that he lost by only 2,000 votes; hence, a relatively small group had much leverage. The second was that the theme of Merson's victory seemed to be to stop growth. As one ardent Merson man put it, "Around here an environmentalist is someone who built his mountain cabin last year." The same theme was repeated in the successful attack on the Winter Olympics in Colorado's referendum of November 7, 1972. A similar sentiment has been strong in Oregon where people are still invited to visit but no longer urged to stay and make their homes--quite the contrary. Similarly in California, as Emil Mrak reported of the governor's conference in May 1972: "There was a strong emphasis on the need to deemphasize growth . . . it was even suggested that we cease the production of . . . power, with a view of discouraging people from entering the state. . . ."[5]

The direct appeal to selfish interests makes the environmentalist cause politically viable. There was a lesson to learn in the effect of Upton Sinclair's The Jungle, which he wrote to awaken the public conscience about the subhuman lives of immigrant workers in Chicago's stockyards and packing houses at the turn of the century, but the message to the middle class was that their food might be poisonous. What emerged politically was support for Harvey Wiley's Pure Food and Drug law. Ordinarily, I suspect, the appeal has to be directly to gut issues before the inchoate mass will be galvanized.[6] In this way, environmentalists will be able to scare congressmen as effectively as the National Rifle Association with its extremely specific enemy-- federal gun control legislation.

An excellent example of the importance of appeals to intensely personal interests is supplied by the Willamette River Valley, which contains 13 percent of Oregon's land and 70 percent of its population. In 1962 the Willamette was said to be the most polluted river in the Pacific Northwest. By 1970 it was one of the cleanest. Fishing was better than ever. Boating was once more attractive and even swimming was safe. The transformation was begun by a newscaster named Tom McCall who put on a television program called "Pollution in Paradise." The legislature launched an investigation. Four years later McCall ran successfully for governor on an environmentalist program and then presided over a policy, vigorously enforced, to clean up the river. Municipalities and businesses were forced by fines to provide primary and secondary sewage treatment. When Boise Cascade threatened to move, the Department of Environmental Quality got a court order, whereupon the company repaired its pollution control system and reopened. Two things seem important. Strong public support could be generated in a concentrated population intensely interested in the amenities provided by a clean river. Second, the pulp and paper companies were somewhat locked in by the fact that 40 percent of the nation's softwood timber is in Oregon.

There may be other factors explaining the recent rise of environmentalist legislation in Congress and state legislatures. The appeal of environmentalist ideals for their own sake must be acknowledged. In addition, environmentalist issues have been attractive as a diversion from the nation's nearly unsolvable and hateful problems. The Vietnam war ground away at terrible costs of every kind, but it seemed quite out of political control. Race relations were producing frightening clashes. Violence grew, poverty remained, and urban blight festered. Many of these interrelated problems seemed virtually intractable. How tempting to forget these politically risky issues and turn to cleaning up the environment!

One must also remember that there is always a question how far lawmakers actually intended to go in environmental

as in other policy. It was more than a generation after
the Civil Service Act was passed before the Civil Service
Commission had more than the most meager financing or any
reforms became visible to the naked eye. After the Interstate Commerce Act was passed in 1887, a score of years went
by before the Interstate Commerce Commission was given effective powers to regulate railroad rates. The Sherman
Antitrust Act was passed in 1890. Not until the late 1930s
was the Antitrust Division of the Department of Justice provided with a million dollars in its annual budget. Probably the most important single act in conservation or environmentalist history was congressional authorization to the
president in 1890 to withdraw public lands to establish national forests. Almost certainly Congress did not know what
it was doing and would have rejected the clause if it had.
When President Theodore Roosevelt vigorously used the power,
Congress withdrew it. The famous conservation movement of
the early 1900s produced almost nothing more than rhetoric.
It was largely the same in the New Deal. The Soil Conservation Service got its chance largely because it helped to put
the unemployed to work--and Hugh Hammond Bennett brilliantly
exploited the opportunity. The Soil Conservation and Domestic Allotment Act of 1936 was a masquerade of price support
and production control as a conservation measure. The Tennessee Valley Authority was unique; but its very success
proved an effective bar to the extension of the valley authority idea elsewhere in the United States.

On January 1, 1970, the Environmental Protection Act
created the Council on Environmental Quality in the Executive Office of the president and required it to report on
proposals for legislation and other action, providing detailed analyses of environmental impacts that would result
and recommending changes to bring proposed actions into line
with the Act. Query: did Congress really know what it was
doing?

PUBLIC OPINION IN REVERSE: THE
POTENTIALITY OF A BACKLASH

The foregoing analysis suggests the possibility of a
public backlash against environmental programs. In the same
way that the political basis of the drive for environmentalist policies is in the citizens' gut reactions to smog,
stench, noise, garbage, and swill, citizens may also respond
adversely if environmental programs appear to threaten their
jobs or their pocketbooks. Emil Mrak's title, "Environmental Quality vs. Food Supply," suggests the conflict.[7] Farmers are restricted by regulations that may be conflicting,

when issued by different governmental agencies, on the use of agricultural pesticides, fungicides, and herbicides; on the disposal of containers for these materials; and on the disposal of agricultural wastes in general. Farmers are worried by threatened rises in the prices of fertilizers and of materials for plant and animal protection. Similarly, food processors may be subject to regulatory threats that create economic uncertainty. The California State Water Control Board proposed to fine the City of Sacramento $6,000 a day for effluents pumped into the Sacramento River by food canning companies. A way was found by the city and the county to avoid the fine, but if it had been imposed, the canneries might have closed down, in which event jobs would have been lost and the market for tomatoes unsettled. If so, the conditions for a backlash may have been created.

The conditions may also emerge in Colorado. Commenting on the environmentalist's share in Congressman Aspinall's defeat, a local political scientist said that while many of his colleagues were "hung up on the environment," they also protest that the state legislature is not giving the university enough money. "But unless we have economic growth, how can the legislature provide the money? They don't put these two things together."

Many examples of backlash come from labor. The Pulp, Sulphite, and Paper Mills Workers in Wisconsin went fishing in the Flambeau River when a state program to require the pulp mill to clean up its wastes brought on a threat to move; their aim was to show that fishing was excellent! The United Steelworkers local in El Paso helped a smelting plant get more time to clean up discharge into the atmosphere. Teamsters, Glass Bottle Blowers, and Steelworkers helped prevent the New Jersey Legislature from imposing restrictions on nonreturnable containers: 30,000 jobs were claimed to be at stake. The United Papermakers in Holyoke, Massachusetts, replaced their job-safety campaign with one to "save jobs by halting the ecology steamroller."

A report of evidence of backlash in the states in April 1972 cited a Wisconsin State Representative, the Chairman of Maine's Environmental Improvement Commission ("There's an impression that Chambers of Commerce, to a degree, have decided to fight back. . . ."), the antienvironmentalist efforts of Missouri legislators, the foot-dragging of the governor of Vermont, growing anti-antipollution pressures in Arizona, and the effectiveness of mining interests in southeastern states in preventing strip-mining control.[8]

OTHER ADVERSE POLITICAL TRENDS

Perhaps encouraged by evidence of backlash, political opponents of environmental programs or, at least, those wanting to water down and soften the environmentalist impact are at work. Through Texas congressmen and senators, oil companies got an exemption under the Federal Water Pollution Control Act so that they could continue to pump water of any quality into the ground for water drive. Their reason: The states were already regulating the quality of water pumped into ground. The Environmental Protection Agency implied--but with understandable prudence only very softly--that Texas was not doing the job.

Because of the striking success of Governor McCall in cleaning up the Willamette River, his rather different influence on the approval of the Atomic Energy Commission's (AEC) proposed Trojan Nuclear plant at Portland is noteworthy. Apparently, the governor's assistant for Natural Resources intervened to squelch the state geologist's request for further study on the susceptibility of the proposed site to earthquakes. In this complex picture some very large interests were at stake. As one admittedly disgruntled engineer who may have lost his job over his efforts to slow the development said, "Once you've got the license to build the thing, you've generated $235 million worth of inertia." A postponement was forced, however, by a Federal Appeals Court's ruling requiring AEC to reexamine the evidence in a suit by environmentalist groups.

In this atmosphere of rising opposition and growing doubts, the political dispositions in the administration and Congress may change. When President Nixon signed the Environmental Protection Act of January 1, 1970, he expressed his conviction that in the 1970s America would "pay its debts to the past by reclaiming the purity of its air, its waters, and our living environment. It is literally now or never." By September 23, 1971, he was talking somewhat differently. "We are committed to cleaning up the air . . . and the water. But we are also committed to a strong economy and we are not going to let the environmental issue be used . . . to destroy the industrial system that made this the great country that it is."

The president may have worked through the Office of Management and Budget (OMB). In February 1972 Senator Thomas Eagleton asked Administrator William D. Ruckleshaus if the Environmental Protection Agency (EPA) had agreed to let the OMB take over the final approval of state plans to meet federal air quality standards set by the Clean Air Act of 1970. The implication was that the OMB would more nearly reflect the president's tilt toward business and away from environmental purity than would EPA. Ruckleshaus was understandably somewhat equivocal in his answer. In the same Senate Hearings (of the Air and Water Pollution Subcommittee) it was suggested that the EPA--in response to White House pressure generated by copper interests--had modified its rulings requiring the copper smelting industry to remove sulfur dioxide from its emissions.[9]

More evidence was provided by Robert Kahn when he resigned from the Council on Environmental Quality to return to the <u>Christian Science Monitor</u>, September 5, 1972. Wholehearted federal agency compliance with environmental laws still lagged, he said; and he singled out for criticism the Federal Power Commission and the Department of Transportation. (The leverage enjoyed by such agencies is explained by Richard E. Neustadt's analysis of bureaucracy.)[10] Kahn praised the White House for its constructive proposals on the environment but lamented that these tended to bog down in Congress. Kahn was especially critical of the forced reliance of the Council on Environmental Quality and the EPA on an appropriations process that was subject to great influence by the agricultural appropriations subcommittee.

In a somewhat different vein, Robert Bendiner scored both Congress and the president for lagging on environmental issues. If President Nixon's rhetoric was impeccable and his proposals often good, he failed to follow them up with effective pressure on Congress. His aides were either inept or intent on putting on the brake, especially when the OMB detected that new policies would cost money--in all this it must not be forgotten that any OMB is the president's agency and exactly reflects what he wants. Congress, on the other hand, was wide open to Nixon's rebuke that it was out of line with citizen's demands for action. Rivalries among committees were often responsible--a struggle between Senators Jackson and Muskie threatened the Land Use Policy Bill in the Senate; and Congressman Aspinall's amendment to the bill to include a giveaway of public lands almost doomed it in the House. Effective legislation to control strip mining had a fighting chance in the House but required a minor miracle in the Senate. And so it went. Robert Bendiner ended on an interesting note in light of interpretations of public opinion advanced earlier: The trouble is "that the country doesn't realize how much it would win because, for all their mobility, Americans, like every other people, concern themselves overwhelmingly with their local terrain--when they do not take its advantages completely for granted."[11]

THE NEED FOR A DIFFERENT POLITICAL FRAMEWORK

Analysis to this point suggests the need for a new political framework. Environmental problems have aggravated until they force the addition of a new dimension to our politics. Political policy formation--now much more than earlier on--must examine the relationships among proposed programs or the secondary effects of proposed undertakings. The "environmental impact statements" imply that the single-purpose agencies that our system has created and nourished shall be forced to consider a much wider range of consequences of their actions than has been their wont. Caldwell recognized the need in criticizing the narrow approach to policy and calling for an integrated attack on problems; Mrak, in criticizing "reductionism" and calling for a "broad spectrum approach."[12]

There is genuine concern that an unrestricted application of the principle of the environmental impact statements will cripple and disrupt the economy and forcefully deprive many groups and individuals. Principles and courses of action must be intensively sought that balance costs and benefits or gains and losses both in the environmental fields and in the attainment of stable economic growth. This is what Mrak means by the "rule of reason" or Perry R. Stout by urging that we develop a sense of the statistical probabilities to guide our policies.[13] Arthur Maass, one of the leading political scientists on water policy, has pointed out that the transformation of the Corps of Engineers from a single-purpose to a multipurpose agency, with all the interagency clearances required by the new departures in environmental policy, threatens to extend the planning period between the inception of projects and the beginning of construction by 22 years![14] If Mrak is properly concerned about the past tendencies toward reductionism (the reduction of complex data or phenomena to simple terms), the swing of the pendulum in the opposite direction may threaten a reductio ad absurdum!

The obvious answer to the fragmentation of policy that is inimical to the environmentalist approach is to enlarge the powers of the president to integrate and coordinate policy. To this end the EPA was created, and its integrating functions seemed for a time to be drawing strong reinforcement from the Nixon administration's vigorous use of the OMB. Nevertheless, the presidential coordinating power conflicts with the genius of Congress, which is to control programs by dividing them up and parceling them out among committees--as can be illustrated by the politics of agriculture interpreted as a case study of Neustadt's theory of bureaucracy.[15] On the other hand, if the president is simply permitted to override Congress, then the checks on presidential dictatorship will, indeed, be greatly enfeebled if not demolished.

For these reasons, I urge consideration of fundamental constitutional changes to strengthen the bonds of party between president and Congress--both to empower the president and also to constrain him by forcing him to face an organized and integrated opposition. The fact that this argument currently confronts a divided government with a Republican president and a Democratic Congress should not prevent an examination of the case for fundamental reforms.

That examination cannot be made in detail here.[16] In addition, however, to improving the coordination of policy and the ability of the government to set priorities without simply abandoning ourselves to presidential dictatorship, such a consolidation of political power (as well as the power of opposition) should also relieve the burden placed on the courts by the frustration of the more directly political branches of government. On issue after issue, environmentalist groups appeal to the courts, just as civil rights groups do. Being somewhat insulated from politics, the courts are able to act effectively. In civil rights the courts have been empowered not only by recent statute law but also by constitutional guarantees of the principle of equality. And yet these guarantees have not saved the courts from a severe loss in public prestige, if Louis Harris is to be believed, from 51 percent of the public who expressed a "great deal of confidence" in the Supreme Court of the United States in 1966 down to 28 percent in 1972.

The environmentalist recourse to the courts, if decisions become associated with declines in the economy and the consequent threat to jobs, may further weaken the judicial branch. This may be all the more true because the politicians may not have intended their legislative acts to be so vigorously enforced. We need a political system capable of making its proper decisions more promptly in order to relieve the courts from the excessive burden of making political decisions because the ordinary processes of politics are in default. The courts have their essential functions, especially the judicial guardianship and application of the Bill of Rights; and these functions should not be jeopardized because the courts are called on to do the political jobs that ought to be done elsewhere in a properly organized polity.

If an examination of environmentalist questions for their political significance leads to a proposal for fundamental political change, then we must return to the issue raised by the environmentalist myths noted in the opening paragraphs of this chapter.

As a political scientist, I am convinced that political myths are essential just as I am impressed by the general adequacy of our present political myths, given some reinterpretation and changes of emphasis especially as they touch representative government. I agree that the concern for the environment is based on the recognition of real dangers. But I am also concerned about the new ecological myths that are being offered, and thus I feel an obligation to try to fit these proposals into the thought patterns of traditional political science.

RELATIONSHIP OF THE ENVIRONMENTALIST MYTH TO THE TRADITIONAL AMERICAN POLITICAL MYTHS

In his conclusion, Caldwell's emphasizes that human and humane evolution produces civility, thus enabling people to live together in communities that enjoy free government. Among the many improvements in the quality of life already achieved by human beings none ranks higher than this.

Communities are different from the natural order or the order produced by the struggle for survival. Human beings come together in recognition of shared needs for sustaining life, for maintaining and improving the culture, for protection from enemies. They need rules and organization to keep order, to provide for defense against outsiders, and to take advantage of complementary functions among the members. For Aristotle, it may be argued, the resulting community polity was a natural growth controlled by the principles of teleology; but in his view the flowering of human beings according to their nature required the active use of the uniquely human characteristic of reasoning and making choices. B. F. Skinner to the contrary, the Aristotelian community is not something that evolves out of conditioned reflexes.

Political communities require myths, that is, statements of principles that have some basis in truth that can be apparent to common experience but that also rest in part on belief confirmed only by faith (and this aspect of the myth may be the most doggedly maintained). American myths include the ideal of equality; the proposition that government is to serve the ends of life, liberty, and the pursuit of happiness; the idea of limited government expressed in the concept of due process of law; and vox populi, vox dei, which, however, needs qualification by the idea of the division of political labor exemplified in representative government (this last needs strengthening, as Paul Ehrlich pointed out in a recent lecture). To this set of myths it now seems necessary to assimilate something representing the new concern for the environment, perhaps drawing on

189

Caldwell's final chapter on the environmentalist ethic. But it can be no more than assimilated. It cannot replace the components of the received myths that are essential to maintain the civil community. Concern for the environment cannot preempt the bonds that brought men together into the community originally, especially the need to maintain order, to secure protection from enemies, and to control power in the name of liberty.

In addition to the myth, something needs to be done to accommodate the virtually limitless time span preferred by the environmentalists to the time span of the political community.[17] By their nature political communities have time spans. How long? For ours I suggest essentially two generations, perhaps with a weaker outlook to a third generation. The urge to preserve and pass along to the next generation a patrimony and a set of conditions of life somewhat better than currently enjoyed seems fairly strong. It can be realized only in a community. It is, indeed, a fruit of civility. A one-generational time span may not be ideal. But it is within the grasp of common sense; and if it is observed and the patrimony is preserved and improved, it will suffice. One has only to contrast a situation wherein each person strives to consume everything he can lay his hands on during his lifetime, leaving nothing at his death.

THE POLITICS OF ECOLOGY

I believe that this analysis will help put the problems of environmental politics in perspective. It recognizes the challenge of a new myth and incorporates it. Furthermore, it takes account of the present flaws and dysfunctions in the making and execution of policy in the environmental field, discovering that these are essentially political rather than merely administrative--and that they call for some fundamental political changes rather than administrative tinkering.

Let me illustrate with Caldwell's preference (in Chapter 8 of Environment) for federal versus local control. There is no question that federal control is needed, for example, in power and energy policy; how else can we deal with dangers and opportunities in nuclear power or develop a policy for exploiting and conserving petroleum and coal resources? Who but the federal government can cope with smog produced by internal combustion engines? States such as California may take the lead, but 50 sets of standards or even 10 sets are unthinkable.

It is not, however, merely a question of empowering the federal government[18] or even of supplementing a more powerful federal government by the development of regional governments more appropriate to deal with problems of the environment.[19] Rather, the nature of environmental problems requires governmental institutions capable of orienting policies to achieve two or more purposes that must be mutually accommodated. It is no longer enough to encourage the development of forests essentially for timber, of grass lands for forage, of coal lands for fuel, or of farm lands for the production of food and fiber, or, indeed, even of economic growth itself in order to maintain economic stability and high employment. New policies in such areas must take more fully and effectively into account the enhancement of environmental values such as the preservation of moisture and the control of its runoff, the protection of scenic beauty, and the diminution of air and water pollution.

I realize that the development of what might be called an organic policy to take into account the multifaceted needs of the community and its environment is what the EPA aims to accomplish with impact statements. And yet I question whether this requirement, given the continuation of our present organization and division of political power, will be effective toward the end it has in view--or whether, if it is effective, it will not produce stasis. Certainly the past tendency in the national government has been to create agencies that, whatever their theoretical responsibility for considering a broad spectrum of effects, develop and solidify their political strength and support by pursuing single-purpose goals--examples are the Army Engineers in building dams, the agricultural price-support and production control agencies in shoring up farm incomes and protecting farmers from the economic effects of surpluses, or the Federal Highway Administration in building super-highways.

The dynamics of our governmental system strongly favor administrative agencies in proportion as they are able to make their objectives accord with those of influential interests in Congress, state legislatures, and the economy. The consequent concentration of support for single-purpose agencies (or, at least, of agencies with very narrow purposes) has been enormous. Unless the dynamics of the system are changed, efforts to introduce new policies by means of legislation are almost certainly doomed to be disappointing. Nor will it suffice within the present political system to improve devices of formal administration,[20] to expand the use of economic incentives,[21] or even to increase partisanship and to enhance the role of political parties.[22]

Rather, fundamental constitutional changes are necessary if our polity is going to be able to cope effectively with the issues of the environment--just as they are re-

quired if we are to maintain a strong presidency but subject
it to effective political controls, bring the burgeoning
bureaucracies (particularly the military bureaucracy) under
firm political direction that is itself centralized and accountable, and redefine and restructure a more practicable
and rewarding role for public opinion.[23]

NOTES

1. Phillip O. Foss, ed., _Politics and Ecology_ (Belmont,
Calif.: Wadsworth, 1972), "Prologue," p. 8.
2. Rachel Carson, _Silent Spring_ (Boston: Houghton,
Mifflin, 1962), pp. 146-53.
3. See Chapter 9, by Harrison Dunning, of "The Effects
of Agricultural Pesticides in the Aquatic Environment, Ir-
rigated Croplands, San Joaquin Valley," (Davis: University
of California, Food Protection and Toxicology Center, 1972).
4. Lynton Caldwell, _Environment: A Challenge to Modern Society_ (New York: Doubleday, 1971).
5. "California's Changing Environment," Occasional
paper, Office of the Chancellor Emeritus, University of
California, Davis, 1972.
6. There are occasional exceptions. In the 1940s and
1950s the Echo Park controversy arose over a proposed dam
on the Green River, part of the upper Colorado Basin development, which would have flooded part of the Dinosaur National Monument. One factor in the eventual defeat of the
proposal was an unusually wide public antipathy. George
Bender, a Republican congressman in Ohio, told an executive
session of the House Interior and Insular Affairs Committee
in 1954 that everyone in Ohio seemed vehemently opposed to
the dam. He had just gone through a statewide primary in
which the first question after the speech was almost inevitably about his stand on Echo Park! Owen Stratton and
Phillip Sorotkin, _The Echo Park Controversy_, an Inter-
University Case Study (University, Ala.: University of
Alabama Press, 1959), p. 93.
7. Occasional Paper, Office of the Chancellor Emeritus, University of California, Davis, 1972.
8. Numerous studies have shown the effectiveness of
local political interests in checking environmental programs
for Lake Tahoe. See, for example, Geoffrey Wandesforde-
Smith and William E. Felts, "The Politics of Development
Review in the Lake Tahoe Basin," (Davis: Institute of Governmental Affairs, University of California, May 1973).
9. Compare the California legislation on air pollutants from automobiles, "the nation's strictest controls,"

passed in 1968 over the opposition of "the automobile industry, automobile clubs, and even the federal government" because of the insistence of "the media, private groups, and many in southern California's 'smog belt.'" Alvin D. Sokolow, "AB 357: The Passage of California's 'Pure Air' Law. . . ." (Davis: Institute of Governmental Affairs, University of California, 1970).

10. This extremely important interpretation of modern American politics is "Politicians and Bureaucrats," in The Congress and America's Future, ed. David B. Truman (Englewood Cliffs, N.J.: Prentice-Hall, 1965).

11. Robert Bendiner, "The Environment of Politics," New York Times, September 11, 1972.

12. Emil M. Mrak, "Research Needs for Environmental Quality," Occasional Paper, Office of the Chancellor Emeritus, University of California, Davis, 1972.

13. Perry R. Stout, "Fertilizers, Food Production and Environmental Compromise" (Santa Barbara, Calif.: Center for the Study of Democratic Institutions, 1971, unpublished paper).

14. Arthur Maass, "Public Investment Planning in the United States: Analysis and Critique," Public Policy XIX (1970).

15. Charles M. Hardin, Food and Fiber in the Nation's Politics, Vol. III, Technical Papers, National Commission on Food and Fiber (Washington: Government Printing Office, 1967).

16. Charles M. Hardin, Presidential Power and Accountability: The Need for a New Constitution (to be published by the University of Chicago Press in 1974).

17. Without endorsing all his interpretations, I must say that the use of orientation toward the future to distinguish among social classes in Edward C. Banfield, The Unheavenly City (Boston: Little, Brown, 1968) is very illuminating. See especially Chapter 3.

18. Theodore J. Lowi, for example, argues that the obstacles presented by federalism to achievement of national policy have already been flanked. The End of Liberalism (New York: W. W. Norton, 1969), p. 75. See also Morton Grodzins, in The American System, ed. Daniel J. Elazar (Chicago: Rand-McNally, 1966).

19. See Edwin T. Haefele, "Environmental Quality as a Problem of Social Choice," in Environmental Quality Analysis, ed. Allen V. Kneese and Blair T. Bower (Baltimore: Johns Hopkins University Press, 1972; published for Resources for the Future), p. 323.

20. Caldwell, op. cit., Chapter 8.

21. See the conclusion of Vernon W. Ruttan's instructive presidential address to the American Agricultural Economics Association, "Technology and the Environment," in <u>American Journal of Agricultural Economics</u>, December 1971.

22. Haefele, op. cit., p. 323.

23. In this argument I am in general sympathy with James MacGregor Burns, <u>The Deadlock of Democracy</u> (Englewood Cliffs, N.J.: Prentice-Hall, 1963), Chapter 14; with Grant McConnell, <u>Private Power and American Democracy</u> (New York: Alfred A. Knopf, 1966), Chapter 10; and with E. E. Schattschneider, <u>The Semi-Sovereign People</u> (New York: Holt, Rinehart and Winston, 1960)--except that I would favor much more sweeping constitutional reforms.

15

PUBLIC OPINION
AND THE ENVIRONMENT:
AN ISSUE
IN SEARCH OF A HOME

J. Fred Springer and
Edmond Costantini

The decade of the 1960s witnessed the elevation of so many new political issues into public prominence--Vietnam, campus unrest, drugs, busing, urban crime, abortion--that followers of American public opinion were left reeling. Some pundits saw the makings of new majorities in the new patterns of conflict--"emerging," "silent," "real" majorities bound to alter the traditional character of the political landscape in some long-term way. Others saw the kaleidoscopic nature of public opinion in the 1960s as a temporary phenomenon: "contemporary disarray" was temporary disarray, with the issues blossoming in that decade likely to wither on the vine in the next.

As the 1960s came to a close, yet another new issue seemed to capture the public fancy, with corresponding attention devoted to it in the arenas of public policy making. With Earth Day in 1970, the environment had "arrived" as a major national issue. Time magazine characterized it as "The Issue of the Year."[1]

Although the public and its representatives had been activated in earlier times by a concern for environmental quality, interest was typically fleeting and the concern waned when confronted by competing interests and values.[2] The present-day ecology movement is, likewise, seen by many to reflect little more than another passing apprehension within the dominant cultural theme of individual and material exploitation of the natural environment. The public

---

The authors are grateful to the National Science Foundation (under grant #GI-22) for its support. They offer their appreciation, too, to Ms. Pat Farid and Ms. Sydney Ann Springer for their assistance.

base of the movement is too narrow, the interest it can gen-
erate too transient, and its adversaries too powerful for it
to become a durable and effective political force. Anthony
Downs argues that environmental concern is an excellent example of the type of issue that moves very rapidly through
the "issue-attention cycle" in public opinion. He predicts
its hasty demise because "First, the majority of persons in
society are not suffering from the problem nearly as much as
some minority. . . . Second, the sufferings caused by the
problem are generated by social arrangements that provide
significant benefits to a majority or a powerful minority of
the population. . . . Third, the problem has no intrinsi-
cally exciting qualities--or no longer has them."[3]

The purpose of this chapter is to assess the place of
environmental concern within the matrix of American public
opinion--the depth and scope of that concern; from whence,
among various subpublics, it springs; and the nature of its
relationship to other, more long-standing or established
components of the nation's opinion system. In the process
we hope to shed some light on the potential that environmental issues have for effective and long-term political expression, realizing of course that conclusions can only be
speculative and tentative. After all, the present concern
for environmental quality is of such recent vintage that the
analyst interested in assessing the durability of that concern is deprived of that most helpful of tools--hindsight.

The present analysis reviews a fair portion of the accumulating array of empirical data on public opinion and the
environment. We refer liberally to the findings of others,
point occasionally to some questionnaire data collected for
a project with which we have been associated on environmental politics at Lake Tahoe, and present preliminary results
of our own analysis of data generated in 1972 by the University of Michigan Survey Research Center (SRC) as part of its
continuing strategy of surveying national population samples
in connection with presidential elections.

THE DIMENSIONS OF PUBLIC CONCERN

"A miracle of public opinion," exclaims Hazel Erskine
in noting the "unprecedented speed and urgency with which
ecological issues have burst into American consciousness."[4]
We have in environmental concern, observed Walter Rosenbaum,
"that rare political phenomenon, a genuinely new issue in
American civic life."[5]

There is a surfeit of public opinion data revealing how
environmental problems were suddenly elevated in the late

1960s to a place among the issues most bothering the nation.
For example, a comparison of Gallup surveys taken in 1965
and 1970 reveals a 300 percent increase in the percentage of
Americans who identified air and water pollution (considered
as a single issue) among the three problems they most wanted
government to attend to during the following two years.
None of the nine other issues about which respondents were
polled evinced anything approaching a change of such magnitude: Whereas an interest in government action on pollution
increased from 17 percent to 53 percent, the next most vola-
tile issue--crime--increased only 15 percent between the two
polls, from 41 percent to 56 percent.[6] Fully 63 percent of
the SRC's 1972 respondents expressed the strongest agreement
with the proposition that "government should force private
industry to stop polluting."[7] Indeed, public consensus was
greater on this issue than on all but three of the eleven
issues on which public opinion was gauged by the SRC. And
on no issue was opinion more favorably inclined toward an
active role for government.[8]

Naturally enough the growing receptivity to government
initiatives designed to stem pollution seems to have paralleled a growing belief that the pollution problem is serious.
For example, Harris polls of 1967 and 1970 reveal a 14 percent increase over the three years in the proportion of the
public who felt there was "a lot of" or "some" air pollution
"around here." Not only had 70 percent of the public come
to feel that way about air pollution at the time of the
April 1970 poll, but over two-thirds also felt water pollution in their vicinity was "very serious" (47 percent) or
"somewhat serious" (22 percent).[9] A June 1970 Opinion Research Corporation poll confirmed the Harris findings, revealing that 69 percent of the public felt air pollution was
"somewhat" or "very serious" in their area, while 74 percent
felt that way about water pollution. As seen in Table 15.1,
the 1970 percentages represented new highs and were achieved
after four years during which the public grew more and more
to perceive the seriousness of these two forms of pollution.

State or local polls in various parts of the country
have also revealed high levels of concern over environmental
problems. Of the respondents in a 1970 Minnesota poll, 87
percent agreed that life as we know it today will "be in
serious trouble if nothing is done about pollution."[10] In
the same year a Harris survey found that 98 percent of Oregon residents felt that pollution was one of the most serious problems facing their state.[11] A similar 1970 Harris
poll undertaken in Washington found that 56 percent of a
random sample of that state's residents volunteered pollution when asked to identify the serious problems facing the

state.[12] Telephone interviews with 170 Illinois residents
in 1971 revealed that air and water pollution were perceived
to be immediate problems by 95 percent and 91 percent respectively.[13] A 1970 survey of approximately 200 North
Carolina residents revealed that over two-thirds of the respondents felt pollution was a serious problem in their
state.[14] A 1971 poll conducted in the Chicago area on life
there found pollution picked as a "particularly important"
problem more than any other issue.[15]

TABLE 15.1

Percent of Public Seeing the Problems of Pollution
as Very Serious or Somewhat Serious, 1965-70

Year	Air Pollution		Water Pollution	
	Total Sample	Big-City Residents	Total Sample	Big-City Residents
1965	28	52	35	45
1966	48	70	49	59
1967	53	76	52	62
1968	55	84	58	73
1970	69	93	74	89

Source: Hazel Erskine, "The Polls: Pollution and Its
Costs," Public Opinion Quarterly 36 (Spring 1972): 121.
See also J. Clarence Davies III, The Politics of Pollution
(New York: Pegasus, 1970), p. 79. The polls were conducted
by the Opinion Research Corporation (ORC). The question
was: "Compared to other parts of the country, how serious,
in your opinion, do you think the problem of air/water pollution is in this area--very serious, somewhat serious, or
not very serious."

Americans not only feel that their environment has been
damaged, they also believe it is continuing to deteriorate.
Thus, the April 1970 nationwide Harris poll referred to
above found that over half the respondents felt air and
water pollution in their vicinity was getting worse while
only 3 percent saw improvement over the most recent few
years.[16] The pattern of response was virtually identical in
Harris' 1970 poll in the State of Washington: approximately
half the respondents felt air pollution (50 percent) and
water pollution (53 percent) had become more of a problem
than they were a few years earlier; substantially lower

percentages (4 percent on air pollution and 12 percent on water pollution) felt they had become less of a problem.[17]

The evidence is impressive--as Americans entered the 1970s there was widespread concern across the country that serious and growing problems surrounded man's relations with his environment. However, a finding of agreement that environmental problems do exist, are serious, and are worsening is not sufficient in gauging the importance of environmental issues in the American public mind. An additional question is the saliency of environmental concern in the larger spectrum of public issues. As Don Dillman and James Christenson point out, "the significant question is not simply whether or not people are concerned, but where protection of the environment ranks in their value hierarchy."[18]

A review of mail questionnaire polls undertaken by various congressmen in 1971 reported that in 23 polls asking such a question, "the environment rated as the most important issue [facing the nation] only once, but in the top three 13 times."[19] National polls--more representative in character than congressional polls, with samples less likely to reflect the views of the activist, politically concerned stratum in America--find the environment placed somewhat lower on the nation's agenda of priorities. A special September 1973 Harris poll undertaken on behalf of the Senate Subcommittee on Intergovernmental Relations--the first national opinion poll ever to be commissioned by Congress-- revealed that pollution/overpopulation was judged to be the nation's biggest problem by 11 percent of the public; it ranked sixth among the issues presented, well behind inflation (64 percent), lack of integrity in government (43 percent), and crime (17 percent), but nearly on a par with welfare (13 percent), federal spending (12 percent), and taxes (11 percent).[20]

Gallup's monitoring of public perceptions of the nation's most important problems provides evidence on this matter. Respondents are asked to indicate, without benefit of cues or listing of alternatives, what they consider to be the nation's most serious problem. Environmental problems (air and water pollution, ecology, etc.) made their first appearance as a significant focus of concern in 1970 when, as Table 15.2 indicates, 4 percent of a national sample felt that they constituted the most serious problem facing the nation. Since that appearance, concern for environmental problems has persisted but has been regularly seen as less important than such issues as national security, economic well-being, welfare, and law and order. As a single issue, the environment has not been ranked as the most serious national problem by more than 7 percent of the national population.[21] Nor has its relative importance increased over the first three years of this decade, indicating that a plateau of concern may have been reached. While the 1972 SRC data revealed widespread agreement that government should act to halt industrial pollution, when asked to identify the nation's most important problem only 4 percent of those polled named issues identified with the environmental movement (principally pollution and population).

TABLE 15.2

The Public Picks the Nation's Most Important
Problem: The Place of the Environment

	Rank	Percent		Rank	Percent
1970			1972		
February	9	4	April	6	6
September	6	6	June	7	4
1971			July	6	5
February	6	7	September	6	4
March	6	7	1973*		
June	10	4	February	6	14
October	10	2	May	5	9
December	6	5	September	7	8

*Findings reflect first and second choices of respondents.

Source: Gallup Opinion Index, No. 60, June 1970; No. 76, October 1971; No. 78, December 1971; No. 88, October 1972; No. 100, October 1973.

The relatively low saliency of environmental concerns in relation to other pressing national problems raises questions about the extent of the public's willingness to support aggressive policies aimed at improving environmental quality. Available evidence indicates public support for current public expenditure levels on pollution control and a willingness to increase these expenditures at the expense of certain competing policy areas. A mid-1971 Harris poll revealed that the public was less inclined to support cuts in government expenditures for pollution control than any other program area, with their disinclination to cut such expenditures standing in marked contrast to their support of cuts in Vietnam spending, foreign aid, space exploration, welfare and defense spending, in that order.[22]

Similarly, a review of congressional polls on the subject found that the protection of the environment, along with combating crime, was felt to most deserve increases in federal appropriations and to least deserve appropriation cuts, with defense, welfare, and space exploration funding especially low in the public's spending priorities.[23]

The approval of shifting governmental spending priorities does not necessarily imply a willingness among citizens to make personal financial sacrifices in pursuit of a purer environment. Harris has reported growing willingness over recent years to accept a $15 per year tax increase to finance federal pollution control programs, with a 44 percent approval in 1967 increasing to 54 percent in 1970 and to 59 percent in 1971.[24] However, the amount of increased personal expenditure that is acceptable appears to be quite limited. In a 1971 Harris poll in New York State, 66 percent of the respondents rejected a $200 annual increase in total family expenditures to reduce pollution. The highest amount acceptable to a majority (60 percent) was $50 per year.[25]

Many observers feel that the public does not appreciate the extent of the personal financial burden that would be imposed by stringent environmental controls. Harold Sprout laments that despite escalating concern for the environment, "I can find little evidence that any large numbers are ready as yet to pay a high personal price to achieve environmental goals."[26] Cecile Trop and Leslie Roos note that "the public seems to feel that the federal government should get involved, but as of 1970 consumers were not willing to make major sacrifices to finance environmental quality programs."[27] Though the preservation and enhancement of environmental quality has certainly entered the American political arena, its exact niche in the larger array of public priorities remains uncertain.

Indeed, the exact range of specific issues encompassed by the environmental movement is itself ambiguous. According to Rosenbaum, "polls indicate that the public's concern for the environment [is] generally confined to pollution and [does] not commonly embrace numerous other environmental issues that experts consider serious, such as solid waste management, noise control, better land management and conservation of open spaces and resources."[28] A 1969 Gallup survey supports this contention: When respondents were asked to choose the most important environmental problem from a list of seven alternatives, air and water pollution proved to be of predominant concern (36 percent and 32 percent, respectively). Pesticides (7 percent), open space (6 percent), wildlife preservation (5 percent), and soil erosion (4 percent) fell well behind.[29]

The public, then, seems particularly concerned about pollution among the broad range of issues potentially encompassed by environmental concern, issues ranging from the genetic effects of pollutants to the removal of highway billboards to planned parenthood. The underlying connection between the apparently diverse issues is presumably an overarching and relatively abstract conception of the nature of man's total relation to his environment, best captured perhaps by certain symbolic terms--"Spaceship Earth" or "ecosystems" or, simply, the "quality of Life"--applied by ardent environmentalists. While available public opinion data do not permit an identification and illumination of such overarching concepts--if, in fact, they exist in any general sense--they do permit conclusions with respect to the linkage between some of the issue concerns associated with the environmental movement. Thus, for example, we may classify the components of environmental concern under three broad problem headings: conservation or preservation of natural resources, pollution, and overpopulation. The general public's concern for each may be independent of the others, suggesting that any overarching conceptual umbrella is, at best, meaningful only as an ideological symbol for a relatively small number of environmental activists and intellectuals. A study by Louis Tognacci et al., of 141 randomly selected residents of Boulder, Colorado elicited independent expressions of concern--measured by scale items-- in each of these three issue areas. There is a strong pattern of intercorrelation evident between the scales and between each of them and a scale generally measuring the perceived importance of "a pure environment." As the authors note, "some scales share such a marked degree of common variance that it is difficult to argue empirically for the uniqueness of these measures."[30] In other words, assessments in individual issue areas regarding the environment may substantially reflect a more generalized concern for the state of the environment.

Similar findings emerged from a survey of students at the University of Oregon. Seven individual items expressing attitudes on natural resource utilization, pollution, overpopulation, and individual rights to a clean environment were combined to form a scale measuring a general concern for environmental rights.[31] In a study of political elites involved in decision making in or affecting the Tahoe Basin it was found that responses to individual questionnaire items including the loss of scenic resources, erosion, noise

pollution, air pollution, and aesthetic pollution were sufficiently related to comprise an "environmental concern"
scale. Additionally, responses on the concern scale were
highly associated with responses on an environmental action
scale, comprised of various items involving specific policy
proposals designed to deal with the environmental problems
in the region.[32] Thus, while pollution may evince the most
urgent expressions of concern about the environment, available evidence indicates a concomitant sensitivity to associated problems in man's relation to other aspects of his
environment.

THE SOCIAL BASIS OF PUBLIC CONCERN

     The elevation of environmental concern to a prominent
place on the public's issue agenda is evident. But who are
the people and what are the factors most responsible for
that elevation?
     Many observers have characterized the environmental
movement as an upper-middle-class phenomenon.[33] McEvoy
notes one important implication to be drawn from a finding
of generally higher concern for environmental problems among
those of higher socioeconomic status: "unlike many contemporary social issues such as race, welfare and poverty . . .
the environmentally concerned segment of the society is
relatively powerful in terms of its access to the economic
and political resources of our democracy." That is, those
high in concern are in a relatively good position to trans-
late that concern into political decisions.[34]
     Table 15.3 presents data relating demographic charac-
teristics to two aspects of environmentalism--expressed concern for problems of environmental degradation and responsiveness to government action against industry designed to
stem pollution. Respondents with little education and with
very low incomes subscribe relatively weakly to environmentalist values. The reasons are not difficult to imagine:
Those whom affluence has eluded are likely to regard such
matters as clean air, pure water, and the preservation of
scenic resources as luxuries until more elemental needs are
satisfied.[35] Interestingly, however, the relationships between socioeconomic status and environmentalism displayed in
Table 15.3 are relatively weak.[36] This is especially true
with respect to receptivity to government antipollution efforts, suggesting that middle-class concern for the environment may be attenuated when it comes to translating that
concern into ideologically unpalatable programs of government regulation of industry, and/or suggesting that the

TABLE 15.3

Demographic Correlates of Environmental Concern

	Gallup (1969) Deeply Concerned		SRC (1972) Most Favoring Government Anti- pollution Action	
	N	Percent	N	Percent
National results	(1,503)	51	(1,172)	63
By age				
18-20 years	--	--	(67)	66
21-34 years	(403)	51	(397)	69
35-49 years	(476)	50	(297)	61
50 years and older	(605)	52	(411)	59
By education				
College	(395)	62	(376)	63
High school	(748)	52	(607)	66
Grade school	(352)	39	(188)	58
By annual income				
$10,000 and over	(449)	58	(523)	63
7,000-9,999	(336)	53	(219)	68
5,000-6,999	(237)	55	(145)	65
under 5,000	(463)	41	(257)	60
By size of community*				
1,100,000 and over	(277)	51	--	--
250,000-999,999	(296)	52	(180)	72
50,000-250,000	(235)	55	(193)	62
2,500-49,999	(233)	52	(445)	63
under 2,500	(462)	46	(336)	60

*High categories for SRC data are 50,000-349,999 and 350,000 and over.

-- not available.

Source: The 1969 Gallup Survey is reported in James McEvoy III, "The American Public's Concern with the Environment," Environmental Quality Series No. 4 (Davis: University of California, Institute of Governmental Affairs, February 1971). All other data in the table are from the authors' compilations.

relative lack of environmental concern among the lower
classes may be partly counterbalanced by higher receptivity
to government initiatives to solve social problems in general, including the problem of pollution.

The data presented here do not permit analysis of what
is undoubtedly a rather complex relationship between social
class and environmentalism. Thus, for example, the survey
of Lake Tahoe's "elite"--comprised almost entirely of relatively high-status persons--indicated that while extent of
education was highly correlated with environmental concern,
there was an inverse relationship between income and concern.
The anomaly was explicable by the fact that those with business occupations, relatively high in income and low in education, were low in concern while those in the professions
or in the government service, relatively high in education
but low in income, were high in concern.[37] Additionally it
may be that class relates to different aspects of environmental degradation differently. Thus, Davies proposes:

> The correlation between high education and
> income and concern about water pollution may
> relate to the differing degree of demand for
> various forms of recreation--swimming, fish-
> ing, sightseeing--which are likely to be en-
> dangered by pollution. Those with higher
> incomes engage in such activities more than
> those with lower incomes and they are more
> concerned about the [water] pollution prob-
> lem.[38]

If the present data support only tenuously the notion
that environmentalism is class-related, they are also somewhat less than conclusive with respect to the contention
that it is highly related to age. While it is true that
those under age 35 are substantially more likely to approve
government antipollution efforts than those older, there is
no evident pattern among the remaining categories.

Demographic correlates tell us something about who is
concerned, but in themselves do not explain how or why the
sudden focus of opinion on the environment. Indeed, the
weakness of the demographic correlates suggests that powerful explanations will be only indirectly associated with
them. The association between environmental attitudes and
urban residence suggests one such explanation of increasing
environmental concern. As the ORC data presented in Table
15.1 suggest, big-city residents are more likely than other
Americans to see both air and water pollution as serious
problems, with their relatively high concern over air

pollution being especially evident. That environmentalism increases with community size is typical of poll findings.[39] The data presented in Table 15.3 do not disconfirm such findings in that rural residents appear low in concern and low in their receptivity to government antipollution efforts, while such receptivity (although not concern) is clearly highest among big-city residents.

The explanation of rising environmentalism suggested by these findings is an obvious one: Environmentalism is a function of environmental degradation. It is in our growing urbanized areas where such degradation has been most acute, and concern has followed naturally.[40] This notion might account for the pattern of findings displayed in Table 15.1: Big-city residence is substantially more associated with relatively high levels of concern over air pollution than water pollution. After all, as Davies points out, while "there is generally a correlation between the size of the community and the degree of air pollution" with those living in cities hardly able to avoid perceiving the air pollution problem, "one would not expect a significant association between place of residence and water pollution because exposure to water pollution is not normally experienced in the home, except in those rare instances when the taste or quality of drinking water is affected."[41]

Several studies have examined the relationship between degree of concern about environmental problems and the actual level of pollution. Studies by de Groot and Samuels, Schusky, and Smith et al. confirm such a relationship.[42] Others reveal that additional factors are at work. Crenson, for instance, finds that "actual air pollution conditions do have some effect on people's attitudes about air pollution. [But] there are other factors that seem to have an even more substantial impact. . . ." Among these are age, education, income, and race.[43] Dillman and Christenson, in a survey of Washington residents, found that actual pollution was associated with awareness of pollution problems, but was not associated with higher saliency of pollution problems for the individual.[44] The results of a survey of Durham, North Carolina residents leads Murch to suggest that "where pollution is serious and unmistakable, all residents are obliged to acknowledge the fact. But where the immediate environment is less obviously threatened, personal factors . . . become operative to influence how one perceives the threat to his environment."[45]

Clearly, environmental degradation in and of itself does not fully account for the rise in environmental concern. As Downs points out "the change in public attitudes has been much faster than any changes in the environment

itself."[46] Indeed, "the available evidence indicates that,
in spite of . . . new and expanding sources of pollution,
the nation's dirty air problem is in some ways less serious
than it was twenty, thirty, or forty years ago."[47]

Many attempts to explain the rising national consciousness of environmental problems focus on factors that intervene between the actual state of the environment and the individual's awareness. An important, oft-identified influence on public awareness is the mass media, and clearly the
media have "found" the environment in recent years. "Not
since the Japanese attack on Pearl Harbor," says one observer, "has any public issue received such massive support
in all the news media, local as well as national."[48] One
analysis of the articles appearing in the three major weekly
news magazines found environment and pollution the subject
of some 109 articles during the 1960s, eighth among 14 major
issues given substantial attention by these magazines.[49] In
1970 coverage increased markedly: 41 articles appeared in
these magazines in that one year, more than on all but two
topics, campus unrest (52) and Vietnam (44).[50] McEvoy has
conducted a content analysis of articles in the Guide To
Periodical Literature from 1953 to 1969 and identified those
relating to the environment. "The overall increase for the
16-year period was slightly greater than 470%, from 48 to
226 articles."[51] Walter Rosenbaum reports in 1973: "A recent survey of editorials in five leading American newspapers over a 12-month period revealed that environmental
problems (principally pollution) were the major domestic issues of editorial concern."[52]

Other evidence indicates that media sources play a major role in channeling information on environmental problems
and events to the public. When asked about where they recall hearing about pollution or damage to the environment,
73 percent of a sample of North Carolina residents named
television and 62 percent mentioned newspapers.[53]

Davies describes the situation thusly:

> Although degree of pollution may be the
> greatest single determinant of variation
> among different groups in the degree of
> concern about the problem, education ef-
> forts and publicity given to the problem
> would seem to be the best explanation of
> the overall amount of public concern.
> Neither air nor water pollution has gotten
> so much worse in the past few years as to
> account for the great increase in public
> awareness.[54]

207

While mass media and related coverage may contribute significantly to the "overall <u>amount</u> of public concern" over pollution, it may also contribute to the somewhat greater levels of concern among those of higher socioeconomic status, given the relatively high level of media attentiveness among this group. The media-induced awareness thesis raises the possibility that concern about the environment represents an issue that is largely rhetorical, that is, an issue that is not firmly rooted in the experience of the individual.[55]

The relation of attitudes toward the environment and individual experiences is subtle and intricate. The extent of attachment to the community apparently influences the individual's ability or willingness to express active concern about its environmental state. Medalia and Murch, in separate studies, found that within a given community, residents who are generally satisfied are less concerned about pollution than those not so satisfied.[56] Along a similar vein, among those in the structure of elites affecting the future of the Tahoe Basin, nonresidents of the Basin proved significantly more concerned about environmental problems there than residents.[57]

A person's attachment to his community derives from many considerations—employment, friends, aesthetics, housing, family, etc. The admission that pollution is particularly bad in one's immediate area of residence and employment, for instance, could force unpleasant and difficult decisions. "It would demand the respondent to make a decision about whether air pollution was sufficient cause for him to move out of the neighborhood and uproot his friendships and usual patterns of life. In addition he would have to recognize that the health of his family would be impaired if he stayed."[58] It is not surprising that other positive aspects of a person's surroundings might lead him to ignore, and even to deny, the existence of pollution or other immediate environmental problems.[59]

The ways in which individuals assess their surroundings is also influenced by other more general orientations toward life. Costantini and Hanf found that concern for the Lake Tahoe environment increased with the degree to which respondents were critical of the impact of technology of society.[60] Those high in concern were also more likely to express aesthetic appreciation, a belief in the importance of beauty, and to have a high regard for the traditional values of rural life. Thus it would appear that the tendency to espouse environmentalist values is related to several larger aspects of an individual's life-style.

The environmental movement as a comprehensive view of man's relation to his physical environment comprehends many

specific and limited aspects of human activity. As such, it
can mean many things to many people, and the paths to awareness are bound to be various and complex. Thus far, the
study of who is concerned and how their concern is aroused
has produced many suggestive alternatives. Apparently, the
awakening of concern for the environment is a complex process that may include exposure to physical stimuli (pollution, beauty, etc.), and that is mediated by the individual's own relationship to his surroundings.

THE POLITICS OF PUBLIC CONCERN

Public confusion over what constitutes effective action
on environmental problems, and the apparently complex determinants of individual concern, suggest that clear mandates
for specific policies will not emerge from the American public. Indeed, the complex implications of the issue for
other areas of social concern make it very unlikely that
such agreement would be easily forged. "Very simply, each
increase in environmental quality costs something in terms
of other social values foregone, just as economic and other
forms of development must be paid for in terms of environmental values lost."[61]
Competing interests may be expected to prevent easy political solutions to environmental problems. "Despite the
widespread existence of favorable attitudes toward environmental protection, it is clear that a national commitment to
solve environmental problems will run head-on into many traditional values and time-honored practices."[62] It would
seem that, to be successful, the environmental movement must
integrate its goals into the larger constellation of issues
and loyalties that constitute the traditional cleavages in
American politics. The remainder of this analysis seeks to
illuminate the extent to which that political home has been
found, and to what extent it is still a-building.
Though the American political experience has been notable for the absence of specific and divisive ideologies,
the public often divides along imprecise liberal-conservative
lines. In locating an issue's place within the spectrum of
political concerns, we might first assess its support among
self-identified liberals and conservatives. Strong government action on industrial pollution* as revealed in Table

---

*The definition of "strong support" throughout this
analysis is a score of 1 or 2 on the 7-point scale described
in note 7 above; 3-5 represent an intermediate or moderate

15.4, tends to receive support from liberals, as distinguished from moderates and conservatives.* Correlation between environmentalism and liberalism is confirmed by Costantini and Hanf, who find a consistent tendency for environmental concern, and particularly for support of strong government action on behalf of environmental values, to be associated with liberal political predispositions among their Lake Tahoe respondents.[64]

TABLE 15.4

Liberalism and Support for Government
Action on Pollution

Self-identified	(N)	Percent for Strong Government Action
Liberal	(194)	84.0
Moderate	(275)	70.9
Conservative	(256)	69.5

$$x^2 = 13.7,\ 2\ \text{df.},\ p < .01$$

Source: Compiled by the authors.

Liberalism has been associated with the growth of an active and powerful government in twentieth-century America. Possibly, the relative antipathy of conservatives and moderates to government action against pollution is produced by hostility toward big government, rather than a lack of concern about the environment. This possibility was considered and tested. As many of those who felt generally that "government is too powerful" favored strong action on pollution as those who felt that government is "not too strong," 74.9 percent and 72.6 percent respectively ($x^2 = .07$, 1 df, not

___

position and 6 or 7 indicate strong support of industrial discretion, or strong opposition to government action.

*Partitioning the x^2 value for the entire Table 15.4 reveals that significance is entirely due to the difference between liberal identification and moderate or conservative identification taken together. ($x^2 = 14.6$, 1 df, p < .001). Dillman and Christenson find that "self-identification as a liberal or a radical is strongly associated with a higher public value for pollution control."[63]

significant). Thus a general antipathy toward government does not explain positions on this issue.

Traditionally, the great aggregators of issues in American politics have been the two major parties. They may emphasize competence in a certain issue area, such as foreign relations in the Republican party, or economic prosperity among Democrats; or parties may offer alternative approaches to solving an issue of great popular concern. Analysis of the 1972 SRC data reveals a significant relation between strong approval of government action on pollution and Republican, Independent, or Democratic party identification. Though party preference, as shown in Table 15.5, makes a difference in the degree of support for such action, significance is due to a strong tendency for Independents to approve action more than party identifiers.[65] There is no statistically significant difference on the issue between Democrats and Republicans.* We may speculate that the relative reluctance of party identifiers to support strong government action on the environment stems from differing sources. Republicans may harbor ideological reservations, reflecting a conservative stance, while Democrats may worry about the effects of environmental constraint on their traditional "bread and butter" concerns.

TABLE 15.5

Party Identification and Support for
Government Action on Pollution

Party Identification	(N)	Percent for Strong Government Action
Republican	(270)	67.0
Independent	(350)	78.6
Democrat	(452)	72.8

$$x^2 = 10.8, \ 2 \ df., \ p < .01$$

Source: Compiled by the authors.

---

*Partitioning the x^2 value for Table 15.5 reveals a significant difference between Independents and party identifiers ($x^2 = 7.8$, 1 df, $p < .01$), and no significance between the two parties ($x^2 = 2.85$, 1 df, n.s.).

Though Democrats and Republicans express no clear difference in their personal preferences for strong government action on pollution, the public may see a difference in the policy commitments of the two major parties in this area. The SRC respondents were asked to rate the position of each party, as they saw them, on the Government Action on Pollution Scale. The personal preferences of the respondents, and their assessments of each party's position, are displayed in Table 15.6. It is evident that, though both parties are seen as supporting government action against pollution, neither party is calling for the degree of action that the public desires.

TABLE 15.6

Personal and Perceived Party Positions
on Government Action on Pollution
(in percent)

	Personal Position	Perceptions of Democratic Party Position	Perceptions of Republican Party Position
Strong support of government action	73.6	47.8	43.0
Moderate position	15.9	46.6	44.3
Strong opposition to government action	10.4	5.6	12.7

Source: Compiled by the authors.

Furthermore, the discrepancy between public preference and party positions is not explained by differences between party identifiers and the perceived position of the opposing party. Table 15.7 displays assessments of each party's stance for members of each party and Independents. The individual's party identification makes no significant difference in the assessment of either the Democratic or the

212

Republican position on the issue. The only noticeable tendency is the lower rating of the GOP position by independents.*

TABLE 15.7

Party Identification and Perceptions of Party Positions
on Government Action on Pollution

	(N)	Perceived Position of Republican Party (percent)	Perceived Position of Democratic Party (percent)
Republican	(175)	48.2	49.1
Independent	(250)	37.9	47.2
Democrat	(335)	44.7	48.3
		$x^2 = 5.94$, 4 df., n.s.	$x^2 = 4.36$, 4 df., n.s.

Source: Compiled by the authors.

Further evidence that the two major parties are not perceived as having clearly distinguishable stands on the role of government in pollution abatement is displayed in Table 15.8. If the public perceived that the parties tend to favor opposition positions on the regulation of pollution issue, or if they were to see either party assuming a position opposed to their own, negative correlations would appear. (For example, if Democrats felt that, in contrast to their own party, the Republican party opposed government action on pollution, negative correlations would appear in the first and third columns of the bottom row in Table 15.8). The positive coefficients that do appear attest to the fact that the issue does not polarize party identifiers and that the parties are not perceived as having assumed opposing positions on the issue. The Independents again stand out, seeing the strongest similarity between party positions and much less correspondence between their own position and that of either party. Republicans display the greatest agreement with their own party, but do not distinguish between parties

---

*Partitioning, however, reveals that the lower rating of the GOP by Independents is only minimally significant ($x^2 = 4.7$, 2 df., sig $< .10$).

as much as Democrats. Democrats and Republicans, though
they find no great conflict between the two parties on the
issue, tend to be much closer to their own party than to the
opposing party.

TABLE 15.8

Correlation of Personal and Party Positions
on Government Action on Pollution

	(N)	Democratic with Republican Party Positions	Personal Position with Democratic Party Position	Personal Position with Republican Party Position
Total sample	(801)	.40	.27	.21
Republican	(172)	.39	.17	.40
Independent	(247)	.52	.29	.23
Democrat	(329)	.31	.33	.10

Note: All correlations (Pearson's r) significant at
better than .05.

Source: Compiled by the authors.

If the American public has looked to political parties
to initiate government antipollution efforts, or to engage
in a dialogue on alternatives to government action, it has
looked in vain. While the Democrats are seen as slightly
more inclined to government action on pollution, the differences are slight compared with the general impression of
"foot-dragging" by both parties. The pattern is most clearly expressed by the Independents, who desire stronger action, find great agreement between the parties, and see a
considerable gap between their own preferences and those of
the parties.[66] Party identifiers tend to place their own
position somewhat closer to their own party, even though
they do not see great differences between the parties and
do not see the position of the other party as opposite or
antagonistic.
Supporters of strong government action on pollution
tend to be self-identified liberals, but they do not con-
spicuously represent either major party, nor do they find
a clear distinction between party positions on the issue.

This constellation of opinion suggests that environmental
problems may represent a new challenge that has not been
clearly articulated in the "ideologies" of the parties.
Possibly, environmental issues cut across old interest
groupings[67] and, thus, represent one of the new "nonaligned"
issues that are difficult for parties to address within
their traditional frameworks.[68]

Correlations between support for government action on
pollution and responses to other issue questions included in
the 1972 SRC survey reveal a consistent, though slight, tendency for such support to be associated with positions that
could appropriately be considered "liberal" in character.
However, an examination of the correlations in Table 15.9
also reveals the absence of a strong association between
opinions on the environmental issue and opinions on any
other issue covered by the survey. Only support for government action against inflation is, on the whole, more independent of individual attitudes on other issues of public
concern.[69]

Except for its slightly "liberal" cast, support for
governmental antipollution activity is essentially "nonaligned" with respect to the other issues of public concern
included in Table 15.9. This underscores the ambiguous position of the environmental issue in the personal and collective priorities of the American people. The existence of
an "ecological crisis" is widely attested to, and the need
for governmental action acknowledged; but a high priority
for solving environmental problems has not been established,
and the public does not seem to foresee great personal sacrifice in attaining solutions.

The nature of the issue, which encompasses many specific problems, contributes to the difficulty of forging a
clear public mandate for government action. While pollution
and overpopulation may be of the utmost importance for future
generations, they do not have the self-evident impact of
poverty, crime, and other immediate issues. The public has,
to a great extent, "learned" to be concerned about them.
Recreational facilities, beauty, open space--all require
affluence and opportunity to be appreciated and valued.
Thus, environmental quality is related to the public's needs
in complex ways, and the basis for widespread political support is uncertain.

The response of political leadership has reflected the
realities of public opinion on the issue. Active and aggressive policy has been demanded by individually dedicated
"environmentalists," with parties on the whole espousing
general support of environmental protection, but backing
away from the active pursual of environmental goals at the

TABLE 15.9

Environmental Concerns: Effect on Issue Alignment
(Pearson's r)

Correlations of Issue Positions

	2	3	4	5	6	7	8	9	10	11
1. Government action on pollution	.06	.14	.13	.07	.15	.09	.08	.18	.10	.09
2. Vietnam withdrawal		.06	.28	.28	.15	.23	.23	.25	.25	.33
3. Inflation			-.10	.00	-.03	.13	.02	.06	.05	.01
4. Legal marijuana				.28	.18	.14	.33	.28	.23	.43
5. School busing					.13	.32	.29	.32	.25	.39
6. Women's equality						.09	.11	.17	.15	.17
7. Guaranteed jobs							.24	.41	.31	.34
8. Criminal rights								.37	.32	.43
9. Minority group aid									.41	.45
10. Urban problems										.41
11. Campus unrest										

Source: Compiled by the authors.

expense of other national priorities. The public perceives
the lack of distinction between party positions and their
generally favorable, though moderate, position on antipollution regulation.

Currently, environmental concern appears more as a national wish than a hard political commitment. The growth
and extent of this commitment, and the lines of political
combat, will become clearer as the costs and benefits of environmental policy become more evident to decision makers
and the public. Hopefully, the environmental awakening of
the late 1960s has provided a foundation of awareness upon
which political commitments and environmental policies of
the 1970s can build.

NOTES

1. _Time_, January 4, 1971, pp. 21-22.
2. As Samuel Hays puts it, "Single-purpose policies,
impractical from the point of view of the conservation ideal
of maximum development through scientific adjustment of competing uses, became the predominant pattern because they
provided opportunities for grass-roots participation in
decision-making." _Conservation and the Gospel of Efficiency_
(New York: Atheneum, 1972), p. 275.
3. Anthony Downs, "Up and Down with Ecology," _The Public Interest_ 28 (Summer 1972): 38-50. The quote appears on
p. 41.
4. Hazel Erskine, "The Polls: Pollution and Its
Costs," _Public Opinion Quarterly_ 36 (Spring 1972): 120.
5. Walter R. Rosenbaum, _The Politics of Environmental
Concern_ (New York: Praeger, 1973), p. 7.
6. Gallup Poll _Index_, June 1970, p. 8. According to a
January 1971 Harris poll, 41 percent of the public felt that
pollution was one of the "two or three top problems" deserv-
ing attention by the new congress, with only the state of
the economy felt to be a more pressing problem. Erskine,
op. cit., p. 125.
7. Responses to the Government Action on Pollution
Scale were elicited through a seven-point scale with two
anchoring statements. The distribution of responses was
as follows:

1. Government should force industry to stop polluting	63.3%
2.	10.3
3.	6.7
4.	6.8
5.	2.4
6.	1.5
7. Industries should handle pollution in their own way	8.9

Except where noted, the analysis of the 1972 SRC (University of Michigan) survey is based on a national sample of approximately 1,200 randomly selected respondents. Interviews were conducted between September 1972 and February 1973.

8. Extent of agreement or consensus is measured by the standard deviation of responses on each of the eleven issue scales on which the question format paralleled that presented in note 4 above. The issue statements, standard deviations, and mean scale scores follow. The higher the mean score, the greater the agreement with the issue statement, and a mean of more than 4.0 demonstrates that the public is more likely to support the statement than its opposite. The statements below represent what would commonly be considered the liberal pole of the issue scale. The high mean for opinion on the pollution scale demonstrates the strong verbal support of the public for government action in this area, greater than for any other issue.

	Standard Deviation	Mean
Government should force industry to stop polluting	1.91	5.85
Government action against inflation	1.57	5.68
Women and men should have an equal role	2.27	4.49
Government should guarantee jobs and good standard of living	1.97	4.33
Withdraw completely from Vietnam right now	1.98	4.32
Protect the legal rights of the accused	2.12	3.83
Government should help minority groups	1.97	3.76
Sympathetic with students and faculty in campus unrest	1.86	3.13
Decrease poverty and unemployment to ease urban unrest	2.09	3.11
Make the use of marijuana legal	2.16	2.64
Bus to achieve school integration	1.66	1.79

9. Erskine, op. cit., pp. 121, 123-24.
10. Ibid., p. 124.
11. Riley Dunlap, Richard Gale, and Brent Rutherford, "Concern for Environmental Rights Among College Students," American Journal of Economics and Sociology, January 1973, p. 56.
12. Louis Harris and Associates, Inc., The Public View of Environmental Problems in the State of Washington, a report prepared for Pacific Northwest Bell Telephone Co., February 1970, p. 12.

13. Rita James Simon, "Public Attitudes Toward Population and Pollution," <u>Public Opinion Quarterly</u> 35 (Spring 1971): 98.

14. Arvin W. Murch, "Public Concern for Environmental Pollution," <u>Public Opinion Quarterly</u> 35 (Spring 1971): 101.

15. "Pollution Map Public Concern, Survey Reports," Chicago <u>Tribune</u>, November 1, 1971, S-1.

16. Erskine, op. cit., p. 124.

17. Louis Harris and Associates, op. cit., pp. 26, 34.

18. Don A. Dillman and James A. Christenson, "The Public Value for Pollution Control," in Social Behavior, Natural Resources and the Environment, ed. William Burch, Jr. et al. (New York: Harper and Row, 1972), p. 237.

19. John Blodgett, <u>The Environment and Grass Roots Sentiment</u> (Washington, D.C.: Library of Congress, Congressional Research Service, March 1, 1972), p. CRS-3.

20. Reported in <u>Newsweek</u>, December 10, 1973.

21. Other studies have yielded similar results. Simon, op. cit., p. 94, found that 13 percent of her Illinois respondents saw population, food shortage, or some aspect of the nonhuman environment as the most important problem in the United States. An additional 10 percent mentioned these problems as next most important. Simon concludes that "considering the amount of publicity that the population and/or pollution problems have received, and the high priority assigned to them by the national administration, neither the 23 percent nor the 13 percent appears impressive."

22. Louis Harris, "Priority Favored for Domestic Needs," Washington <u>Post</u>, August 15, 1971.

23. Blodgett, op. cit., p. CRS-6f.

24. Louis Harris, "Pollution Reaction Grows," Chicago <u>Tribune</u>, July 26, 1971.

25. Louis Harris, <u>The Public's View of Environmental Problems in New York</u>, a report prepared for the New York State Council of Environmental Advisors, May 1971.

26. Harold Sprout, "The Environmental Crisis in the Context of American Politics," in <u>The Politics of Ecosuicide</u>, ed. Leslie L. Roos, Jr. (New York: Holt, Rinehart and Winston, 1971), p. 44.

27. Cecile Trop and Leslie L. Roos, Jr., "Public Opinion and the Environment," in Roos, op. cit., p. 61.

28. Rosenbaum, op. cit., p. 15.

29. James McEvoy III, "The American Concern with Environment," in Burch et al., op. cit., p. 226.

30. Louis Tognacci et al., "Environmental Quality: How Universal is Public Concern," <u>Environment and Behavior</u> 4 (March 1972): 73-86, 79.

The correlations between scales were as follows, with each correlation significant at the .01 level of confidence, two-tailed:

	Conservation	Pollution	Overpopulation
Importance of a pure environment	.49	.45	.38
Conservation		.81	.64
Pollution			.62

31. Dunlap et al., op. cit. Use of the same scale items in an as yet unreported study (Tahoe Research Group, Institute of Governmental Affairs, University of California at Davis) of an environmental action group, the League to Save Lake Tahoe (of whose members, 267 were randomly sampled) yielded additional evidence of the undimensional qualities of the scale. The average item/intercorrelation of scale items was .30 in the latter study, compared to .29 in the University of Oregon study.

32. Edmond Costantini and Kenneth Hanf, "Environmental Concern and Lake Tahoe," Environment and Behavior 4 (June 1972): 209-42. The average item/scale correlation for the individual components of environmental concern was .73.

33. The relationship between social class and other demographic variables, on the one hand, and environmentalism, on the other, has been demonstrated--sometimes only tenuously--in many studies. See Dillman and Christenson, op. cit., Costantini and Hanf, op. cit., Erskine, op. cit., J. Harry, R. Gale, and J. Hendee, "Conservation: An Upper-middle Class Social Movement," Journal of Leisure Research 1 (1969) 246-54; J. Clarence Davies III, The Politics of Pollution (New York: Pegasus, 1970), p. 80; McEvoy, op. cit., pp. 214-36.

34. McEvoy, op. cit., p. 226.

35. Richard Neuhaus writes most directly to the general issue. Not only is environmentalism considered by Neuhaus to be "a seductive diversion from the political task of our time"--the fight against poverty and economic inequality--but much that is on the environmentalist agenda will adversely affect in a direct way the interests and aspirations of the poor and underprivileged. See his In Defense of People (New York: Macmillan, 1972).

Davies makes a related point in explaining the rise of public concern over pollution: "At a time when America is deeply divided on fundamental political questions, an issue like pollution which at least verbally unites everyone is not only of political value to the officeseeker but also of psychological value to members of the general public. Thus, people may stress concern with pollution as a way of avoiding thinking about more divisive matters." Davies, op. cit., p. 82.

36. Correlations (Pearson's r) between demographic variables (uncollapsed) and support of government antipollution action for the 1972 SRC data are all statistically significant (p<.05) but of a small magnitude.

	Age	Education	Income	Size of Community
Government action on pollution	-.166	.119	.054	.078

37. Costantini and Hanf, op. cit., pp. 224-27.
38. Davies, op. cit., p. 81. Davies does not suggest that income is unrelated to concern about air pollution. If concern for water pollution is experience-based, concern for air pollution is learned through media-attentiveness and formal education, each a function of income. Both concerns, it is suggested, are directly associated with income--but the avenues to those concerns are different.
39. See Erskine, op. cit., pp. 121-28.
40. Richard Means discusses the "myth" that only a rural environment creates a genuine sensitivity to problems of encironmental degradation. Actually, he argues, problems of waste disposal, air pollution, the relationship of land and space to human behavior, and other environmental matters most manifest themselves in the city. Thus environmentalism has urban roots. See his "Public Opinion and Planned Changes in Social Behavior: The Ecological Crisis," in Burch et al., op. cit., pp. 206-08.
41. Davies, op. cit., pp. 79, 80.
42. I. de Groot and S. Samuels, People and Air Pollution: A Study of Attitudes in Buffalo, New York (Buffalo: New York State Department of Health, Air Pollution Control Board, 1962); J. Schusky, "Public Awareness and Concern with Air Pollution in the St. Louis Metropolitan Area" (Washington, D.C.: HEW, Public Health Service, May 1965); W. S. Smith, J. J. Scheuneman, and L. D. Zeidberg, "Public Reaction to Air Pollution in Nashville, Tennessee," Journal of the Air Pollution Control Association 14 (1964): 445-48.
43. Matthew A. Crenson, The Un-Politics of Air Pollution: A Study of Non-Decisionmaking in the Cities (Baltimore: Johns Hopkins University Press, 1971), pp. 13-14. Crenson cites one of the early studies of public opinion and pollution, where it was found--among St. Louis' respondents interviewed in 1963--that post-high-school education was more strongly associated with concern over air pollution

than other factors, including exposure to high concentra-
tions of such pollution. (Thomas McMullen et al., "Air
Quality and Characteristic Community Parameters," a paper
delivered at the 1967 Annual Meeting of the Air Pollution
Control Association, Cleveland, Ohio.)

44. Dillman and Christenson, op. cit., pp. 247-49.

45. Murch, op. cit., p. 103.

46. Downs, op. cit., p. 38.

47. Crenson, op. cit., p. 11.

48. Sprout, op. cit., p. 49.

49. G. Ray Funkhauser, "The Issues of the Sixties: An
Exploratory Study in the Dynamics of Public Opinion," Public
Opinion Quarterly 37 (Spring 1973): 66-67. An additional
36 articles were devoted to population which, if added to
the environment/pollution articles, would still leave the
issue ranked eighth--behind Vietnam (861), race relations/
urban riots (687), campus unrest (267), inflation (234),
mass media (218), crime (203) and drugs (173).

50. Ibid., p. 68.

51. McEvoy, op. cit., p. 218.

52. Rosenbaum, op. cit., pp. 13-14.

53. Murch, op. cit., p. 102.

54. Davies, op. cit., pp. 81-82.

55. Dillman and Christenson, op. cit., p. 250, cite
evidence suggesting the effect of the mass media in successfully inducing people to be concerned about pollution in
spite of pollution being perceived as a minor problem in
their own local community. Davies argues that the mass
media are especially effective in generating concern for air
pollution: "People have to be taught that air pollution is
bad for their health. One may even have to be taught to
consider air pollution aesthetically unattractive. Thus,
unlike such problems as unemployment or crime or poor housing, perceptions of air pollution as a problem is heavily
dependent upon exposure to channels of information. . . ."
Davies, op. cit., p. 80.

56. N. Z. Medalia, "Air Pollution as a Socio-environ-
mental Health Problem: A Survey Report," Journal of Health
and Human Behavior 5 (Winter 1964): 154-65; Murch, op.
cit., p. 103.

57. Costantini and Hanf, op. cit., p. 228.

58. I. de Groot, "Trends in Public Attitudes toward
Air Pollution," Journal of the Air Pollution Control Association 17 (1967): 679-81.

59. In relation to recreation, Lucas found that individual users of a wilderness canoe area differed in their
perception of the area's attractive qualities, and even in
their definitions of what constitutes wilderness. These

differences were related to the type of recreational activity pursued by the responsents, for example, canoers, fishermen, day-campers, etc. Thus, the nature of the attachment to the area helped determine the evaluations made and the standards applied. See Robert C. Lucas, "Wilderness Perception and Use: The Example of the Boundary Waters Canoe Area," Natural Resources Journal 3, no. 3 (January 1964): 394-411.

60. Costantini and Hanf, op. cit., pp. 236-37.

61. Edmond Costantini and Kenneth Hanf, The Environmental Impulse and Its Competitors: Attitudes, Interests, and Institutions at Lake Tahoe (Davis: University of California, Institute of Governmental Affairs, Environmental Quality, October 1973).

62. Dunlap et al., op. cit., p. 45.

63. Dillman and Christenson, op. cit., pp. 253-54.

64. Costantini and Hanf, "Environmental Concern and Lake Tahoe," op. cit., p. 233.

65. Dillman and Christenson, op. cit., pp. 253-54.

66. The general pattern indicates lack of confidence in the will of the parties to deal with the pollution issue. This lack of confidence is especially evident among the 4 percent (n=33) of the SRC sample who identified environmental degradation as the most important problem faced by the country. Relatively few members of this most concerned group feel that either the Republican party (34.8 percent versus 43 percent of the general public) or the Democratic party (39.1 percent versus 47.9 percent) support strong government action. Over half (51.7 percent) feel that the parties are no different in their capacity to solve the environmental problem. Only 13.3 percent feel the government would be "very helpful" in solving environmental difficulties. As a final statement of pessimism, 54.8 percent of this group felt that environmental problems will "always be with us." The serious concern of these individuals over environmental degradation may be aggravated by their belief that government is unwilling or unable to help.

67. Grant McConnell, among others, contends that the environmental movement transcends familiar lines of social and political cleavage. See his "The Political Context of the Environmental Movement," a paper prepared for the 1970 John Muir Institute Conference, "Forum for a Future," Aspen, Colorado.

68. For a discussion of "nonaligned issues," see Richard E. Dawson, Public Opinion and Contemporary Disarray (New York: Harper and Row, 1973).

69. The measure of association with other issues employed here is the average correlation of each issue with

all the rest.   The resulting average coefficients were:

Inflation	.06	Guaranteed jobs	.24
Government action on pollution	.10	Solving urban problems	.25
Women's equality	.13	Minority group aid	.29
Vietnam withdrawal	.22	Criminal rights	.30
School busing	.23	Sympathetic with students	.30
Legal marijuana	.23		

16

ON DOING THE DEVIL'S WORK IN GOD'S COUNTRY: LEGISLATURES AND ENVIRONMENTAL POLICY
Geoffrey Wandesforde-Smith

ENVIRONMENTAL POLITICS AS A MYSTERY PLAY

On returning from a vacation among the woods and lakes of northern Wisconsin in the summer of 1973, Rice Odell discovered that Congress and assorted special interests had been doing the Devil's work. In God's country, amid the trees, water lilies, and bald eagles, Odell had renewed his sense of perspective, a perspective based on "beauty, honesty and the environmental fitness of things." The insights he subsequently acquired into events on Capitol Hill led him to his typewriter. He promptly denounced in the August 1973 issue of the Conservation Foundation's Letter both the substance of several environmental policy decisions taken by Congress in previous months and the way these decisions had been made.[1]

Scrutiny of previous issues of the publication edited by Odell reveals that Congress is often cast as the villain in what might be called the medieval mystery-play view of environmental politics. The administration is also a frequent agent of the Devil, sometimes aiding and abetting congressmen in the formulation of legislative compromises that, "however necessary from a pragmatic political standpoint,

Preparation of this chapter was supported in part by a grant from the California Water Resources Center under the matching grant program of the Water Resources Research Act of 1964, and in part by a grant from the division on Research Applied to National Needs of the National Science Foundation to the Tahoe Research Group. The assistance of Ms. Pat Farid is also acknowledged.

may still be bad legislation from a public interest standpoint." The heroes and heroines of these monthly scripts
are the courts and a variety of citizen groups, the latter
possessing the power on occasion to save some portion of
God's country despite makeshift organization, shoestring
budgets, and opponents whose expediency knows no bounds.

There is, of course, more than a grain of truth to the
mystery-play approach to understanding the formulation of
environmental policy. Environmentalists have attempted to
find friends wherever they could since their cause attained
widespread popularity in the late 1960s, and their success
among those who populate the major political institutions at
the state and federal levels has been mixed. In their use
of the courts they have been suspected of trying to achieve
legislative and administrative objectives by the back door,
their critics on this score operating on the not-altogether-
accurate assumption that the courts are unresponsive to public opinion and hence overly protective of minority interests. But the judicial defense of environmental interests,
particularly the interest in a strict interpretation of the
National Environmental Policy Act (NEPA),[2] has been encouraging to a movement that has found few consistent allies
among legislators and bureaucrats. Not even Senator Henry
Jackson, chairman of Interior and Insular Affairs, principal
sponsor of NEPA, and "Mr. Environment" for many years in the
Senate, could be counted on when the time came to defeat the
Alaska pipeline project and this despite the very real possibility of adverse environmental consequences for his home
state of Washington.

The courts have also ridden herd on the administration,
a traditional refuge for environmentalist bêtes noires such
as the Corps of Engineers, the Bureau of Reclamation, and,
more recently, the Atomic Energy Commission. More than 20
years ago, Arthur Maass identified a symbiotic relationship
between bureaucrats, legislators, and resource development
groups.[3] The policy subsystems represented by this trinity
have proven resilient as well as unholy, advancing the Devil's work not only on the nation's rivers and watersheds but
also in the forests, parks, and wilderness areas. Reform of
administrative structure and standard operating procedures
has yielded some benefits, most notably greater opportunities for those environmental groups with the requisite resources to participate in the administrative process.[4] However, there is still cause for environmentalist rejoicing
when the budgets of some agencies are reduced and others re-
directed.[5]

The major weakness of the mystery-play approach is its
lack of sophistication, and in this respect, as K. N. Lee

has noted, it is not unlike much of the academic literature on environmental politics.[6] Once Congress and the administration have been cast as villains, it is very difficult to give them credit when credit is due. The tendency is rather to beat on them even harder, insisting that both make radical changes in policy. The usefulness of the environmental lawsuit as a blunt instrument for reducing in the short run the value of the congressional pork barrel, and for delaying agency action, has probably been sufficient to persuade some environmentalists that it is worthwhile waiting for extensive institutional restructuring and redirection to occur. However, this optimism conceals a further weakness of the mystery-play approach, namely that it anticipates a resolution of the plot that, no matter how attractive it may be as dramatic political fiction, is simply unrealistic. The plot calls for the "money-men and industry leaders" to abandon their lobbying and advertising, and what Odell calls "ill-considered compromise, expediency, hypocrisy, and cramped, special interest vision," and to rally around his public interest standard.[7] Even assuming for the sake of argument that Odell has a corner on the public interest, his scenario presupposes a conversion of miraculous proportions. In reality, the Devil is not as black as he is painted and the tasks of environmental politics are less in the realm of miracle working than in the fashioning of the institutional and policy alternatives that occupy what Lee identifies as a largely unexplored middle-ground between radical restructuring and incrementalism. It is in this context that legislative activity needs, ideally, to be examined.

The fact is that in the last few years Congress and the state legislatures have been very active in shaping new policies and institutional changes. Analytically, the problem is that once the morality-play approach to understanding these changes is abandoned, and the alternative assumption that incrementalism prevails is rejected, there remains no single or fully satisfactory theoretical explanation of events and behaviors. Before commenting further on this problem, though not as a prelude to detailing its solution, it will be helpful to briefly review some of the studies that have been made.

THE LESSONS OF PREVIOUS RESEARCH

There is, of course, an established tradition of scholarship that deals with legislative behavior in the United States. Political scientists have devoted considerable attention to the United States Congress at several levels of analysis[8] and some of this work has treated environmental policy issues. State legislatures have also been studied from a variety of theoretical perspectives. Research employing the concept of role[9] and studies that use aggregate data within a systems framework to analyze policy outputs[10] are perhaps the most notable additions to the literature in recent years. However, at the state level there are relatively few studies addressed specifically to the consequences of legislative behavior for environmental policy.

Environmental Policy and State Legislatures

Turning first to the states, one recent study not authored by political scientists argues that there is an unfortunate tendency among some observers to believe that legislative responses to environmental issues are inadequate because legislators are captured by special-interest lobbyists.[11] "But," say the authors, "it is an inescapable fact that legislators hear the public interest side of the story as well." They conclude that legislators make choices about policy "according to individual conscience, partisan considerations, and affinity with lobbyists." Of these variables they find on the basis of a simple statistical analysis of votes cast in the California Legislature in 1969 and 1970 that partisanship is very important in determining legislative behavior. More specifically, they find that "not only do Democratic legislators tend to support environmental protection more than Republicans, but Democrats also seem to evince a higher degree of support as a result of party cohesion than do Republicans."

Since the authors are representatives of environmental interest groups, they are disappointed by the influence of party affiliation on environmental voting. They see "a compelling need . . . to develop an ecologically valid politico-ethical perspective which cuts across party lines." It is unfortunate that the design of their study does not allow the relationship between party affiliation and environmental voting to be compared with that between the nature of a legislator's district and environmental voting, which they also consider, to see which is stronger. Their study also does not test the influence of partisanship while controlling for other variables, such as region, age, ideology, and length of service.

Another recent study, also dealing with California but focusing on policies for preserving agricultural and open-space lands, finds that there is no significant partisan or sectional dimension to conflict over legislative proposals

related to special tax assessments for open-space land.[12]
However, there is significant rural-urban conflict. The relationship between legislative voting and party affiliation
is significant on measures dealing with the planning, acquisition, or regulation of open-space land, although for the
bills considered in the study this relationship "explains"
only 12 percent of the variation in voting. The author concludes that "only rural Republicans have continued to be
relatively active in sponsoring legislation related to special assessment. The attention of urban legislators--espe-
cially Democrats--has turned to programs for government planning, acquisition and/or regulation of open-space land."[13]

This conclusion based upon California data should be
tested and reexamined in other states. Race Davies suggests
that

> when roll call voting is strongly related to
> partisan affiliation, a rapid change in the
> relative strength of political parties can
> have an important effect on the possibili-
> ties for developing a legislative coalition
> strong enough to enact or kill proposals.
> When the section and type of district from
> which legislators come is significantly re-
> lated to their votes on a certain type of
> measure, changes in the concentration and
> distribution of population may have an im-
> portant bearing on levels of support and
> opposition in the Legislature.[14]

These hypotheses might also be tested in other states and on
issues other than those relating to agricultural and open-
space land.

State legislation dealing with land use is an attractive focus for study for several reasons. State legislatures, with some exceptions, are not known for their innovative responses to social problems, and yet state initiatives
in land use regulation over the past few years have been described as a quiet revolution. Fred Bosselman and David
Callies present several case studies to show how "the feudal
system under which the entire pattern of land development
has been controlled by thousands of individual local governments" is being overthrown.[15] Their research does not begin
to bear upon the kinds of questions about state legislative
behavior that Davies suggests are important.

However, some interesting conclusions emerge from their
work. One is that the states are aware of growing interest
at the federal level in land use control and the formulation

of a national land use policy. The willingness of state legislatures to respond to external pressure, in part to forestall federal preemption and in part to put their houses in order to take advantage of federal funds for land use planning, is reminiscent of the state legislation passed in anticipation of congressional approval of the Water Resources Research Act of 1964 and the Water Resources Planning Act of 1965.* Second, it is evident that state legislatures approach land use policy from a variety of perspectives and have varied objectives in mind. In Maine and Colorado, for example, legislation has reflected the annoyance of groups that have discovered the diminishing possibilities for country living. In Massachusetts the concern is with the availability of suburban land for low- and moderate-income housing. In California, New York, and New Jersey, legislation has been directed at areas of critical environmental concern with a view to bringing them under unified management that respects their ecological integrity. In other words, within the general (and often undifferentiated) category of state land use policy, legislative agendas reflect a wide variety of what have been referred to elsewhere as issue contexts.[16]

Third, the Bosselman and Callies study shows that state legislators are grappling with some perennial problems while at the same time trying to cope with the ostensibly new issues raised by environmentalists. The reshaping of land use policy has heightened traditional conflicts over state-local jurisdiction and patterns of state administrative organization, for example. The finding is that the resolution of these conflicts follows no uniform pattern. What Bosselman and Callies do not say is who benefits and who loses from the various jurisdictional and organizational arrangements that have emerged from the legislative process. It may be too early to tell, in which case their conclusion that state organization for land use policy should adopt the form of "a new line agency directly under the governor" would seem to be premature.[17]

---

*The pattern is one in which, prior to enactment of federal legislation providing funds for assistance to the states for programs that help meet national policy goals, the states create new institutions, or change the official purposes of existing ones, in order to qualify for assistance grants. The requirement that the states receiving monies designate a state agency as responsible for a particular program is presumed by Congress to push the states toward necessary and desirable institutional reform. Whether the reforms are really necessary and whether they actually lead to improved performance are questions that Congress rarely stops to ask.

Another striking feature of the case studies on state land use policy is the diversity of the communities of interest that come before the legislatures.[18] Their conflicting demands cannot always be resolved--a fact that belies the morality-play view of the supremacy of prodevelopment interests in legislatures, particularly when the environmentalists have the strength to take the issue directly to the electorate. A descriptive study of legislative behavior in California traces the history of state policy for coastal land use regulation and details the legislative impasse that led to the placing of an initiative measure on the 1972 general election ballot.[19] On matters of agricultural and open-space land policy in California, legislative proposals have been modified to the degree necessary to gain consensus. With respect to the coast, consensus within the legislature was unattainable and the issue was referred to the people. This pattern has been repeated, both in California and other western states, in recent years.[20]

The pattern is one that raises some interesting questions about how to deal with externalities, a matter that is of particular interest to students of environmental public policy and, as Larry Wade has noted, is of general theoretical interest to students of policy outcomes.[21] Wade discusses the fate of Proposition 18, a measure on the November 1970 general election ballot in California. It would have allowed, at the option of local governments, diversion of one quarter of state gasoline tax revenues from highway construction and maintenance to programs aimed at developing alternative transportation systems. Wade notes that one possible conclusion from a study of Proposition 18, which was defeated, is that "the public itself was more vulnerable than the legislature to manipulative interest groups working through a well-endowed public relations effort." Thus, even when environmentalists have the political muscle to make an end-run around the legislature, it may be strategically wiser to seek conflict resolution through the regular channels of representative government. In contrast to the disappointment with the legislature's ability to cope with environmental externalities that emerge from the McCloskey and Zierold study, Wade writes as follows: "While the political process as a whole was not receptive to reform, the response of the legislature was encouraging. For this reason, an overly pessimistic assessment of the possibility of redressing our environmental neglect is unjustified. Ironically, for democrats, perhaps such problems may not be solved through an aroused and mobilized electorate but, if at all, by the political elites who dominate our political institutions."[22]

There is also on the positive or optimistic side of the ledger a study of the California Pure Air Act of 1968.[23] This legislation is worthy of note "because of the political context in which (it) was proposed, developed, and passed." The study demonstrates that the behavior of legislators on this issue was not significantly influenced by either the national government, already noted as a source of state policy innovations, or by the state executive branch. More generally, the passage of this air pollution control law contradicts "two well-accepted generalizations about the course of American federalism." They are (1) that policy innovation is more typical of the national than the state government, and (2) that state legislatures are essentially review-oriented bodies, inclined to follow or resist policy direction from state executives but not inclined to initiate new policies. This study also points to the importance of staff and research resources in state legislatures as influences upon behavior, and to the importance of individual legislators in formulating strategies to overcome the "maze of obstacles" that confront a bill after it has been introduced.

There is little published research dealing with states other than California, although legislatures across the country have responded to a variety of environmental issues.[24] The issue of state government organization, mentioned earlier, is the focus of nine case studies sponsored by the Ford Foundation. These studies warrant mention here because, although they address the question of legislative behavior qualitatively rather than through survey data or roll-call analysis, they lead to some forceful conclusions. Observing that state legislatures are generally subject to the domination of chief executives and administrative agencies, the authors urge legislators to invest more time and money in staff and investigative hearings. Their comments on state legislation are harsh as well as sweeping:

> Environmental bills rarely include significant, specific policy guidance to the administering agencies or the courts. Rather, laws are loaded with platitudes about beautifying everyone's environment in all ways, for all uses, all the time. Instead of making policy choices and setting priorities, these bills sound like campaign speeches, which they often become.
>
> The vaguely written laws are dumped in the lap of appointed executive officials or state bureaucrats, who then make the basic

policy decisions. In this way, legislators
abdicate their responsibility to make fundamental value judgments affecting their constituents and trade-offs among environmental
and other competing public goals.[25]

This is no more than an environmental variation on a
familiar theme in the "good government" literature on state
politics. Inasmuch as it is not supported by evidence that
lack of staff and funding are key variables in an explanation of legislative performance, and inasmuch as the argument fails to recognize that symbolic reassurance can be an
important legislative outcome, the assertion that state legislatures have abdicated their responsibilities cannot be
taken seriously. There is clearly room for additional research on state legislatures and environmental policy, including research that spells out the trade-offs that are
made "among environmental and other competing public goals,"
and research that avoids the initial assumption of Elizabeth
Haskell and Victoria Price, namely, that legislators are
presently incapable of making reasonable trade-offs when the
future of God's country is at stake.

Congress and Environmental Policy

At the federal level, two early studies of environmental legislation appeared in a volume on congressional policy
making for urban areas.[26] Some of the findings reported by
Kent Jennings are reminiscent of the California studies.
Reviewing the period from 1956-61, he states that "partisanship directly or indirectly was decisive in establishing the
configuration of voting in the House (on water pollution
control bills), in contrast to the rather undifferentiated
pattern by type of district." He notes that support for the
legislation was generally high among Democrats, with significant defections by southerners, and opposition generally
high among Republicans, with a few Republicans breaking party ranks but with no clear pattern of nonconformity. Jennings is persuaded that neither urban nor nonurban interest
groups played a major role in influencing congressional behavior. "To a great extent," he writes, "the water pollution control program as it stands today was congressionally
inspired and constructed." He also stresses the extraordinary influence of one man, Representative John Blatnik of
Michigan, on the evolution of the program.
    In the same volume, Randall Ripley's analysis of air
pollution control legislation also points to the crucial

role of Congress in formulating policy. Ripley argues that, left to its own devices, "the executive would have produced legislation less far-reaching in its provisions than what was produced with the help of Congress." In this case congressmen were responding to several key individuals, both lobbyists and colleagues, and their behavior showed a remarkable resilience to the large industrial interests that are so often assumed to be influential. In an essay that seeks to generalize from the studies by Jennings and Ripley, and others in the book, Frederic Cleaveland notes that they confirm the findings of much previous research, namely that political party is most likely to be the decisive factor in congressional voting behavior. They also suggest that there is a significant cleavage along ideological lines attributable to the fact that so many of the issues dealt with involved expansion of federal government activities and an increase in federal spending. This ideological dimension of congressional behavior is one that could be expected to appear across a wide range of environmental issues in the light of the demands frequently made for a larger governmental role in problem solving. The overall framework of Congress and Urban Problems might usefully be applied to state legislatures as a preface to comparisons of congressional and state legislative treatment of environmental policies.

The case studies in Congress and the Environment are more critical of congressional treatment of environmental issues than those by Jennings and Ripley.[27] They range beyond legislation dealing with pollution control to include the Wilderness Act, national park and lakeshore legislation, the Land and Water Conservation Fund Act, highway beautification, and the formulation of a national environmental policy. Most of the studies are critical of the influence of special interests on Congress and argue that the seniority system and committee structure make it difficult for environmental protection interests to have their preferences taken into account. The conclusion suggested by the essays collectively is that Congress could and should do a better job of responding to environmental problems, although the implicit assumption that congressional perceptions of the issues should match those of the authors is questionable.

Indeed, in a study by Michael Kraft it appears that congressmen have varied attitudes toward, and understanding of, environmental issues.[28] On the assumption that the greater the attention paid to environmental problems by political elites, and the greater their tendency to think about these issues in terms of critical ecological threats, the more likely they are to promote sound ecological policies, Kraft interviewed almost the entire membership of six

234

congressional subcommittees. He found striking differences
in the attention that congressmen give to environmental issues. He also found that congressmen fall into three types
on the basis of their orientation toward these issues; some
perceiving them in terms of pollution control, some in terms
of recreational opportunities and resource conservation, and
some in terms of the ecological threats identified by scientists who take a holistic, global view of environmental
problems. Kraft establishes tentative relationships between
these types and roll-call voting, although he cautions that
the contribution of issue orientation to an explanation of
voting behavior must be weighed against that of other variables used in previous research, such as party and presidential leadership, the influence of committee chairmen, interest group pressure, and constituency opinion.

Of course, many congressmen conduct polls to help them
maintain a degree of correspondence between their own perceptions and those of the public. In 81 congressional polls
conducted in 1971, respondents generally supported stronger
measures to control pollution and indicated a willingness to
pay for stricter controls. However, on specific issues, as
might be expected, some congressmen chose to vote against
their constituents' wishes. The question of whether or not
to continue federal subsidy for the supersonic transport
(SST) plane was a major and fully debated environmental issue before Congress in 1971, for example. Constituent opinion on the issue was tapped in polls conducted in 20 congressional districts, and, as Table 16.1 shows, respondents
were opposed to continued subsidy in all but one of these
districts.[29] However, on two crucial roll-call votes about
one-third of the 20 representatives voted to support the
subsidy by voting against the Yates amendment to delete the
SST subsidy from the Department of Transportation appropriations bill in March 1971 and for the Boland amendment rein-
stating SST funding in the second supplemental appropriations bill in May 1971. The names of those representatives
casting pro-SST votes are capitalized in Table 16.1. The
table also shows the ranking accorded these 20 congressmen
by the League of Conservation Voters (LCV) on the basis of
the votes cast by each one on 15 issues regarded by the LCV
as key environmental issues.[30] The table is meant to be il-
lustrative rather than conclusive. It is indicative of the
varying intensity of opinion among voters in several congressional districts with respect to a single issue. In addition, if representatives with absences (Halpern and Michel)
and representatives who may have cast pro-SST votes before
soliciting constituent opinion (Byron and Carney) are excluded from the table, it appears that four of the five

TABLE 16.1

Constituency Opinion and Roll-Call Voting
on the SST Subsidy, 1971

Representative	SST Roll Call Votes[a]		LCV 1971 Ranking	Percent of Constituents Who Favor SST Subsidy[b]		
	March '71	May '71		Yes	No	No Opinion
ARCHER (R-Tex)	N	Y	290	42	52	6
ASHBROOK (R-Ohio)	N	Y	365	14	--	--
Broomfield (R-Mich)	Y	N	166	25	--	--
Burke (R-Fla)	Y	N	198	38	62	--
BYRON (D-Md)	N	Y	191	28	52	20
CARNEY (D-Ohio)	N	Y	153	19	69	12
W. Ford (D-Mich)	Y	N	15	22	78	--
Halpern (R-NY)	Y	absent	138	42	41	13
Hathaway (D-Me)	Y	N	92	15	85	--
Helstoski (D-NJ)	Y	N	21	32	60	8
McCLORY (R-Ill)	N	Y	276	39,30[c]	61,70[c]	--
McKevitt (R-Colo)	Y	N	191	27	70	3
Michel (R-Ill)	Y	absent	333	30	65	5
Monagan (D-Conn)	Y	N	84	30	70	--
Riegle (R-Mich)	Y	N	38	12	76	12
SCOTT (R-Va)	N	Y	292	40	53	7
Seiberling (D-Ohio)	Y	N	30	17	74	--
Stanton (D-Ohio)	Y	N	165	19	71	8
Udall (D-Ariz)	Y	N	47	26	69	4
WHITE (D-Tex)	N	Y	249	37	59	--

[a]The LCV approved of a Yes vote in March and a No vote in May.

[b]Figures may not add to 100 percent because of rounding errors or missing data.

[c]First figure is for male respondents, the second for females.

Sources: Congressional Research Service and League of Conservation Voters.

remaining House members voting against constituent opinion
were Republicans. It also appears that all five remaining
pro-SST votes came from members with low environmental rankings by the LCV (Archer, 290; Ashbrook, 365; McClory, 276;
Scott, 292; and White, 249). Both SST votes were close, the
Yates amendment passing by a vote of 217-203 and the Boland
amendment being adopted by a vote of 201-195 (only to be
nullified by subsequent congressional action). The data in
the table cannot account for many variables, such as the influence of pro-SST lobbying by the administration. Moreover,
it should be evident that the relative influence of party,
presidential leadership, constituency opinion, and overall
attitude toward environmental issues as denoted by the LCV
rankings is extremely difficult to unravel even with reference to a single issue.

The complexity of the often cross-cutting pressures
surrounding environmental voting in Congress has not prevented the LCV from drawing some simple conclusions from its
roll-call analyses. With the goal of proving that environmental issues can help decide elections, the LCV has injected
its limited money and manpower into selected congressional
races. Since it played a role in defeating Representative
Wayne Aspinall of Colorado, who ranked 405th in the 1971 LCV
standings and failed to win his 1972 primary election, the
LCV has enjoyed increased stature among a small group of environmental lobbying organizations that have developed since
1970. The information disseminated by these groups, as well
as that distributed by older organizations such as the National Wildlife Federation, can be most helpful to students
of Congress and environmental policy, provided it is taken
with a grain of salt.[31]

At the end of the 92nd Congress, for example, the National Wildlife Federation looked over the record of "the
first full Congress in what has been called the Environmental Decade" and concluded that on balance it had to be considered a disappointment.[32] It transpires that the Federation's lack of enthusiasm stems more from what Congress
failed to do rather than what it achieved. To someone with
a less jaundiced eye, the 92nd Congress must be counted
among the stauncher defenders of God's country. It passed
the Federal Water Pollution Act Amendments, the Federal Environmental Pesticides Control Act, the Coastal Zone Management Act, the Marine Protection, Research, and Sanctuaries
Act, and the Noise Control Act. In addition to these five
major pieces of legislation, the 92nd Congress established
five new national recreation areas, two new national parks,
a new national river, and a new national seashore. It added
nine new units to the National Wilderness Preservation System

and passed several measures for the protection of fish and wildlife. The 92nd Congress, it is true, did not approve a national land use policy, did not pass any major legislation dealing with energy conservation, and failed to deal with bills pertaining to strip mining, solid wastes, and the use of Highway Trust Fund money for rail mass transit. It is also true that, from the environmentalist viewpoint, the legislation that was approved is less than perfect. Nevertheless, the Conservation Foundation was moved to conclude in its December 1972 review of recent legislation that "Congress has enacted basic legislation designed to control most types of pollution. . . . it will now turn more to broader questions involving land use and energy."[33]

SOME BROADER QUESTIONS

The information made available by environmental interest groups about the treatment of environmental policy issues by Congress and state legislatures can have a narcotic effect on the student of politics. One can become so enthralled by the week-to-week and month-to-month accounts of legislative infighting, and so bent upon staying on top of the latest victories and defeats, that a concern for the substantive questions that interest the Conservation Foundation and other groups replaces a concern for broader theoretical questions. In terms of an earlier metaphor, the narcosis may be attributable to the fact that the scripts of medieval mystery plays make more exciting reading that the academic literature. The reason for this is that the interest-group newsletters are more suggestive of the range of phenomena political scientists would like to explain than the research that has been published. A careful empirical study of legislative voting on environmental issues is very properly concerned with relating votes cast to independent variables such as issue orientation, party identification, type of district, constituency opinion, and executive leadership. And such a study can be tied to a larger literature on legislative politics that uses similar methodology. However, there are possibilities for linkages to previous research that do not rely upon the systematic collection and analysis of data on roll-call votes and legislator attitudes and interests, even though the legislature and the legislative process are foci of research. Not all the possibilities can be touched on here. However, some are worth noting.

The attack launched on Representative Aspinall by the LCV is a reminder that individual legislators and legislative committees are a fruitful focus of research. Aspinall was widely suspected of being too receptive to the mining and other development-oriented special interests in his home state and district, and of using his chairmanship of the House Interior and Insular Affairs Committee to frustrate environmentalist objectives. Yet there is no careful analysis of this central figure in the drama of environmental politics, no scholarly record of who got what, when, and how as a result of Aspinall's maneuvering, and no examination of the consequences for the functioning and organization of other committees of his unwillingness to allow the House Interior Committee to become an environmentalist sounding board. Case studies, including that by Jennings already noted, point to the importance of interindividual and intercommittee relations in the shaping of legislation. Other studies suggest that these factors may be especially important in the outcome of bills not marked by sharp partisan or interest-group conflict.[34]

The attention given by the Conservation Foundation to the money gap, or the discrepancy between monies authorized for environmental programs and monies appropriated, suggests other lines of inquiry related to previous research on both budgetary decision making and legislative-executive relations. While the pattern of congressional appropriations appears to follow the incremental model associated with Aaron Wildavsky,[35] the pattern of authorizations shows radical shifts and raises questions about the symbolic uses of environmental politics. The politics of funding environmental programs is complicated by the frequent lack of coincidence between congressional priorities and executive priorities as reflected in the annual budget requests. These complications have become especially fascinating during Republican tenancy of the White House and Democratic control of Congress since 1969.[36] In some cases the conflict is dramatic and the potential consequences of disagreement between Congress and the administration are easy to predict. Thus, the funding for water pollution control programs, authorized by Congress at $24.6 billion for fiscal 1973 and fiscal 1974 in the Water Pollution Control Act Amendments, provoked a bitter confrontation with President Nixon during the 1972 presidential election. The president described the authorization as unconscionable and said it would lead to higher taxes. When Congress overrode his veto of the bill, Nixon returned to the attack in preparing his January 1973 budget message, announcing that in the interests of holding down federal spending and trimming waste and red tape in government programs he would ask for $5 billion rather than $11 billion to fund the construction of waste water treatment plants, the largest single environmental item in the federal budget. The National League of Cities and the U.S. Conference of Mayors complained that the reduction of funds would make it impossible for local governments to meet the standards and deadlines imposed by the 1972 legislation. Their comments also pointed to another consequence, namely increased competition among environmental and other programs for scarce local funds.

In other cases the impacts of budgetary decisions and legislative-executive policy conflict are more undertain, in part because they are related to vague or implicit policy goals or because they may trigger second or third order effects that are difficult to foresee. To cite but one example, the federal budget for fiscal 1974 may portend some significant but largely undeclared shifts in policy for the National Forests. Funding increases over fiscal 1973 are requested for timber sales administration and management, and for management of mineral claims and leases, both programs that presage greater development of Forest Service lands. On the other hand, reduced appropriations are requested for reforestation and stand improvement, development of advanced logging techniques, forest and range management research, pollution abatement, and the construction of forest roads and trails. It is difficult to tell whether these proposals, if accepted by Congress, would erode the environmental quality of the National Forests, or would lead in the case of the reduced road and trail appropriations, for example, to the charging of higher timber prices or the submission of lower bids for federal timber by private companies. There would seem to be room for studies of the impact of federal legislation that might be helpful to Congress and others in the evaluation of budgetary and other legislative decisions, particularly when the conflict between congressional and executive policy goals is subdued or obscured.

There are also some intriguing questions raised by economists about legislatures and environmental policy in the context of the larger political system. Edwin Haefele has argued that decisions involving environmental quality are problems of social choice and therefore problems that economists are particularly well-qualified to analyze. Having asserted that existing governmental structures bear "little relationship either to representative government, the party system, or to social choices," he offers ideas for institutional redesign. Legislatures are to play a key role in his scheme of things. Says Haefele:

> We are moving now to a time when legislative
> government, using technical and administra-
> tive advisory committees, is needed. For

when true social choices are at stake, nothing less than legislatures making these
choices will suffice in our system of representative government. The spectacle of
executive personnel attempting to assess the
public interest through public hearings or
to divine appropriate actions through committees "representing" all interests from
housewives to steel mills is an outrage in
the pure sense--it does violence to our system of government. In a technical sense it
does not aggregate individual preferences
correctly into social choices.[37]

Haefele yearns for the seventeenth and eighteenth cen-
turies, when the American colonists were skilled at designing representative legislative bodies to resist the domination of executives appointed by the crown. His yearning is
sustained by a paper that examines representative government
in terms of utility theory. The paper demonstrates "that
the congruence between the election results of a properly
functioning two-party system and the decision of a legislature composed of the same voters extends at least through
all non-trivial permutations of the two issue-three voter
cases (eight examples) and the three issue-three voter
cases (432 examples)."[38] The reader might wonder how this
conclusion from formal analysis holds up in situations where
the electorate and the legislature are composed of different
voters subject to differing constraints and influences,
where the legislature has more than 500 members, as does
Congress, and where the number of issues available for vote
trading is considerably in excess of two or three.
Notwithstanding such questions, Haefele's conclusions
are interesting in that they recall conclusions reached by
others from quite different premises. He observes, for example, that reestablishing strong legislatures in the colo-
nist tradition will require "sweeping out many twentieth
century habits, . . . among them the excessive dependence on
seniority and the abuses of the committee system, and creation of some twentieth century research capabilities within
the legislatures."[39] He also takes on the pork-barrel politics of the congressional public works committees. It is
not the principle of pork-barrel politics he finds objection-
able, nor the character of the committee members. The problem is rather that Congress is using a natural resource,
water, as a specie of political exchange at a time when the
intended beneficiaries of the exchange (local or regional
communities) are losing faith in the value of the specie

(dams, flood control projects, and irrigation and navigation facilities). The solution Haefele proposes is to decentralize decisions on public works projects to the states, regions, and localities, leaving Congress to decide how much money the nation should allocate for public works and how it should be distributed to the subnational decision centers.[40] The advantages of this solution are obscure inasmuch as water continues to be used as specie. The geographical reach of the decision makers has been shifted, substituting local concerns for considerations of national policy, although Haefele does not explain why local people are best equipped to make decisions about water. Nor does he volunteer the logical extension of his argument, which is presumably that other congressional decisions involving resources of the physical environment should also be decentralized. Nor does Haefele contemplate the possibility that at least some of his local jurisdictions are going to form a coalition with the object of persuading Congress to allocate more money than is needed for water development, or to overallocate to some regions rather than others. Haefele appears to have overstated the decentralization argument suggested to him by his own brand of economic reasoning. Most students of water resource policy, including many economists, would argue that the real problem is that of persuading all decision makers to place a much higher value on water as a specie, and even to value water differently than in the past by giving formal recognition to its utility as a superior good.[41] Simply shifting water resource decisions from national legislators to local legislators is unlikely to produce this reevaluation.

Another recommendation advanced by Haefele is that new representative governmental structures be created at the regional level to deal with both intrastate and interstate environmental problems that do not respect the boundaries of established governing units. Haefele would like to see regional officials elected by the people of the region. However, in none of the regional agencies so far created has this pattern been followed. The usual procedure is for the members of a regional agency or commission to be appointed to represent whatever mix of federal, state, and local government interests seems appropriate for the problem at hand. Most regional entities do not have legislative functions. For example, federal-state river basin commissions, river basin interagency committees with federal and state members, and multistate regional economic development commissions are essentially administrative entities performing coordination and planning functions on behalf of federal and state executive agencies.[42]

Some recently created regional agencies, however, do have legislative functions and are specifically designed to bring local and nonlocal officials together for the purpose of solving environmental problems. In contrast to regional bodies created as extensions of the executive, which usually have a decision rule of unanimous consent, these new regional environmental planning and management agencies use a less restrictive decision rule, such as simple or extraordinary majority. Thus, roll-call votes are taken and it is possible to study the voting behavior of the members of these regional legislatures. One such study is notable for the preliminary test it makes of the Schattschneider-Caldwell hypothesis concerning the behavior of local and nonlocal officials when confronted by the same environmental decision problems.

In the literature of environmental politics, the behavior of local government officials is generally, though often implicitly, analyzed within a framework outlined by E. E. Schattschneider.[43] The thesis is that every organization, including government institutions, embodies a policy bias. In the case of local governments the bias is usually assumed to be one that favors economic growth and development over other interests and values. Lynton Caldwell has elevated this assumption to the status of a general proposition:

> Politics at the local level tend to become
> highly personal, and economic interests be-
> come intermeshed with friendships, enmities,
> and a variety of other self-interest motiva-
> tions, which greatly complicates efforts to-
> ward environmental control. As a general
> proposition (and hence not invariably valid),
> it may be said that the strength of environ-
> mental exploitation is most easily brought
> to bear on local government, whereas environ-
> mental protectionists mobilize most effective-
> ly at the national level.[44]

It follows from this proposition that local officials will behave differently with respect to environmental issues than nonlocal officials such as those who have state and federal constituencies. Caldwell writes of the tendency for local officials to be "friendly to economic interests" and "hostile to noneconomic interests, which are perceived as threatening progress, development, jobs, and enhanced land values. . . ." He concludes, somewhat caustically, that the quality of American public life is degraded because so many local officials "are permitted to engage in anti-public action that is 'corrupt' without being actually illegal."[45]

In common with other observers, Caldwell argues that greater responsibility for environmental control should be vested with nonlocal governments. They are thought to possess the functional prerequisites for exercising effective control, including appropriate areal jurisdiction, money, competent technical and administrative personnel, political support, and "the relative objectivity that adequate solutions to environmental problems require." While it has been shown that local and nonlocal officials do indeed have different attitudes toward a wide range of environmental problems,[46] the question of whether local and nonlocal officials behave differently in response to the same problems has received almost no attention.

For the most part, local and nonlocal officials function in distinct political environments or arenas. Even within a single policy area--for example, water pollution control--that is of concern to all levels of government, the behavior of local and nonlocal officials is subject to widely varying political and institutional constraints. To some extent formal and informal communication and interaction among officials at different levels of government tend to produce agreement about the problems they face and the available action alternatives.[47] However, this is not sufficient to permit comparative analysis of their behavior with respect to a given set of issues. Ideally, the behavior of local and nonlocal officials would be compared while controlling as much as possible both for the nature of the issues involved and the character of the political arena within which the behavior occurs. In a situation where local and nonlocal representatives are brought together and required to act as regional officials, both controls are operative. It should be possible in these circumstances to discover whether, over a common set of issues and within the same political arena, there are local/nonlocal differences in behavior. Recent experience in the Lake Tahoe Basin has provided an opportunity to test for such differences.

The Tahoe Regional Planning Agency (TRPA) was established by an interstate compact between California and Nevada in 1969.[48] Its principal charge is to prepare and implement a plan for the conservation and orderly development of an interstate region of some 500 square miles that sits astride the California-Nevada border in the high Sierras and is dominated by one of the largest and clearest high-altitude lakes in the world. Its creation can be seen as a response to the failure of local government to deal with the environmental problems at Lake Tahoe. The eleven-member board created by the Tahoe Regional Planning Compact is comprised of one person appointed by each of the five county boards of supervisors and the South Lake Tahoe City Council, one member from outside the Basin appointed by each of the state governors, the administrator of the California Resources Agency, the director of the Nevada Department of Conservation and Natural Resources, and one presidential appointee who is not a voting member.

The assumption underlying the 1969 Lake Tahoe legislation is that there is a fundamental conflict at work in decision making that affects the environment of the Basin. The conflict can be simply and somewhat crudely characterized as one between (1) local, business-oriented interests principally motivated by a desire to see continued growth and development in the Basin regardless of the environmental consequences, and (2) nonlocal, environmentally oriented interests motivated by a desire to see the remaining beauty of the Basin preserved for future generations regardless of the economic consequences to those residing or investing there at present. A second assumption naturally follows from the first and also underlies recent calls for further institutional restructuring at Lake Tahoe, namely that the behavior of the TRPA's Governing Body since its creation has reflected this conflict. It is this second assumption--that locals and nonlocals on the Governing Body have behaved differently-- that the recent study attempted to examine.

The study analyzed 856 roll-call votes taken by the TRPA Governing Body from April 1970 to January 1973. The issue of whether or not the six local and four nonlocal members of the Governing Body bring distinctly different perspectives to the Agency is most clearly joined when votes are differentiated in terms of their consequences for environmental quality. A procedure was devised to identify those divided Agency votes that, on their face, were likely to have an impact on the physical environment of the Basin. These selected votes were then used to test the key hypothesis of the study, namely that nonlocal members would be more proenvironmental in their voting behavior than locals. Table 16.2 shows the environmental voting record of each member of the Governing Body on 129 issues. It is clear that the local/nonlocal distinction obtains only among the California members of the Agency. On the Nevada side, the member with the highest percentage of proenvironment votes is a nonlocal. However, the member with the second highest percentage is a Nevada local and there is clearly no local/ nonlocal pattern among the Nevadans. Indeed, the Nevadans as a whole were considerably less proenvironment in their voting than the Californians, the former casting 36 percent of their 596 votes on the 129 issues in a proenvironment direction and the latter 47 percent of their 604 votes on the same issues.

TABLE 16.2

The TRPA and Environmental Voting, April 1970 to January 1973

	Member*	Proenvironment	Antienvironment	Abstain	Absent	Percent of Votes Cast Proenvironment
California nonlocal	A	97	26	4	2	76
	B	84	42	2	1	66
California local	C	32	80	2	15	28
	D	40	76	5	8	33
	E	33	78	3	15	29
Nevada nonlocal	F	49	64	5	11	42
	G	42	83	4	0	33
Nevada local	H	47	62	7	13	41
	I	44	84	1	0	34
	J	30	69	5	25	29

*There were membership changes affecting four of the ten seats on the board during the period covered (one including only a single month). The figures presented here are computed by seat and do not take turnover into account.

Source: Edmond Costantini and Kenneth Hanf, The Environmental Impulse and Its Competitors: Attitudes, Interests and Institutions at Lake Tahoe, Research Report No. 29 (Davis: University of California, Institute of Governmental Affairs, October 1973), p. 56.

The failure of the local/nonlocal distinction to illuminate the voting behavior of the Nevada members of the TRPA
may be attributable to a number of factors. These are explored elsewhere, together with a review of the limitations
of roll-call analysis when applied to a small legislative
body, like the TRPA, that must deal with complex environmental issues in a rapidly changing political environment.[49]
The point to be made here is that the design of new legislative institutions at the subnational level cannot proceed on
the basis of the impressive generalizations found in the existing literature and epitomized by the Schattschneider-
Caldwell thesis. Whether the behavior of TRPA members would
have been substantially different had Haefele's recommendation been followed, and the members elected from regional
districts, is a matter for speculation. Arguments for changing regional agency decision rules and membership to favor
nonlocal and presumably proenvironment interests are equally
speculative, and their presumed advantages must be weighed
against the political costs of tinkering with the TRPA, including the risk of losing even the semblance of regional
government for the Tahoe Basin. The fact is that the design
of new institutions is a complex problem not likely to be
solved until more is known about what makes existing institutions work the way they do.

CONCLUSION

Experience with the TRPA suggests a concluding comment
on legislatures and environmental policy. The members of
the TRPA were given the task of implementing policy as well
as formulating it, and as a consequence their behavior as
legislators cannot easily be distinguished from their behavior as executives. To some extent, of course, the behavior of members of Congress and the state legislatures
also evidences an intermixing of legislative and executive
functions. The problem for the student of behavior is to
incorporate this mixing into a suitable analytical framework. The temptation is to treat the behavior of legislators in policy formulation and policy implementation processes separately, but in the case of the TRPA, where the
same individuals are formally charged with making and administering policy, this strategy has obvious weaknesses.
At least the constitutional separation of legislative and
executive powers at the state and federal levels lends a
formalistic credence to the pursuit of separate but presumably related lines of inquiry into policy formulation and
policy implementation, one focusing on legislators and the

other on administrators and executive agencies. The weakness here is that students following one line of inquiry may tend to treat the political actors and events central to the other line of inquiry as no more than incidental to an explanation of policy outputs and policy impacts, whichever is the object of research.

The search for a suitable analytical framework is further complicated by introducing phenomena beyond those associated with the interrelationship of legislative and executive behavior. As preceding paragraphs have suggested, the study of legislatures and environmental policy must take account at some level of the role of the courts, various interest groups, political parties, and public opinion. And it must do so by going beyond the popular but simple-minded assertion contained in the current ecological slogan that everything is related to everything else. The challenge is being taken up by political scientists who are not primarily identified as students of environmental politics. Their work can only be noted here in a tantalizing final footnote.[50] But perhaps those who are primarily interested in the politics of environmental problems and unhappy with the simplicity of the mystery-play model will be tempted (by the Devil?) to read further.

NOTES

1. Conservation Foundation Letter, August 1973.
2. Frederick R. Anderson, NEPA in the Courts: A Legal Analysis of the National Environmental Policy Act (Baltimore: Johns Hopkins University Press, 1973).
3. Arthur Maass, Muddy Waters: The Army Engineers and the Nation's Rivers (Cambridge, Mass.: Harvard University Press, 1951).
4. Helen M. Ingram, "Information Channels and Environmental Decision Making," Natural Resources Journal 13 (January 1973): 150-69.
5. See, for example, the comments on the federal budget for fiscal 1974 in Conservation Foundation Letter, February 1973.
6. K. N. Lee, "Options for Environmental Policy," Science 182 (November 30, 1973): 911-12.
7. The phrases quoted here appear in the Conservation Foundation Letter, August 1973, pp. 1 and 8. It would be wrong to suppose that Odell is alone in his use of phrases such as these or that he is being singled out for special treatment. His August 1973 commentary happens to bear on the general theme of this chapter. Other morality-play

scripts appear regularly in Not Man Apart, a publication of the Friends of the Earth, and the Sierra Club Bulletin, for example. From time to time they are also found in publications such as Harper's Magazine, The Atlantic Monthly, Fortune Magazine, and Playboy, and either reproduced or cited in books of readings edited by political scientists.

8. A selection of some of the best work on Congress appears in Nelson W. Polsby, ed., Congressional Behavior (New York: Random House, 1971). Most of the principal works are listed in the bibliography in Leroy N. Rieselbach, Congressional Politics (New York: McGraw-Hill, 1973).

9. The classic work on legislative roles is John C. Wahlke, Heinz Eulau, William Buchanan, and LeRoy C. Ferguson, The Legislative System (New York: John Wiley, 1962). For an extremely useful introduction to research on state legislatures, see Malcolm E. Jewell, The State Legislature: Politics and Practice, 2d ed. (New York: Random House, 1969).

10. The principal works are cited and reviewed in Thomas R. Dye, Understanding Public Policy (Englewood Cliffs, N.J.: Prentice-Hall, 1972), Chapter 11.

11. J. Michael McCloskey and John H. Zierold, "The California Legislature's Response to the Environmental Threat," Pacific Law Journal 2 (July 1971): 575-602.

12. Race D. Davies, Preserving Agricultural and Open-Space Lands: Legislative Policymaking in California, Environmental Quality Series No. 10 (Davis: University of California, Institute of Governmental Affairs, June 1972).

13. Davies notes that legislation instituting land use regulation has been most successful when dealing with sub-regions of the state, such as San Francisco Bay and the Lake Tahoe Basin. Case studies of legislative behavior with respect to these two regions appear in Note, "Saving San Francisco Bay: A Case Study in Environmental Legislation," Stanford Law Review 23 (January 1971): 349-66, and Raymond G. Davis, Regional Government for Lake Tahoe: A Case Study, Environmental Quality Series No. 2 (Davis: University of California, Institute of Governmental Affairs, November 1970).

14. Davies, op. cit., p. 61.

15. Fred Bosselman and David Callies, The Quiet Revolution in Land Use Control (Washington, D.C.: Government Printing Office, 1972, for the Council on Environmental Quality). See also the special issue on state land use policy of State Government 46 (Summer 1973): 134-207.

16. Raymond A. Bauer, "The Study of Policy Formation: An Introduction," in The Study of Policy Formation, ed. Raymond A. Bauer and Kenneth J. Gergen (New York: The Free Press, 1968), pp. 16-20.

17. Bosselman and Callies, op. cit., p. 325. At least they recognize that their ideal solution to the problem of organizational design is the one usually found in state and local government textbooks, and therefore one that bears closer evaluation.

18. On the theoretical significance of this point, see Vincent Ostrom, "Human Fallibility, Political Theory, and the Environment," Policy Studies Journal 1 (Summer 1973): 205-08.

19. Fred C. Doolittle, Land-Use Planning and Regulation on the California Coast: The State Role, Environmental Quality Series No. 9 (Davis: University of California, Institute of Governmental Affairs, May 1972).

20. See, for example, William H. Rodgers, Jr., "Ecology Denied: The Unmaking of a Majority," in Inside the System, ed. Charles Peters and John Rothchild, 2d ed. (New York: Praeger, 1973), pp. 247-56, and Conservation Foundation Letter, December 1972. The origins and uses of the initiative measure in several of the western states are discussed in the individual state chapters in Frank H. Jonas, ed., Politics in The American West (Salt Lake City: University of Utah Press, 1969). See also Raymond E. Wolfinger and Fred I. Greenstein, "The Repeal of Fair Housing in California: An Analysis of Referendum Voting," American Political Science Review 62 (September 1968): 753-69.

21. Larry L. Wade, The Elements of Public Policy (Columbus, Ohio: Charles E. Merrill, 1972), pp. 57-65.

22. Ibid., p. 64.

23. Alvin D. Sokolow, AB 357: The Passage of California's "Pure Air" Law in 1968, Environmental Quality Series No. 3 (Davis: University of California, Institute of Governmental Affairs, November 1970).

24. For useful summaries of recent state activity, see the chapters on this subject in the second, third, and fourth annual reports of the Council on Environmental Quality. The reports are published in August or September each year by the Government Printing Office.

25. Elizabeth H. Haskell and Victoria S. Price, State Environmental Management: Case Studies of Nine States (New York: Praeger, 1973), p. 264. The states dealt with in the book are Illinois, Minnesota, Washington, Wisconsin, New York, Vermont, Maine, Maryland, and Michigan.

26. M. Kent Jennings, "Legislative Politics and Water Pollution Control, 1956-61," and Randall B. Ripley, "Congress and Clean Air: The Issue of Enforcement, 1963," in Congress and Urban Problems, ed. Frederic N. Cleaveland et al. (Washington, D.C.: Brookings Institution, 1969), pp. 72-109 and 224-78. See also James L. Sundquist, Politics

and Policy: The Eisenhower, Kennedy and Johnson Years
(Washington, D.C.: Brookings Institution, 1968), Chapter 8.

27. Richard A. Cooley and Geoffrey Wandesforde-Smith,
eds., Congress and the Environment (Seattle: University of
Washington Press, 1970).

28. Michael E. Kraft, "Congressional Attitudes Toward
the Environment: Attention and Issue-Orientation in Ecological Politics" (unpublished Ph.D. dissertation, Yale University, 1973), and "Political Science, Ecology and Political Change: Congressional Attitudes Toward the Environment,"
a paper delivered to the 1971 American Political Science
Association, Chicago.

29. John E. Blodgett, The Environment and Grass Roots
Sentiment (Washington, D.C.: Congressional Research Service,
March 1972), pp. 8-9. Data derived from polls conducted by
congressmen among their constituents must be treated with
great circumspection. Sampling procedures, sample sizes,
and the wording of questions tend to be highly variable.

30. Prior to the congressional elections of 1970 and
1972, the League of Conservation Voters had distributed a
poster-size sheet entitled "How Your Congressman Voted on
Critical Environmental Issues." Some of the data in Table
16.1 are taken from the sheet issued before the 1972 election.

31. A publication especially worth noting is Conservation Report, published weekly when Congress is in session
and available without charge from the National Wildlife Federation, 1412 Sixteenth Street, N.W., Washington, D.C. 20036.

32. National Wildlife Federation Conservation Report,
no. 33 (October 20, 1972), pp. 350-51.

33. Conservation Foundation Letter, December 1972, p. 1.

34. Anderson, op. cit., pp. 4-14; Terence T. Finn, "Conflict and Compromise: Congress Makes a Law, The Passage of
the National Environmental Policy Act" (unpublished Ph.D. dissertation, Georgetown University, 1972); Richard N. L. Andrews, "Environmental Policy and Administrative Change: The
National Environmental Policy Act of 1969 (1970-1971)" (unpublished Ph.D. dissertation, University of North Carolina,
1972), pp. 76-109.

35. Aaron Wildavsky, The Politics of the Budgetary
Process (Boston: Little, Brown, 1964).

36. The consequences of changes in administrations for
budgetary decisions considered by program rather than by
agency, and the possibility that they may be nonincremental,
are among the points discussed in Peter B. Natchez and Irving
C. Bupp, "Policy and Priority in the Budgetary Process,"
American Political Science Review 68 (September 1973): 951-
63, esp. 956-57.

37. Edwin T. Haefele, "Environmental Quality as a Problem of Social Choice," in _Environmental Quality Analysis: Theory and Method in the Social Sciences_, ed. Allen V. Kneese and Blair T. Bower (Baltimore: Johns Hopkins University Press, 1972), p. 285.

38. Ibid., p. 292. The earlier paper by Haefele is "A Utility Theory of Representative Government," _American Economic Review_ 61 (June 1971): 350-67.

39. Haefele, "Environmental Quality," op. cit., p. 323.

40. Ibid., pp. 285 and 324.

41. The term "superior good" is used by Kneese and Bower in their Introduction to _Environmental Quality Analysis_, op. cit., p. 4. It is there defined as a good the demand for which rises more than in proportion to increases in income.

42. Two recent reports are useful introductions to the form and purposes of contemporary interstate and intrastate regional institutions: Advisory Commission on Intergovernmental Relations, _Multistate Regionalism_ (Washington, D.C.: Government Printing Office, April 1972), and Advisory Commission on Intergovernmental Relations, _Regional Governance: Promise and Performance, Substate Regionalism and the Federal System_, Vol. 2 (Washington, D.C.: Government Printing Office, May 1973).

43. E. E. Schattschneider, _The Semi-Sovereign People_ (New York: Holt, Rinehart and Winston, 1960).

44. Lynton K. Caldwell, _Environment: A Challenge to Modern Society_ (New York: Natural History Press, 1970), p. 215.

45. Ibid., p. 216.

46. Edmond Costantini and Kenneth Hanf, "Environmental Concern and Lake Tahoe," _Environment and Behavior_ 4 (June 1972): 209-42; Lettie M. Wenner, _Attitudes of Water Pollution Control Officials_ (De Kalb: Northern Illinois University, Center for Government Studies, January 1973).

47. Jack L. Walker, "Diffusion of Innovations Among the American States," _American Political Science Review_ 62 (September 1969): 880-99.

48. This discussion follows that in Edmond Costantini, Geoffrey Wandesforde-Smith, and Laurence Baxter, _Regional Agency Voting Behavior: The Tahoe Experience_, Research Report No. 30 (Davis: University of California, Institute of Governmental Affairs, January 1974).

49. Ibid.

50. The middle-range analytical frameworks that seem to be needed to pull together and to relate the various phenomena of concern in the broader view of legislatures and environmental policy suggested in this chapter are the

kind of frameworks sought by Theodore Marmor: frameworks that "shape the field of vision, determine the level of detail, color the objects viewed, and limit the range of consideration." The Politics of Medicare (Chicago: Aldine, 1973), p. 96. Marmor applies three such models, following the work of Graham T. Allison in Essence of Decision: Explaining the Cuban Missile Crisis (Boston: Little, Brown, 1971). Marmor correctly advises of the advantages to be gained by resisting the temptation to see Allison's three models as mutually exclusive and he is sensitive to the implications of emphasizing one or another model in terms of the recommendations likely to follow from analysis. Of the three models suggested by Allison and applied to a case study of legislative policy formulation by Marmor—the rational actor model, the organizational process model, and the bureaucratic politics model—the last would seem to have great applicability to the study of legislatures and environmental policy. The model is succinctly outlined, as are some of the key relationships that bind together its elements, in Morton H. Halperin and Arnold Kanter, "The Bureaucratic Perspective: A Preliminary Framework," in Readings in American Foreign Policy: A Bureaucratic Perspective, ed. Halperin and Kanter (Boston: Little, Brown, 1973), pp. 1-42. There are few systematic attempts to treat legislatures and legislative behavior in the context of organization theory. One such attempt is Raymond G. Davis, "The Administration of Politics: Staff Structures in the California Legislature" (unpublished Ph.D. dissertation, University of California, Davis, 1972).

CHAPTER

17

ENVIRONMENTAL POLICY
AND CONSTITUTIONAL LAW
Stuart S. Nagel

The purpose of this short chapter is to describe the
kinds of constitutional law issues that are most likely to
be raised in discussions of environmental policy alternatives. The issues can be grouped into those relating to
whether the environmental policies satisfy constitutional
requirements with regard to (1) affirmative constitutional
authorization and proper allocation of governmental power
between governmental units, (2) negative constitutional restrictions of a civil liberties nature other than due process, and (3) due process or fair procedure. The chapter
mainly uses air and water pollution as examples, but what
it says could generally apply equally well to solid waste,
noise, or radiation pollution, or land use planning and
conservation.

GOVERNMENTAL POWER

In order for the federal or state government to pass
legislation regulating the environment, it is legally necessary for the policy makers to be able to point to some
clause in the federal Constitution authorizing the type of
regulation involved. For the federal government, the most
relevant clause is likely to be the interstate commerce
clause since (1) air and water pollution cross state lines,
(2) air pollution in the form of smog interferes with safe
interstate auto and air transportation, (3) air and water
pollution make people sick, thereby decreasing their produc-
tivity and the flow of goods in interstate commerce, and
(4) water pollution interferes with interstate commerce by
way of hurting commercial fishing, agriculture, and industrial water supplies.

For the state governments, the most relevant clause is the Tenth Amendment, which in effect says the states can do whatever reasonable legislators would consider relevant to promoting the health, safety, and well-being of the people of the state so long as there is no conflict with lawful federal legislation or provisions related to portions of the Bill of Rights or other constitutional prohibitions on state action.

The taxing and spending clause can be used to enable the federal government to get at within-state matters that cannot be so readily reached by the interstate commerce clause. The federal government can do so by providing grants to state and local governments to fight pollution and requiring the states to do things of a local nature in order to receive the money. This is constitutional so long as the grant requirement is designed to cause the money to be spent to promote the general welfare of the people in the state or local area involved, which should be easy to establish given the harm to health, safety, and well-being that comes from pollution.

Other less likely clauses that the federal government can use as a basis for authority include the power of the president to enter into international antipollution treaties and the power of Congress by way of the necessary and proper clause to implement those treaties. In addition, Congress could probably resort to section 5 of the Fourteenth Amendment, which gives Congress the power to pass legislation appropriate for enforcing equal protection under the law which may be violated when state and local governments regulate pollution worse in the inner city than in outlying areas.

If some legislative power and some judicial power is delegated to an antipollution administrative agency, then this sometimes raises an issue of whether the principle of separation of powers has been violated. The principle will, however, generally be considered satisfied (1) if reasonably clear guidelines or standards are provided, and they are capable of being amended by the legislature as a restraint on its delegation, and (2) if the courts are free to overrule the administrative decisions that conflict with administrative, statutory, or constitutional guidelines.

If the states pass air or water pollution legislation, then doing so may raise a federalism (or national versus state) constitutional question under Congress' interstate commerce power or the supremacy clause. That kind of issue is likely to be resolved in favor of the states but only if Congress has explicitly or implicitly authorized them to do so, or if Congress has said nothing, and the problem is local in nature rather than one requiring more uniform national treatment, and the state legislation is not unreasonably burdensome on interstate commerce.

CIVIL LIBERTIES RESTRICTIONS

If a statute classifies activities by the type or degree of pollution and subjects them to different legal treatment, then those who are more harshly treated may claim a violation of the concept of equal protection. Such classifications, however, will be upheld if the more harshly treated activities are the activities that reasonable legislators could consider as being the most harmful or the most capable of being remedied. Legislators need not attack all social problems simultaneously.

If antipollution legislation applies penalties to facilities already built, then does that violate the ex post facto concept prohibiting penalties applied to behavior that was not illegal at the time the behavior was done? The courts are likely to find no ex post facto violation so long as the penalties only apply to future pollution regardless when the basic facilities were built.

If the antipollution law provides that each day pollution occurs constitutes a separate offense subject to separate penalties, then does that constitute a violation of the clause prohibiting double jeopardy for the same crime? The courts would probably find that each day can be considered to be a separate transaction unlike the simultaneity present in a mass killing. The double jeopardy clause is also more likely to be satisfied if there is only one trial, and if there are breaks in the pollution as when the chimney or effluent spout is not running continuously.

If antipollution legislation provides for searches without a warrant then does that violate the search and seizure clause? The courts are likely to uphold periodic inspections to correct pollution equipment defects rather than to incriminate, especially where innocent third parties might be harmed, as in welfare recipient inspections, although housing inspectors are required to get area search warrants with a showing of probable cause to suspect violations. Randomly stopping cars, however, may represent an unreasonable search unless a notion of implied consent is resorted to analogous to the inspection of airline passengers or the use of drunkometers on auto drivers.

If the antipollution law requires a business firm to buy expensive equipment that does not add to its income but reduces its income-producing funds, then does that in effect represent confiscation of property without just compensation? The courts have held that there is no literal confiscation unless the property is taken over for use as a public facility, especially if the business firm is still making a profit anyhow.

FAIR PROCEDURE

If a polluter is ordered to stop his pollution pending a hearing rather than after he has had a hearing, then is due process violated? The courts are likely to say that this is not an unfair sequencing of events since the public should not suffer from the continued pollution while lengthy hearings and appeals have to be held. In addition, ordering the polluter to stop his pollution does not necessarily mean he has to go out of business or even necessarily suffer any great economic loss, especially if the hearing is held quickly. This situation is distinguishable from the desperate welfare recipient who is entitled to a hearing before a welfare termination.

If an administrative agency holds an adjudication hearing to determine whether there has been a pollution violation, then due process is generally satisfied if the accused has been given notice, an opportunity to call his witnesses, an opportunity to cross-examine his accusers, a judge who is not under the administrative control of the prosecutor, and an opportunity for judicial review. The accused need not be provided with a jury trial, a free attorney, or the same rules of evidence as are used in court, especially if the administrative decision is subject to a complete retrial as part of the judicial review. If an administrative agency holds a rule-making hearing to make new rules governing the substance or procedure of the agency, then due process is generally satisfied simply by giving notice to interested parties so that they may have the opportunity to present testimony.

Sometimes antipollution statutes do not contain precise details as to what constitutes a pollution violation. This may raise the issue of whether the statute violates the due process prohibition on unreasonable vagueness designed to enable violators to know in advance what they will be held liable for. The courts, however, have been flexible in recognizing that it may be unreasonable to expect absolute precision and have allowed phrases like "excessive fumes or smoke" in referring to automobile exhaust pollution.

Sometimes antipollution procedures provide that when the occurrence of pollution by the accused has been established in the proceeding, the burden of justifying the pollution then shifts to the accused. So long as the accused only has the burden of going forward with counteracting evidence so as not to in effect lose by default, then the due process requirement is still satisfied whereby the overall burden in case of ties is on the prosecution side.

Related to the problem of fair procedure is the problem of court jurisdiction. There is no violation of due process if the federal courts require an exhaustion of state court remedies where state legislation is involved, or an exhaustion of administrative remedies where a meaningful administrative grievance procedure is provided. Likewise there is no violation of the constitutional jurisdiction of the federal courts for Congress or the courts (1) to limit citizen suits against polluters to cases only involving certain kinds of damages, provided the classification is not arbitrary, or (2) to limit requests by polluters for injunctions against enforcement agencies to situations where they have been proceeded against.

In addition to the constitutional law arguments that are sometimes made in environmental policy litigation, the arguments more often made in courts below the Supreme Court relate to statutory interpretation and common law judge-made principles. These include such matters as how to apportion damages among multiple-defendant polluters; how to calculate the time expired when time limitations are placed on the bringing of lawsuits; what constitutes a tort like trespass, nuisance, or negligence; what kind of an injunction order is reasonable under the circumstances; and what constitutes a waiver or consent to pollution on the part of a complaining plaintiff.

In addition to constitutional law issues, the public law field of political science also cuts across environmental protection problems by virtue of the field's concern for such issues as how to maximize compliance with the law, empirical comparisons between court adjudications and administrative adjudications, the role of private lawsuits versus governmental lawsuits, prospective standard setting versus a more ad hoc case-by-case approach, and other matters relating to the operation of the legal process.

REFERENCES

Edelman, Sidney. The Law of Air Pollution Control (Stanford, Conn.: Environmental Research and Applications, 1970), pp. 56-95.

Grad, Frank. Environmental Law (New York: Matthew Bender, 1971).

Platt, Rutherford H. "Toward Constitutional Recognition of the Environment." 56 American Bar Association Journal, 1061-64 (1970).

Pritchett, C. Herman. The American Constitution (New York: McGraw-Hill, 1968).

Roberts, E. F. "The Right to a Decent Environment: Progress Along a Constitutional Avenue." In Law and the Environment, ed. Malcolm Baldwin and James Page (New York:
Walker, 1970).

Rosenthal, Albert. "Federal Power to Preserve the Environment: Enforcement and Control Techniques." In Environmental Control: Priorities, Policies, and the Law, ed.
Frank Grad et al. (New York: Columbia University Press,
1971).

CHAPTER

18

THE END OF ILLUSION:
NEPA AND THE LIMITS
OF JUDICIAL REVIEW
Walter A. Rosenbaum

Few measures emerging from Congress in recent years seemed more promising to ecologists than the National Environmental Policy Act of 1969 (NEPA). It was often called "the Magna Carta of ecology," sometimes the "great equalizer" in the long conservation struggle, even "the Big Bertha" of the environmental movement. These were not necessarily extravagant expectations in light of NEPA's language. In sweeping terms, it committed all branches of the federal government to an unprecedented regard for environmental protection.[1] Moreover, it rested upon the federal administration a heavy weight of responsibility for implementing this pledge, much to the satisfaction of many ecologists who believed federal agencies had been derelict in their environmental duties; these agencies were now mandated through the preparation of "environmental impact statements" to a very explicit, elaborate set of procedures to assure that environmental consequences were calculated and considered before any major federal actions affecting the environment were taken.[2]

Equally important, the law was written so that its guardianship could rest in part with the federal courts, for the strict standards of environmental consideration it ordered were judicially enforceable.[3] This appealed to many ecologists who believe the courts are now more likely to assure administrative fidelity to environmental responsibilities than will any purely administrative review procedures. Indeed, among politically knowledgeable ecologists, faith in NEPA was heavily pinned to this judicial oversight.

More than 200 district and appellate court decisions relating to NEPA have now been written, with new ones emerging on an average of one a week; though litigation will continue indefinitely, the judicial record is firm enough to reveal unmistakable trends in the courts' interpretation of NEPA and it is appropriate to ask what the record discloses about this judicial stewardship. For ecologists, two issues are paramount. Have the courts held the administrative branch to the stringent procedural standards specified by NEPA? And has judicial enforcement accomplished the law's broad intent? In short, what impact has judicial enforcement of NEPA produced on the federal administration?

The answers reveal the most optimistic expectations for NEPA as largely a fabric of illusions. Federal judges have indeed construed NEPA so as to produce a pervasive, sometimes radical alteration in the administrative procedures for making environmental decisions but, at the same time, they have largely refused to use NEPA to alter the substance of the decisions. This means that administrators, while compelled to take elaborate precautions to assure that they understand the environmental consequences of their acts, often need not be bound by the information. The result is largely a triumph of procedural ritual approaching, all too often, a parody of the law's intent. Moreover, NEPA's failure to produce dramatic policy alternations has not deflated the political pressure to emasculate it. Rather, there is a growing movement on Capitol Hill to lighten NEPA's judicially imposed procedural burdens on the administration, largely because numerous congressmen and administrators allege that judges have enmeshed too many vital programs (and beloved pork-barrel projects) in interminable litigation and procedural complexity.

It may still be possible to liberate NEPA from political emasculation or degeneration into a purely procedural interpretation; we shall consider several possible remedies. To evaluate the merit in such remedies it is necessary to describe briefly the apparent intent of NEPA and then to examine how the courts have constructed its important substantive and procedural provisions.

THE SHAPE OF EXPECTATIONS

The important administrative provisions of NEPA are found in two sections. Section 101 declares "a national environmental policy" in extended, rather vague terms. First, there is a sweeping policy commitment made for all federal institutions:

> The Congress . . . declares that it is the
> continuing policy of the Federal government,

> in cooperation with State and local govern-
> ments . . . to use all practicable means
> and measures . . . to create and maintain
> conditions under which man and nature can
> exist in productive harmony, and to fulfill
> the social, economic and other requirements
> of present and future generations of Ameri-
> cans.[4]

This broad policy is then sharpened in a manner that appears
to create a specific substantive duty for all federal officials: "it is the continuing responsibility of the Federal
government to use all practicable means, consistent with
other essential considerations of national policy, to improve and coordinate federal plans, functions, programs, and
resources" to the end that the nation may accomplish certain
policy goals.[5] Included in this list are a trusteeship for
succeeding generations, an assurance of a "safe, healthful,
productive and esthetically and culturally pleasing" surrounding, attaining the widest range of beneficial uses of
the environment without degradation and many additional policies; less important than the details is the existence of
these as specific, enumerated responsibilities.

   In Section 102 the act declares explicit procedures to
be followed by administrative agencies in implementing the
act's general purpose. It orders "to the fullest extent
possible" that the "policies, regulations and public laws of
the United States shall be interpreted and administered in
accordance with the policies set forth in this Act."[6] Among
other duties, Section 102 mandates that all federal agencies
include in any proposal for actions "significantly affecting
the quality of the human environment" a document since known
as an "environmental impact statement" (EIS). An EIS must
discuss five matters:[7]

1. the environmental impact of the proposed action;
2. any adverse environmental effects that cannot be avoided
    should the proposal be implemented;
3. alternatives to the proposed action;
4. the relationship between local short-term uses of man's
    environment and the maintenance and enhancement of long-
    term productivity; and
5. any irreversible and irretrievable commitments of re-
    sources that would be involved in the proposed action
    should it be implemented.

NEPA's sponsors repeatedly insisted that Sections 101 and
102 would become an "action-forcing" mechanism within the

administration. Part of these enforced duties, apparently,
would be the substantive ones detailed in Section 101 and
for this reason, presumably, the language "to the fullest
extent possible" was added to Section 102 to emphasize that
the duties of Section 101 were mandatory.[8]

In any case, there was nothing discretionary intended
in Section 102. According to a NEPA sponsor, Senator Henry
Jackson (D-Washington), the preparation of impact statements
was an unavoidable procedural task intended to force upon
administrators an environmental sensitivity; it was "unwaver-
ing" in its insistence that "all relevant environmental values and amenities (be) considered in the calculus of project
development and decision-making";[9] the EIS would be "a statutory foundation to which administrative agencies may refer
. . . for guidance in making decisions which find environmental values in conflict with other values."[10] Since NEPA em-
braced all agencies, including those without previous statutory authorization to ponder environmental implications of
programs, it was hoped that NEPA would dissipate the "mission orientation" that commonly impelled agencies to a zealous promotion of their own programs with scant concern for
environmental consequences.

It was obvious that the courts would face a long, difficult task in interpreting NEPA. It enumerated a wealth of
new, often vague duties frequently lacking operational guidelines; administrators were not always sure what was required
of them, even when a faithful effort to comply was made (often there was no such effort). Then, too, NEPA's partisans
were sure to press litigation to assure that NEPA's intent
was scrupulously observed. In general, noted Judge Henry
Friedly in an early case, "NEPA is so broad, yet opaque,
that it will take even longer than usual fully to appreciate
its impact."[11] Environmentalists calculated that this litigation would largely work to their advantage. It would mean
that NEPA's implication rested, in good measure, with a far
less "political" institution than the executive agency. According to this logic, NEPA ordained the kind of public-
rights consciousness that administrators often disregarded,
usually by giving paramount attention to bureaucratic values
and political pressures emanating from Congress and clientele groups. "The administrative process," suggests environmental lawyer Joseph Sax, Jr., "tends to produce not the
voice of the people, but the voice of the bureaucrat--the
administrative perspective posing as the public interest."[12]
In contrast, argues Sax, judges are "political outsiders"
more capable of an even-handed, public-minded approach to
legislation. Moreover, judicial enforcement of NEPA was
also attractive because the litigation could be initiated

by environmentalists themselves, thereby giving them a means of _forcing_ issues upon administrators and offering a viable alternative to reliance upon the administrative process for a hearing of grievances. The result of this judicial avenue of enforcement should be, in the end, greater administrative responsiveness to NEPA:

> Litigation, then, provides an additional
> source of leverage in making environmental
> decision-making operate rationally, thought-
> fully, and with a sense of responsiveness to
> the entire range of citizen concerns. . . .
> The more leverage citizens have, the more
> responsive and responsible their officials
> and fellow citizens will be.[13]

All this was still a matter of faith. An enormous latitude of discretion lay open to the judges in deciding what NEPA meant in operational terms, for the legislative record that might serve for guidance was virtually absent and the terms of the law were quickly submitted by federal agencies and NEPA's partisans to extremely varied, often widely divergent interpretation. Most agencies delayed or evaded compliance as long as possible. Almost every major part of the law would have to be litigated with all the possibilities for unexpected interpretations this promised.

The very early litigation over NEPA quickly put to rest a number of preliminary issues that had to be settled before the fundamentals could be debated. The courts, for example, established the right of environmental groups to "standing" under the law, affirmed the retroactivity of the legislation to include many projects authorized and/or partially completed before its enactment, and affirmed NEPA's judicial reviewability under the Administrative Procedures Act.[14] The courts have now concentrated upon NEPA's substantive and procedural duties. One critical issue is whether NEPA establishes a substantive duty for administrators to protect the environment and, if so, what standards the bench will use in deciding when this duty is properly discharged. The answers currently developed by the court cannot be very encouraging to conservationists.

THE EROSION OF SUBSTANCE

Washington's bureaucracy today presents an impressive facade of compliance with NEPA. More than 40 agencies have reported operational procedures complying with NEPA's "impact statement" provisions and following presidential guidelines for statement review. The total cost of federal EIS preparation in fiscal 1972 exceeded $20 million; the Atomic Energy Commission currently assigns 200 employees to this task, which cost the Commission $6 million and the Department of the Interior over $8 million last year.[15] After some early misadventures, agencies are demonstrating great proficiency in producing substantial, highly professional impact statements, occasionally running to elephantine proportions (the Interior's nine-volume EIS for the Alaskan oil pipeline contained 2,500 pages, weighed 18 pounds, and allegedly cost $25 million). Moreover, approximately 25 federal projects are currently enjoined by federal courts until their developers comply with NEPA guidelines.

Unfortunately, NEPA's procedures prevail more often than NEPA's objections. In general, the federal courts have largely released agencies from strict compliance with the substantive duties apparently mandated in Section 101 while still insisting upon meticulous regard for the preparation of impact statements according to Section 102; the result, if not the intent, is to give wide latitude for agencies to promote environmentally destructive projects that appear inconsistent with NEPA's Section 101. This situation arises mainly because judges have largely interpreted NEPA's substantive duties to be a proper "consideration" or "balancing" of environmental and nonenvironmental costs of agency projects, an obligation often becoming little more than a ceremony with scant effect upon ultimate decisions; then--in keeping with the traditional judicial reluctance to overturn administrative decisions on discretionary matters--the courts have adopted standards for reviewing these decisions that strongly favor the agency's freedom of action.

An important early case in setting this trend is Environmental Defense Fund v. Corps of Engineers (1971) involving a challenge to a partially complete impoundment across Arkansas' small, scenic Cassatot River.[16] In this case, environmentalists asked the court to interpret both Sections 101 and 102 by alleging that the Engineers had failed to discharge their substantive duties under Section 101 and their procedural duties under Section 102. Regarding Section 102, the court declared that the Engineers had an obligation to demonstrate "good faith" in following each of the steps for impact statement preparation--an interpretation that later cases have largely sustained. More important was the final ruling of the court of appeals on the meaning of Section 101. In one perspective, the court appeared to be approaching Section 101 so that its total objectives would be regarded as substantive duties enforceable by the bench:

The unequivocal intent of NEPA is to require
agencies to consider and give effect to the
environmental goals set forth in the Act,
not just to file detailed impact studies.
. . . Given an agency obligation to carry
out the substantive requirements of the Act,
we believe that the courts have an obligation to review substantive agency decisions
on the merits.[17]

But the actual standard of review adopted by the bench insisted only that administrators demonstrate "good faith"
consideration and balancing of environmental values in making decisions:

Where NEPA is involved, the reviewing court
must first determine if the agency reached
its decision after a full, good faith consideration and balancing of environmental
factors. The court must then determine, according to the standards set forth in 101(b)
and 102(1) of the Act, whether "the actual
balance of costs and benefits that was
struck was arbitrary or clearly gave insufficient weight to environmental values."[18]

Beyond this, the court carefully noted, it could not go,
quoting with approval an earlier case: "Although this inquiry into the facts is to be searching and careful, the
ultimate standard of review is a narrow one. The court is
not empowered to substitute its judgment for that of the
agency."[19] In effect, the logic implies that the court cannot insist that an agency make decisions in accord with the
policy goals of Section 101 but can only assure that administrators have properly calculated environmental costs
(through impact statements) and weighed them. How then are
aggrieved parties to obtain redress when they believe the
eventual agency decision violates the objectives of Section
101? The answer, suggested the trial court in the Cassatot
case, is only through appeal to legislative or executive officials: "The only chance to stop the dam, or to alter the
same, lies in the [plaintiffs'] ability . . . to convince
decision makers as to the wisdom and correctness of their
views."[20]
     The Cassatot ruling strikes the dominant theme in most
current interpretations of Section 101. Thus, in Calvert
Cliffs Coordinating Committee v. United States Atomic Energy Commission (1971), the appellate court again noted that

the "general substantive policy of the Act is flexible."
Said the court:

> [NEPA] leaves room for a responsible exer-
> cise of discretion and may not require par-
> ticular substantive results in particular
> problematical circumstances. . . .
>   Perhaps the greatest substantive im-
> portance of NEPA is to require the Atomic
> Energy Commission and other agencies to
> consider environmental issues just as they
> consider other matters within their man-
> dates.[21]

This reasoning appeared more recently in the final ruling on
the bitter litigation over a proposal for a pump-storage
generating plant on New York's Storm King Mountain and in
five other decisions in the latter part of 1973.[22]
    This approach would be profoundly significant, if only
because it severely restricts the impact of NEPA's policy
goals upon administrative agencies and because it obstructs
the effort of aggrieved parties to challenge agency action
arising under NEPA. But this approach also depreciates the
value of impact statements. Under the prevailing doctrine,
the material in an impact statement need not--indeed, often
will not--govern the decision to which it relates. No matter how strongly a statement may argue against a decision on
environmental grounds, the courts will apparently not intervene so long as there is evidence that environmental matters were carefully considered, that the statement was prepared "in good faith," and that the action was not "arbitrary, capricious and an abuse of discretion." How far this
can reduce an impact statement toward impotence is illustrated in Conservation Council of North Carolina v. Froehlke
(1972) in which conservationists asked the court to enjoin
the Corps of Engineers from completing a small impoundment
across North Carolina's New Hope River. Apparently, the
conservationists had quite convinced the bench that the
project might be an environmental disaster:

> These experts gave very damaging testimony
> as to the future water quality of the New
> Hope Lake; they point out alleged discrepan-
> cies in the cost-benefit ratio as figured by
> the defendants; they question whether the
> project is really needed . . . they fear a
> loss of air quality because of the cutting
> of timber land. . . .[23]

Nonetheless, this "strong evidence which cast doubt on the advisability of continuing the dam project" did not prompt a judicial injunction principally because the Corps had prepared an impact statement in which it dutifully noted and pondered all these objections—indeed, the Corps had included all this damning testimony within the statement! To the court, this fine even-handedness was evidence that the Engineers had honored NEPA's intent to make the statement a "full disclosure" document. As for any other substantive duties arising from Section 101, the court declared it could not "substitute its opinion as to whether the project should be undertaken or not" since the discretion lay with the administrator. Such are the peculiar consequences of neutralizing Section 101 while insisting upon meticulous attention to Section 102.

In essence, the courts have come close to equating the preparation of impact statements with administrative compliance to NEPA's policy goals in Section 101. In light of this, environmentalists have increasingly concentrated upon challenging the adequacy of impact statements alone, hoping to enjoin decisions on grounds of inadequate impact statement preparation. In a sense, this has worked too well. It has not only produced numerous temporary injunctions to halt projects until proper impact statements are prepared, but has persuaded federal judges to impose very stringent standards for the preparation of impact statements. The major problem is that the bench has in recent years applied these very demanding standards to federal licensing agencies, particularly to the Federal Power Commission and Atomic Energy Commission, leading to a growing complaint in Congress that vital federal projects—particularly generating plants needed to relieve the "energy crisis"—are intolerably delayed. Let us examine briefly how this situation has arisen.

THE CALVERT CLIFFS CRUNCH

In 1967 the Baltimore Gas and Electric Company (BG&E) announced its intention to build a huge 1,600-megawatt nuclear generating plant at Calvert Cliffs on Chesapeake Bay. Local residents were outraged; they had not been consulted by BG&E, feared a multitude of environmental hazards from a "nuke," and resented the company's apparent disregard for their interests. Several years of vigorous protest to the Atomic Energy Commission (AEC), whose responsibility it was to license the project, produced no satisfactory administrative remedy; then environmentalists, seizing upon the newly enacted NEPA, went to court, charging that the AEC had violated NEPA's procedural guidelines in issuing a license for the huge "nuke." In July 1971, the U.S. Court of Appeals issued the most significant judicial interpretation yet made of NEPA's procedural provisions; in a stinging rebuke to the AEC, the court announced an extraordinarily rigorous interpretation of NEPA, surprising both sides of the litigation. To the plaintiffs it was "an environmentalist's dream," to most federal administrators it was "the Calvert Cliffs crunch."[24]

The AEC was a very vulnerable target for such a challenge. It is a prime example of a "mission"-oriented agency with statutory responsibilities for both regulating and promoting nuclear power, one that environmentalists believe has been particularly zealous in shunting aside its environmental responsibilities in the interests of the nuclear power industry. Moreover, an enormous number of "nukes" would be affected by the decision, for the AEC then had in its jurisdiction 55 plants under construction and 76 planned, all subject to NEPA. The AEC had also displayed an obvious antipathy toward NEPA procedures, practicing so many blatant evasions of NEPA's clear intent that the court remarked on the agency's "crabbed" interpretation of the law. Beyond all this, Calvert Cliffs was the first interpretation of NEPA procedures by the appellate court and, consequently, was sure to be widely noted and followed in administrative circles.

The great significance of Calvert Cliffs lies in the court's broad declaration concerning what administrative behavior was expected of licensing boards in dealing with policy affected by NEPA. First, asserted the court, NEPA requires that all important environmental considerations be weighed in each such decision at every stage of the decision:

> Compliance to the "fullest" extent possible
> would seem to demand that environmental is-
> sues be considered at every important stage
> in the decision-making process concerning a
> particular action--at every stage where an
> overall balancing of the environmental and
> nonenvironmental factors is appropriate and
> where alternatives might be made in the pro-
> posed action to minimize environmental
> costs.[25]

Moreover, this had to be "a rather finely tuned and 'systematic' balancing in each instance":

> NEPA mandates a case-by-case balancing judg-
> ment. . . . In each individual case, the

particular economic and technical benefits
of planned action must be assessed and then
weighed against the environmental costs; alternatives must be considered which would
affect the balance of values.[26]

The court then indicated what the AEC (and presumably other
licensing boards) would have to do to achieve this "finely
tuned" balancing of interests:

1. The Commission could not waive its responsibility
for evaluating environmental impact to another expert agency
(the AEC had relied upon the Federal Water Quality Administration to certify that federal water quality standards
would be met by the plant).

2. A very ample opportunity had to be given at every
decision-making stage for intervenors to raise issues ger-
mane to the environmental impact of plants.

3. The Commission's Hearing Board could not rely solely upon its own staff reports concerning environmental impact of plants but must "independently consider the final
balance of conflicting factors"--even on noncontested issues.

4. The agency must consider alternative measures even
when it had no authority to implement them.

In short, "the court essentially took the position of
environmentalists . . . that someone is responsible for considering not only power needs but also the impact on the environment of the satisfaction of those needs."[27]

The AEC did not appeal the decision, leaving it to
stand as the guideline for other federal licensing boards
and, perhaps, for other agencies also. One immediate result
was a sudden slowdown in license proceedings for plants representing more than 80 million kilowatts of generating capacity; between March 1971 and August 1972 the AEC had li-
censed only half the "nukes" it had anticipated before Calvert Cliffs. Moreover, the delay imposed large costs on existing facilities for lost capacity; plants in New York and
Michigan were losing in excess of $1 million monthly on this
account.[28] The predictable congressional protest, echoed by
the power industry, was further aroused by some environmental groups carrying to excess their new right as intervenors
in licensing hearings; the immense list of issues they often
raised for licensing boards to ponder seemed little more
than a covert conspiracy to delay licenses as long as possi-
ble--it is a public secret, after all, that some conservationists want "nukes" under no circumstances.[29] Further,
licensing boards may be in an almost impossible situation.
Previously, they could use the solution of procedural or
substantive standards to resolve many issues that ecologists

might raise in proceedings but now, apparently, no standards would be binding; additionally, it was difficult to dispose of some issues by stipulation because, notes one observer, "there is a fundamental disagreement between environmentalists and power advocates as to what is desirable."

Licensing delays continue, costs mount, and the congressional temptation to rewrite Section 102 grows. Indeed, a future omen may already have appeared. Congress, impatient with the litigation halting the Alaska oil pipeline, specifically excluded the project from NEPA's provisions to prevent further challenges under Section 102. In 1974, with a national "energy crisis" upon us, there are sufficiently powerful incentives for Congress to act against NEPA without undue political risk. Thus, the more stringently the court interprets Section 102, the greater the probability that a political backlash will undo even these procedures; whether this takes the form of an amendment weakening Section 102 or an exclusion of particular projects from NEPA by separate bills, the effect will be largely to render NEPA impotent.

FOUR WAYS OUT OF AN IMPASSE

Without arguing the merit in the court's approach to NEPA as we have described it, the result has been to produce a very different administrative impact than many of NEPA's proponents had hoped. First, it does not now seem possible to compel administrators to follow the environmental goals stated in NEPA's Section 101 and it is small wonder, therefore, that commentators have been hard pressed to identify any major policy impact directly attributable to the legislation (except for largely unprovable assertions that NEPA has been effective because many actions or programs were not undertaken). Second, the procedural aspects of NEPA have been carried to such literalness that a political backlash may result. Are there any strategies that might plausibly ease this situation? There are several possible approaches but they have an inherent difficulty: The most potentially successful may not satisfy environmentalists determined to see Section 101 scrupulously observed and those most likely to honor the intent of Section 101 are least likely to be politically feasible. Let us consider these options.

The "Good Faith Consideration" of Impact Statements

Several recent court decisions suggest that the federal courts might be persuaded to apply a stricter standard for

271

administrative compliance with NEPA's procedural provisions
without necessarily forcing the substantive duties of Section 101 upon agencies. This could reduce the administrator's freedom to ignore the environmental data in the statements and, perhaps, might force administrative policy to
conform to good environmental principles when the impact
statements clearly demonstrate that a decision would entail
grave environmental consequences. However, this approach
would not remove administrative discretion in cases where
environmental costs were involved in a project; it would
probably force administrative compliance with Section 101
only when the calculation of environmental costs gives overwhelming evidence that a project's environmental toll greatly exceeds any other benefits.

Essentially, this judicial standard would insist that
administrators demonstrate "good faith" in both the preparation of statements (as is now commonly expected) and in the
consideration of the information. This approach was recently taken in Conservation Society of Southern Vermont v. Secretary of Transportation (1973) and Natural Resources Defense Fund v. Grant (1973).[30] In the Vermont case, the
court fully elaborated an administrative duty far more demanding than simple "good faith" preparation of impact
statements:

> [the] agency preparing the environmental im-
> pact statement must show that it has adequate-
> ly weighed the relevant environmental factors
> in deciding whether and how to go forward
> with the project, and though the agency need
> not show "subjective impartiality" it must
> be demonstrated that, with regard for the
> specific project for which the statement is
> prepared, the agency has weighed "in good
> faith consideration" the environmental im-
> pact of the project and that the agency will
> modify or drop the project if the environ-
> mental costs are sufficient to outweigh the
> benefits of the project.[31]

This approach creates a standard in the grey area between
purely procedural compliance with NEPA and substantive concepts of agency duties under NEPA. It has the virtue of requiring no legislative rewriting of NEPA and would probably
prevent such projects as the one involved in the Froehlke
case from proceeding. But it falls short of insisting upon
full respect for Section 101 and, quite clearly, could not
force administrative decisions in the vast number of cases

where environmental costs in a project are not overwhelmingly greater than the presumed benefits. Environmental purists are not likely to be enthusiastic about this approach mainly because it does not produce a dependable, environmentally protective rule of decision in most, or all, administrative cases they might contest and because it falls short of Section 101's broad policy declarations.

Judicial Remands to Congress

A second strategy, requiring the collaboration of environmental litigants and the court, is the request and grant of a remand to send a project back to Congress for specific authorization. As Sax explains, by a remand "the courts thrust upon the promoter of that project the affirmative obligation to go back to the legislature and obtain specific authorization (if he can get it) that makes clear a decisive public policy to subordinate traditional public use to some private or governmental use."[32] A remand might arise in several circumstances: (1) when the court believes that an impact statement strongly argues against a decision an agency intends to take and the court does not believe it can overturn the decision; or (2) when an agency will not, or cannot, produce a satisfactory impact statement due to lack of time, information, or expertise. This approach, though uncommon and freighted with some tangled legal issues that might cast doubt on its practicability, might offer some advantage to environmentalists. It could force an open, public debate on an issue and remove it from the sequestered administrative or legislative chamber; it might also offer judges a method for countering administrative decisions to which they object without exposing themselves to criticism that they are usurping legislative or executive powers. The major disadvantage, aside from possible judicial reluctance to remand and the time consumption involved in the procedure, is that it would place the ultimate decision back in the political arena where many environmentalists suspect they are least likely to obtain a favorable results.

The first two approaches, in any event, would require no congressional debate or declaration of any affirmative, comprehensive policy positions nor would it reopen a general discussion on NEPA; both approaches leave the initiative with courts and environmental groups. Two other approaches can also be considered. These would have the virtue of removing many of the procedural delays now imposed by court interpretations of Section 102 and might, consequently, reduce congressional opposition to NEPA. Both approaches would also get directly at the need for a declaration of substantive administrative duties under NEPA. The problem is that the decisions must both be made by Congress and this, many environmentalists would assert, makes the result very unlikely to please them.

A Declaration of Environmental Rights

It has sometimes been suggested that Congress ought to declare a set of "environmental rights" for all citizens. The wording would require enormous care and would doubtless provoke much argument among environmentalists, but the advantage would be that such a declaration would remove any doubt about the existence of substantive environmental duties within the administrative branch. This declaration would also bring the duties within the scope of "public trust doctrine" declared and elaborated by the courts as a procedure for coping with administrative mandates to protect some public trust such as environmental protection; these public trust procedures would seem reasonably hospitable to the kind of interests that environmentalists are attempting to protect currently through NEPA. At the same time, this approach depends heavily upon an affirmative, environmentally sensitive declaration of clear congressional policy at a time when the complexities of NEPA have already ired many legislators, the "energy crisis" has arrived, and environmentalists no longer enjoy the political initiative or favor they once possessed. A firm congressional commitment to environmental protection as a public right and an administrative trust would be difficult under the most congenial political climate; it may be impossible today.

A Legislative Declaration of Licensing Criteria

Although less comprehensive in its approach to administrative policy than the other proposals, one strategy that might deflate some current political pressure against NEPA would be a congressional declaration of criteria that licensing boards could use in resolving the environmental issues they must confront in the wake of <u>Calvert Cliffs</u>. The effect of such a declaration would be to relieve licensing boards of deciding, case-by-case and through "careful balancing," how environmental aspects should be handled in licensing applications; some general criteria would be declared and the licensing process possibly accelerated. This approach would also simplify the task of judicial review of licensing proceedings, for judges could presumably determine with relative ease whether the congressionally mandated criteria had been observed. The major risk in such a strategy is common to all proposals that require Congress to reinterpret, amplify, or otherwise amend NEPA or procedures arising from it: The Congress may well enact new policy or procedures that defeat the broad environmental values NEPA attempts to implement. This might certainly happen when Congress is invited to create guidelines for licensing boards to follow in balancing environmental and nonenvironmental considerations in generating plants, impoundments, canal projects, federal highways, or other enterprises that commonly provoke the ire of ecologists.

Regardless of which strategy, or combination of strategies, might be attempted by environmentalists--and these are by no means the only possible solutions--it seems apparent that some concerted, imaginative effort must be made to save NEPA from its present prospect of degenerating into a procedural ritual without substantive effect or becoming a victim to legislative scalpels that will amputate its vital provisions in the guise of making it workable. In brief, environmentalists must awaken to the current miscarriage of NEPA's intent and espouse some new approach that may fall short of a complete resurrection of NEPA's original purpose but may nonetheless permit the courts to preserve a large measure of the original expectations.

NOTES

1. Public Law 91-190, January 1, 1970 (42 U.S.C. 4321-4347), Title I, Section 101.
2. Ibid., Section 102.
3. Enforcement was explicitly provided in the bill through the creation of an administrative review system under the direction of the Council on Environmental Quality (itself created by the measure's Title II) and, by implication, through whatever administrative details might be ordered through the White House. The Council's guidelines may be found in 36 Federal Register 7724 (1971), the president's directive in 35 Federal Register 4247 (1970), Executive Order No. 11, 514. The court's general right to review is established in the Administrative Procedures Act; see, for example, 5 U.S.C. 701 et. seq. (1970).
4. Public Law 91-190, Title I, Section 101(a).
5. Ibid., Section 101(b).
6. Ibid., Section 102(1).
7. Ibid., Section 102(c)(i)-(v).

8.   Such material as exists on NEPA's intent may be found in several sources. See Senate Report No. 296, 91st Cong., 1st sess., 1969; Hearings on S. 1075 before the Committee on Interior and Insular Affairs, 91st Cong., 2d sess., 1969; and especially Conference Report on National Environmental Policy Act, Congressional Report No. 765, 91st Cong., 1st sess., 9-10 (1969). I deliberately use the words "presumably" and "apparently" when dealing with the intent of Section 101 because the intent, while it seems reasonably clear, is still subject to argument on the evidence in the previous documents.

9.   See 115 Congressional Record 29055, 1969.

10.   See 115 Congressional Record 40416, 1969.

11.   New York City v. U.S., 338 F. Supp. 792 (1972).

12.   Joseph L. Sax, Jr., Defending the Environment (New York: Alfred A. Knopf, 1971), p. 56.

13.   Ibid., p. 115.

14.   This early litigation is traced in John R. Sandler, "The National Environmental Policy Act: A Sheep in Wolf's Clothing?," Brooklyn Law Review, Fall 1970, pp. 139-58.

15.   Robert Gillette, "The National Environmental Policy Act: How Well Is It Working?," Science, April 14, 1972, pp. 146-49. On agency implementation of NEPA generally, see U.S. Senate, Joint Hearings on the Operation of the National Environmental Policy Act, 1969-72, 92d Cong., 2d sess., Serial No. 92-H32.

16.   Environmental Defense Fund v. Corps of Engineers, 325 F. Supp. 728, 342 F. Supp. 1211, 470 F. 2d 289 (1972).

17.   Ibid., 470 F. 2d s98.

18.   Ibid., 300.

19.   Ibid.

20.   Ibid., 342 F. Supp. 1217.

21.   Calvert Cliffs Coordinating Committee v. United States Atomic Energy Commission, 449 F. 2d 1112 (1971). A complete examination of the litigation relating to substantive review may be found in Stephen T. Smith, "Environmental Law--Substantive Judicial Review Under the National Environmental Policy Act of 1970," North Carolina Law Review, November 1972, pp. 145-54.

22.   Scenic Hudson Preservation Conference v. Federal Power Commission, 453 F. 2d 463. See also Silva v. Lynn, 482 Fed 2d 1283 (1973); Citizens For Mass Transit Against Freeways v. Brinegar, 357 F. Supp. 1270 (1973); Movement Against Destruction v. Volpe, 361 F. Supp. 1363 (1973); Environmental Defense Fund v. Froehlke, 477 F. 2d 1033 (1973); and Scientist's Institute for Public Information v. Atomic Energy Commission, 481 F. 2d 1079 (1973).

23. Conservation Council of North Carolina v. Froehlke, 340 F. Supp. 226. For comment on this case, consult Bernard S. Cohen and Jacqueline M. Warren, "Judicial Recognition of the Substantive Requirements of the National Environmental Policy Act of 1969," Boston College Industrial and Commercial Law Review, March 1972, pp. 685-704.

24. The implications of this decision have been widely discussed in many professional journals. The legal implications are traced in Ralph F. Fuchs, "Administrative Agencies and the Energy Problem," Indiana Law Journal, Summer 1972, pp. 606-23; Robert Gillette, "National Environmental Policy Act: Signs of a Backlash Are Evident," Science, April 7, 1972, pp. 30-33; Norman J. Landau, "Postscript to Calvert Cliffs," Boston College Industrial and Commercial Law Review, March 1972, pp. 705-17. Two articles quite critical of the ruling are Arthur W. Murphy, "The National Environmental Policy Act and the Licensing Process: Environmental Magna Carta or Agency Coup de Grace?," Columbia Law Review, October 1972, pp. 963-1009; and A. Dan Tarlock, "Balancing Environmental Considerations and Energy Demands," Indiana Law Review 47 (Summer 1972): 645-79.

25. Calvert Cliffs Coordinating Committee v. United States Atomic Energy Commission, 449 F. 2d 1118.

26. Ibid., 1123.

27. Murphy, op. cit., p. 989.

28. New York Times, January 14, 1973.

29. See Murphy, op. cit., pp. 974-76 for illustrations of this tactic.

30. National Resources Defense Fund v. Grant, 355 F. Supp. 280 (1973); Conservation Society of Southern Vermont v. Secretary of Transportation, 362 F. Supp. 627 (1973).

31. Conservation Society of Southern Vermont v. Secretary of Transportation, op. cit.

32. Sax, op. cit., p. 175.

19

THE PUBLIC ADMINISTRATION
OF ENVIRONMENTAL POLICY
Lynton K. Caldwell

Environmental policies belong to a class of issues concerned with the quality of life, for example, with health, education, and public safety.[1] From the viewpoint of economists, the substance of these issues is "public goods." Like pure air and clean water, where available they are available to people generally and their use can seldom be allocated through pricing or rationing.

These issues are distinguishable by their emphasis on social ends from those economic issues tending to emphasize means. But environmental policies, characteristically concerned with systemic relationships (for example, atmospheric pollution), are not easily adapted to meet individual preferences. Environmental goals and standards for pollution control, land use, or wildlife management tend to be generalized throughout the entire political society. Allowance for diversity of preference can sometimes be made, but implementation often calls for regulatory administration and policing, for example, use of off-road vehicles in national forests or preservation of wildlife refuges or wilderness areas.

The great majority of public policies evolve through a cyclical process; perceived need giving rise to practical measures which induce theory which modifies practice. Policy is thus induced through feedback loops linking all stages of the policy process. But the rapid rise of environmental quality as a public issue has frequently resulted in formal policies being adopted in advance of practical experience, and conceptual or institutional filters in the feedback process have often altered the "message" that feedback should have conveyed. Incongruities in public environmental policies have been a result.

THE CYCLE OF POLITICS-POLICY-ADMINISTRATION

The topic of this chapter raises again the pseudo-issue of the relationship of policy to administration.[2] Although once a subject for vigorous debate, comparatively little interest has been shown in the matter for the last quarter century. Currently, a widely held assumption, among political and other social scientists, appears to be that administration is an operational phase of the policy process and occurs at all stages of that process. This means that policy not only precedes administrative application, but that policy is generated during the course of administration. If administration may be defined as "the art of getting things done," then its scope and content will necessarily be as flexible as the methods available to the administrator, the objectives he seeks, and the milieu in which he operates.

The researcher-teacher and writer on politics and public administration thus has a broad and subjectively defined scope for his efforts. The interrelationships between policy and politics and administration may be studied from a great variety of viewpoints and with widely differing emphasis. In the particular case of public environmental policy, the relative novelty of the field and the yet indeterminate character of its organizational structure and administrative procedures force the student to consider its political aspects. There are technical aspects of environmental administration, but to understand their relationship to the politics of environmental policy requires major attention to the political circumstances that caused the particular technical approaches to be used in preference to possible alternatives.

The basic concept of "environment" is of reciprocating relationships between whatever the focus of inquiry may be--in our case modern industrial society--and the matrix of forces and influences with which it interacts.[3] Because "environment" is a relational concept it implies a "circularity" of actions, responses, and reactions. We may therefore visualize the total process of policy as an evolving cycle, which may be entered by the policy analyst at any convenient point, but for which a well-defined beginning or end may not be easily found and may not even exist.

RECIPROCAL RELATIONSHIPS BETWEEN THEORY AND PRACTICE

The relationship between environmental politics (or policies) and public administration may be approached from three viewpoints, all of which must ultimately be considered in any comprehensive study. They are:

1. theory--a formal statement of the policy and the purposes, history, and values or interests that it serves;
2. practive--the actual process of policy implementation
   through administrative agencies or the judicial courts;
   and
3. impact--the effects of both theory and policy on society
   or its subdivisions, and feedback into further policy
   development.

The objective of this threefold approach would be to
identify the _actual_ as contrasted with the _formal_ policy and
to understand the effects of the difference upon policy implementation. The actual is always different from the formal if only in its greater complexity. The meaning of a policy is clarified and elaborated during its administration,
and it can sometimes be argued that the practice _is_ "the policy." This is often the case among pragmatic people such as
Americans, disinclined to develop theory in advance of practical necessity. The American way characteristically has
been to evolve a policy out of the necessities or expedien-
cies of solving a practical problem. In such cases, policy
becomes an ex post facto rationalization of established
practice; the practice must be understood before the theory
can be explained.

But administrative practices are not developed in vacuo;
if not always preceded by well-developed theory they are
based on some form of a priori rationalization. The findings and assumptions accepted by legislators in the drafting
of statutes or by judges in their interpretation may often
be based on "theory" in the popular sense, but it is seldom
"theory" as understood in the more methodologically rigorous
sciences. A large body of social and political "theory" has
not been subjected to controlled or even to objective empirical testing. Such "theories" might more accurately be
called "assumptions." More often tacitly than explicitly
they are bases for policy and administration in such matters
as employment security, crime deterrence, racial integration.
Environmental administration has been based upon a mixed
background of scientifically verified evidence and value
preference rationalization, and the two sources of policy
are often mixed in ways that are confusing to the public and
its political representatives.

The environmental problems with which environmental
politics are currently concerned have arisen largely out of
conflicting public values and objectives. In most cases
economic objectives (for example, in agriculture, mining,
forestry, manufacturing, merchandising, tourism, or energy
production) have entailed environmental effects that have

become increasingly unacceptable to growing numbers of people. Since the mid-1960s a large body of law and administrative practice has been developed on the "theory" or assumption that environmental damage in industrial society is largely a result of accidents, side-effects, or correctable errors in an otherwise sound technoeconomic system. These assumptions have had a controlling effect upon the politics and administration of environmental policy.

The actual causes of the environmental problems of modern society are complex and broad, generalizations yield little insight that is meaningful. Some forms of blight (for example, billboards along the highways) are easily understood and could be remedied, over time, with relatively minimal disruption to the economy. But the extent of avoidable environmental damage from energy extraction, generation, and transmission is not so easily comprehended, prevented, or effaced. The causal factors of nearly all environmental problems are as often technological and behavioral as they are economic. Although economic considerations may account for the particular expressions of technology and behavior, in some countries other factors may be more significant.

Thus the argument that the system of private economic enterprise necessarily degrades the environment fails to account for paralleling environmental problems of socialist regimes and for relatively good environmental conditions in some free enterprise countries. Moreover there may be as many ways in which economic enterprise relates (or does not relate) to the environment as there are economic activities. There are business practices that have had devastating impact upon the environment, but there are others (and especially new forms of enterprise) whose function is environmental protection and enhancement. Particular systems of economic enterprise may and do operate in ways that produce environmental degradation. The primary problem for the analyst of environmental policy is therefore to discover why these systems are environmentally damaging. Without this knowledge, policies rest on no more than conjecture, and administrative action may be ineffectual or even counterproductive.

Reverting to our simple model of (1) theory, (2) practice, and (3) impact, two further observations should be made. The first is that the model is a cybernetic interpretation of policy implementation and adjustment through feedback. But the model does not imply that policy and administration are always governed by a cybernetic process. It is a model for inquiry, not for illustrating political reality.

The second observation explains why the model does not necessarily describe reality. The explanation is found in what Jay Forrester calls "the counter-intuitive behavior of social systems."[4] He points out that our policies and decisions are often based on intuitive assumptions regarding the collective behavior of people and their institutions that are contrary to what actually happens. Forrester has illustrated counterintuitive social behavior by reference to the conspicuous failure of low-cost housing efforts, as presently conceived, to obtain the sought-for improvements in urban environments. He observes that as housing becomes cheaper in aging urban centers the poor move into these areas, where employment is declining. Public efforts to arrest urban decay through low-cost housing have not alleviated the deteriorating situation and have served only to compound it. It seems probable that frustrated attempts to deal with many of the social and environmental ills of modern society have resulted from political adherence to policies based upon what people wish to believe rather than upon how people, and institutions, actually behave.

The value of intuitive judgment in analyzing social problems ought not to be discounted. But some means of testing against results is required if intuition is to be reliable. A danger in intuitively based policy is that it is customarily rationalized and given a doctrinal justification, which its adherents feel committed to defend. When policy fails because social phenomena are behaving counterintuitively, a common tendency is to intensify efforts to force the elusive goals of unsound policy. Indoctrination and training in pursuit of such policies become a form of "educated incapacity," frustrating a truly rational and effective way of dealing with the problem.

The cyclical character of the process of politics, policy, and administration does not therefore imply that it will be cybernetic. Feedback may be blocked or distorted by assumptions and arrangements in society that not only obstruct accurate assessment of the effects of a policy, but may prevent corrective action based upon valid appraisal of experience. A fundamental objective of rational policy should be to ensure full accessibility to the testing, warning, and learning potentialities of feedback loops.

COMPREHENDING THE TASK OF POLICY

To understand how feedback may be filtered, and how perceptions and institutional arrangements may distort the formulation of policy, a simple model may again be helpful (see Table 19.1). Three levels of comprehension may be identified with respect to perceived causes of environmental disorders. Each of these three levels (which, in real life, intergrade) represents a different interpretation of the causes of environmental problems. Each prompts different conclusions regarding the policies that are required and the institutional arrangements and administrative actions that are indicated.

TABLE 19.1

Interpretations of Environmental Impairment:
Levels of Comprehension

Perceived Causes	Explanations	Remedies
I. Incidental: harmful be- haviors or events occur- ring in the normal course of human ac- tivities	Environmental im- pairment attribu- ted to accident and dereliction	Exhortation; ad hoc corrections; clean- up campaigns, in- doctrination and education
II. Operational: errors in program planning and execution	Defective proce- dures require cor- rection; environ- mental standards imposed upon ex- isting procedures	Statutory law; ad- ministrative regula- tions; impact state- ments
III. Systemic: environmen- mental im- pairment "built into" technoeco- nomic systems	Environmental dam- age is inherent in operations of the technoeconomic system	Basic changes in technical and behav- ioral systems; rede- signing of institu- tions and alternative methods and materials indicated

At Level I, environmental problems are perceived as incidental to the normal operations of the technoeconomic system. Environmental disruptions are seen as accidents and miscalculations, extraneous to the system, and are explained as consequences of human failure or neglect. The implications for public policy are not far-reaching. They suggest reliance on admonition, education, and indoctrination to influence human behavior: "Only you can prevent forest fires!" and "Every litter bit hurts!"

Level I has sometimes been called the cosmetic approach to the environment. Its concern has been primarily with the appearance of the physical environment and is characteristically expressed by community clean-up and paint-up campaigns, by planting trees and flower boxes, and by removing billboards from the roadsides. At this conceptual level, legislation is characteristically prohibitory of environmentally degrading acts (for example, littering highways or dumping refuse in streams, etc.). It may also be mandatory (for example, set-back and height restrictions on buildings, required landscaping of shopping centers, etc.). It may impose penalties for oil spills, ban phosphate detergents, and require emission control devices on automobiles; but it does not otherwise interfere with the customary behaviors or operations of individuals or organizations.

The politics of natural beauty associated with the presidency of Lyndon B. Johnson, although concerned with more than environmental cosmetics, had a pronounced Level I emphasis. The 1965 White House Conference on National Beauty, by inadvertence or design, appears to have been a strategy to move the nation from a Level I to a Level II perception of environmental policy. The conference agenda and report reveal a concern with environmental quality extending far beyond the beauty issue into areas of economic, technological, and materials policy. But "natural beauty" was an innocuous approach to a new area of public policy that held profound implications for all sectors of the economy.

Whether because of a limited perception of the issue, or because of the competing demands of both the Vietnam war and the civil rights movement, the Johnson administration never moved far beyond Level I. The expansions of the National Park System, the Land and Water Conservation Fund, the scenic rivers and wilderness programs, and the public attention that Mrs. Johnson helped to direct toward environmental amenities--all were important contributions to the national quality of life. They enlarged and legitimized a new area of politics and policy, and prepared the way for a Level II approach to environmental policy.

At Level II environmental problems are perceived primarily as consequences of inadequate planning and administration. From this viewpoint environmental damage is seen as resulting from a faulty or incomplete definition of organizational goals or missions. A frequent explanation of environmental disruption is failure of the planners of programs and projects to take full account of all the parameters of their proposals. It is therefore unrealistic to seek prevention or correction of environmental damage simply

284

by use of penalties or exhortations; and it is not far-reaching enough to limit standard-setting merely to the output of the activity in question (for example, acceptable levels of effluent discharge, or reclamation of surface mines). Level II perceptions imply intervention in the decision processes and the operational procedures of government and economic enterprise. Intervention is characteristically undertaken through statutory laws, executive orders, administrative regulations, and a limited restructuring of governmental agencies.

The clearest present expression of Level II perception is the National Environmental Policy Act of 1969 (PL 91-190) and more specifically its Section 102 (2)(c) five-point environmental impact statement requirement. This action-forcing provision, in effect, causes the federal agencies to incorporate environmental considerations into their policy and planning operations. The preceding sections of this act specify certain criteria for environmental quality and for that kind of planning that will more likely take account of the full range of quality-of-life values. The NEPA is a statutory intervention into the erstwhile "normal" administrative procedures of the federal agencies. The legislation, although not regulatory in the conventional legal sense, has been implemented by executive orders of the president, by guidelines issued by the Council on Environmental Quality (established under the act), and by the interpretations of the act by the federal courts.

But the National Environmental Policy Act leaves the missions and structures of the federal agencies unchanged. There is no power directly authorized by the act to prevent or to modify any environment-affecting action by any agency of government. Court orders restraining federal projects have been based on agency failure to conform fully to the procedural requirements of the act. Unless the president intervenes (as did Richard Nixon in stopping construction of the Cross-Florida Barge Canal), an agency may proceed with environmentally damaging projects--at least to a point at which opponents may persuade the courts that the substantive provisions of NEPA are being violated unnecessarily and without the justification of "essential considerations of national policy."

In many instances, the inherent limitations upon policy in the Level II approach induce frustration and checkmate. If, after resounding declarations and outpouring of regulations and controls, the quality of the environment fails to improve--or even continues to decline--environmental advocacy may seek more radical remedies. Level III perceptions view the causes of environmental disorder as being rooted in social attitudes and values and expressed through their implementing institutional arrangements. At this level, environmental damage is seen to be an inevitable consequence of normal operations of the technoeconomic system. The solution to the major problems of man-environment relationships is neither in exhortation nor regulation, but rather in the redesigning of social institutions and the reordering of political and economic priorities. Level III solutions are "radical" in the exact meaning of this word, their tendency being to alter values, to redefine the responsibilities of government, and to reinterpret the practical meaning of many so-called human rights.

The systemic level would appear to be more congenial to scientists and engineers than to most other groupings in society. Perhaps the greatest skepticism concerning Level III solutions would be found among lawyers and economists. Among their numbers are many who distrust administrative action, to whom the proper unit of political concern is not society but the individual, and whose judgments are moralistic rather than scientific. They may be no less critical of the attitudinal-institutional systems of present society, but unlike Level III "environmentalists," they would prefer social change in the direction of traditional "liberal" norms of egalitarianism and individualism.

The systemic approach resembles neither traditional conservatism nor liberalism, loosely defined. It does not belong to the right-left spectrum of conventional political ideology, but represents a third position that may conveniently be termed "ecological"; its position, in relation to conservative-liberal polarities, being analogous to the third extremity of a right-angled triangle:

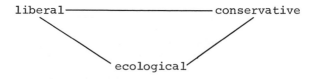

Because of the far-reaching adjustments that the systemic approach may require of presently existing arrangements, it is not likely to win easy popular acceptance. Its persuasive power appears to be roughly proportionate to popular dissatisfaction with the prevailing state of the environment. Peoples and governments cannot be expected to accept Level III solutions except under conditions of distress and duress. For example, the energy crisis of 1973 was necessary to force serious consideration of basic changes in the nation's systems of energy, transportation, and materials allocation that for several decades had been urged without success by informed scientists and engineers.

This three-level model of environmental perception and policy should serve to explain the incoherence of environmental politics, and the apparent inconsistency between professed objectives and administrative implementation. Before a political position can be described as "inconsistent" in any meaningful sense, it is first necessary to specify the criteria for consistency. On environmental issues it may be useful to discover with what other policies or objectives a relationship of consistency may exist. For example, Senator Henry M. Jackson, primary sponsor of the National Environmental Policy Act, has been criticized for an inconsistent support of both the Supersonic Transport, and the Trans-Alaska oil pipeline--each of which was opposed by most environmental-quality groups. But from the viewpoint of a senator from the State of Washington, his positions were mutually consistent--his constituency favored all three policies. By other criteria of logic, Jackson's position may have been contradictory. But the senator's perceptual level was II, not III, and contradictions of this type are characteristic of the operational level. Level III arguments alone are not likely to win public elections except in the event of mass popular anxiety associated with social-ecological crisis.

The energy crisis, in both its contemporary and longer-range aspects, has had a significant inpact upon the political significance of these three perceptual levels. The full impact of the energy situation on public opinion cannot be accurately assessed until the immediate crisis has either passed or become endemic. But its lesson for environmental politics is already clear. American political commitment to environmental quality is still largely at Level I--a nice idea, provided no one is unduly inconvenienced.

The sudden rush of Congress to set aside environmental obstructions to the construction of the Alaska oil pipeline, the readiness of the government to relax environmental standards for air and water quality, and the call by highest public officials for "reasonableness" in environmental controls over surface mining and shale oil development have all been instructive. The lesson is that at perceptual Levels I and II, environmental quality is, politically, a fair-weather proposition. Level III perceivers cannot influence public decisions until, or unless, they control sufficient political power to force serious consideration of systemic changes.

There is, however, evidence to suggest that American reaction to the energy crisis in relation to environmental values may be counterintuitive.[5] Only experience will show the validity of political assumptions that the American people generally will pay any environmental price to satisfy their energy demands. At Level III perception, the energy crisis would seem to be a counterpart of the environmental crisis, both evidence of systemic failure. The remedy for the energy shortage would not be a rape of the environment to get the last available BTUs from an inherently defective energy system. It would rather be a search for a new, renewable, ecology-compatible energy system that was economically feasible.

The state of environmental politics in the mid-1970s seems almost certain to be tumultuous. If environmental quality as a general social goal retains its current popular support, and if the environment itself is badly mauled by government and business in the name of "keeping America moving," some portion of Level I and II "environmentalists" may be pushed, reluctantly, to Level III positions. As neither of the major political parties, nor any of their internal factions, seems responsive to the idea of a systemic restructuring of the American political economy, more people especially at higher levels of education, income, and influence are likely to be alienated from the prevailing political system or at least from its set of slogans, policy biases, and persons occupying leadership positions.

It has been a near truism of political science that when the governing institutions of society weaken under stress and appear incapable of coping with the problems for which they are popularly held accountable, the stage is set for a turnover of political power. When the performance of the socioeconomic system is perceived to be at fault, this political change is more likely to be fundamental and ideological rather than superficial and personal. The political transformation is more in the character of revolution than of coup d'état. But it would be erroneous to infer that revolution in the classic patterns of 1789 and 1917 is indicated.

There is basis for conjecturing that the restructuring of political power in advanced industrial societies is more likely to involve displacements of doctrines and behavior patterns and changes in relationships among institutions than in the replacement of one ruling class by another. The open and interdependent character of modern society makes this kind of change plausible. In a society that depends for survival upon the continuous functioning of its interdependent institutions, systemic change requires administrative mediation and direction. A policy "revolution" in the future may be more properly called "administered change" than "political revolution" even though profound changes in the means and ends of political power may result.

Only at Level III perception does environment become a factor in such fundamental change and then in conjunction with other social and quality-of-life issues. At Level III, environmental deterioration is seen a symptom of deeper societal derangement. The policy goal at Level III is to remove the causes rather than to alleviate the symptoms. At Level III, quality of the environment is inseparable from quality of the economy. Both are aspects of an ecological approach to social behavior. The ecological approach is a logical concomitant of the systemic interpretation of environmental problems and implies a heavy reliance upon administered solutions.

THE LITERATURE AND THE STATE OF RESEARCH

With the assistance of the National Science Foundation, the Environmental Studies Program at Indiana University has surveyed some 2,500 books, monographs, articles, and reports dealing with environmental policy, law, and administration. Publication of this information as a guide to advanced study will provide an overview of the state of the literature at the beginning of 1974.[6]

The sources of published material relative to environmental policy and administration are obviously very extensive. Now material is appearing rapidly and it does not therefore seem useful to single out particular items as the leading works in the field. "Omnibus" reviews of books on environmental politics and administration appeared in The American Political Science Review 66 (June 1972, by Charles O. Jones) and in Public Administration Review 32 (November-December 1972, by Geoffrey Wandesforde-Smith). But these publications totalled only 18 out of a literature with entries numbering in the hundreds.

The interrelating nature of the subject matter makes the literature hard to classify. There are many different ways to categorize the material and no single one is "best" for all purposes. Some approaches to the subject matter and to the literature are, however, more rewarding than others. Except for very limited technical studies, the most productive approach to environmental issues has been through the "systems" concept. Environmental policy research requires a high order of synthesis. It must draw upon all sources relevant to its problems and is therefore multidisciplinary in character. This synthesis must be preceded and succeeded by analyses of the data and of their interrelationships. Environmental studies may conceivably emerge as a metadiscipline if a nucleus of studies in policy, law, and administration grows to a "critical mass." Presently, however, the field of inquiry is in a formative state. Its definition must await the larger conceptualizing and organizing works that are yet to come.

NOTES

1. Environmental Protection Agency, Office of Research and Monitoring, Environmental Studies Division, The Quality of Life Concept: A Potential New Tool for Decision-Makers (Washington, D.C.: Government Printing Office, 1973).

2. Paul H. Appleby, Policy and Administration (University, Ala.: University of Alabama Press, 1949).

3. See Marston Bates, "Environment," in International Encyclopedia of the Social Sciences, V (New York: Macmillan and The Free Press, 1968), pp. 91-93.

4. Technology Review 73 (January 1971) and reprinted in Toward Global Equilibrium: Collected Papers, ed. Dennis L. Meadows and Donella H. Meadows (Cambridge, Mass.: Wright-Allen Press, 1973), pp. 3-30.

Numerous illustrations of counterintuitive behavior may be drawn from environmental policies, but their complexities and long-time effects make them less clearly illustrations than the following examples from the field of crime prevention:

Drug addiction is associated with criminal acts; we "know" intuitively that punishment deters crime. Penalties for possession and sale of addictive drugs are therefore increased and enforcement is stepped up. The obtaining of drugs thus becomes more dangerous and their availability is diminished. The price of drugs correspondingly rises making their sale economically more attractive and forcing drug users to spend more and more money to satisfy their addiction. To meet the cost of drugs the addict must obtain money wherever he can and because his situation tends to preclude most legitimate employment he seeks to obtain money through resort to crime. As a result, intuitive approaches to this aspect of crime prevention may have actually increased the incidence of crime.

5. Analysis of environmental opinions undertaken by Lester Milbrath of the State University of New York at Buffalo in late 1973 did not reveal a shift away from environmental quality priorities.

6. Lynton K. Caldwell and Toufiq A. Siddiqi, Environmental Policy, Law and Administration: A guide to Advanced Study (Bloomington: Indiana University Press, 1974).

20

ENVIRONMENTAL ADMINISTRATION:
NEPA AND FEDERAL AGENCIES

Richard A. Liroff

The National Environmental Policy Act (NEPA) is the most far-reaching environmental statute ever enacted by the United States Congress.[1] It establishes environmental quality as a leading priority by stating a national policy for the environment. It makes environmental protection part of the mandate of all federal agencies, establishing procedures for incorporation of environmental concerns into agency decision making. And it creates a Council on Environmental Quality (CEQ) in the Executive Office of the president to oversee and coordinate all federal environmental efforts.

An indication of NEPA's breadth is readily found in the court actions based upon it; it has been used to challenge successfully a multitude of federal activities ranging from bank chartering to barge canal construction. Environmentalists have stated that NEPA "has done more to preserve and protect the environment than all of the previous environmental protection measures combined."[2] Senator Henry Jackson, the leading architect of the act, describes it as making "fundamental and far reaching changes at all points in the Federal decision making process which touch on environmental questions."[3] This view, however, is not universal; other commentators have been less charitable. A member of the Federal Power Commission, for example, has characterized NEPA as a "paper monster."[4] Life under the law has "approached chaos," claimed the Oil and Gas Journal,[5] while the federal bureaucracy has been reported as feeling that

The research reported in this chapter was supported by a Woodrow Wilson Dissertation Fellowship and a Brookings Institution Research Fellowship. The usual disclaimer applies.

the statute is "the most annoying and troublesome law to be passed in years."[6]

The considerable impact of NEPA and the passions aroused in support of and in opposition to it can be traced in large part to the vagueness of the law. The act has been characterized as being "almost constitutional" in its breadth and lack of specificity."[7] One federal judge has written that its meaning is "more uncertain" than that of most statutes because of the generality of its phrasing,[8] while a second justice commented that it is "so broad, yet opaque, that it will take even longer than usual fully to comprehend its import."[9]

LEGISLATIVE HISTORY

The principal operative section of NEPA has been Section 102(2)(c), requiring federal agencies to prepare environmental impact statements for all major actions that significantly affect the quality of the human environment. The environmental impact statement requirement was added late in NEPA's legislative history, after public hearings on the measure were held.[10] It replaced a provision in earlier versions of NEPA calling for the compilation of environmental "findings." Because the change came so late, little thought was given to the requirements of an environmental impact "statement"--the impacts to be evaluated, the alternative courses of action to be discussed, the timing of impact statement preparation, and so on. Many questions were ultimately to be left to administrative agencies and the courts to resolve.

The courts have played a particularly important role in defining NEPA's administrative requirements. Approximately 400 NEPA-based lawsuits have been filed, and most discussions of the law's requirements have drawn at great length from a series of "leading NEPA cases."[11] The liberal interpretations that the courts have tended to give NEPA have functioned to give environmentalists much greater access to the decision-making processes of mission-oriented agencies than they previously enjoyed. The enjoining of public works projects dear to the hearts of many congressmen raises in some minds the question of whether Congress anticipated that environmentalists would use the courts as a fulcrum and NEPA as a lever for prying open agency decision making to intense public scrutiny. A review of NEPA's legislative history and interviews with staff members active in its formulation suggests that the answer is "no." For example, no mention of a leading role for the courts in the interpretation and implementation of NEPA can be found in congressional debates or reports on the bill. While Senator Jackson recognized that litigation might result from the law, he did not anticipate the volume of litigation that was ultimately to ensue. He and his colleagues should not be faulted, however, for their seeming lack of foresight, for ample statistical evidence exists showing that the environmental law movement at the time of NEPA's consideration was nascent and had not yet become a force to be reckoned with in administrative politics.

THE CEQ

The NEPA bill signed by President Nixon on January 1, 1970, was a vague mandate for action whose implications were far from clear.[12] Its legislative history was meager, but one major theme was interwoven through it—that all federal agencies had an affirmative responsibility to integrally incorporate environmental considerations into their decision making. To coordinate the new federal environmental policy, NEPA established the Council on Environmental Quality.

While NEPA assigned a multitude of duties to CEQ, it did not clearly delegate to the council responsibility for developing guidelines for agency implementation of the statute's procedures. Support for a strong CEQ oversight role could nevertheless be found in NEPA, though legislative history could also be cited that implied a major role in impact statement coordination for the Office of Management and Budget (OMB). A March 1970 Executive Order clarified matters by placing primary responsibility for guiding the environmental impact statement process with the CEQ, and the council proceeded to fulfill its oversight obligation by issuing procedural guidelines for environmental impact statement preparation, issuing supplementary memoranda describing the NEPA process's requirements, reviewing environmental impact statements and holding informal meetings with federal agency officials.

The first CEQ guidelines were almost as vague as NEPA itself. This was the result of the council's attempting to write directions applicable to a diverse, governmentwide range of activities. The guidelines provided little detailed guidance as to the kinds of actions requiring statements, gave scant direction with respect to statement content, and left somewhat ambiguous the matter of NEPA's applicability to ongoing projects. Line agencies were assigned the obligation of defining for themselves within the confines of the guidelines the specific manner in which NEPA should be implemented.

The CEQ guidelines have evolved and have reflected three themes present in NEPA's legislative history. First, evaluation of environmental impacts is the responsibility of all agencies. Second, environmental impact evaluation should be a conscious element of choice processes at all levels of agency review. Third, outside commentators should play an important role in environmental review, and provision must be made for their timely intervention in administrative decision-making processes. The guidelines also expanded on a theme that was implicit in the actions of NEPA's architects--that the public should be provided information with respect to the reasoning that underlies agency choices of action.

Council memoranda circulated to supplement the guidelines provide interesting insight into agencies' implementation of NEPA. Their lengthy discussion of court decisions underscores the considerable role that the courts have played in defining NEPA's requirements. The memos also indicate that the CEQ apparently encountered some difficulty in obtaining administrative procedural compliance with the law, and that its only ultimate sanction was to suggest that agencies would be subject to bad press and legal action should noncompliance continue.

While the council found its various techniques for promoting compliance with NEPA somewhat useful, it nevertheless lacked legal authority to compel a reluctant agency to comply with the act. In addition, its presidential advisory relationship was fragile, its budget was reviewed by a potentially hostile congressional committee, and it had few visible rewards to offer potential constituents. The CEQ's inability to bring about executive agency action consonant with what it deemed to be the requirements of NEPA produced a flurry of lawsuits by key allies of the council, citizen activists. A number of cases can be identified in which the absence of administrative regulations for implementing NEPA, or the promulgation of regulations insufficiently implementing NEPA, led to court decisions faulting agencies for their lack of procedural compliance with the act. In these matters, involving the Atomic Energy Commission, Federal Power Commission, Law Enforcement Assistance Administration, and Bureau of Indian Affairs, environmentalist lawsuits were a vital supplement to CEQ efforts to promote implementation of NEPA.

AGENCY RESPONSE TO NEPA: CONCEPTUAL APPROACHES

NEPA is a fine example of a broadly worded congressional enactment that lacks precise directions for administrators. Its general intent is clear--it in effect calls for increasing the environmental rationality of administrative decision making. It is a comprehensive attack on narrow agency decision-making schemes that can be said to insist that the agencies' satisficing decision-making routines must always incorporate an identification and evaluation of environmental impacts.[13] The function of the impact statement is to lay bare the values, assumptions, and calculations underlying processes of agency choice, the presumption being that if particular environmental costs are neglected or undervalued, increased public participation and interagency coordination will ensure their full and fair evaluation.

But because of its brevity and lack of precision, NEPA has given administrators considerable discretion in deciding how it should be implemented (that is, until their field of action has been circumscribed by the courts). To the extent that these incrementally oriented decision makers have refused to enlarge their frames of reference, have not known how to enlarge them, or otherwise have not met environmentalists' legitimately raised decision-making expectations, they have fueled conflict over NEPA's implementation. At the root of this conflict is the question of what "change" does NEPA require of agencies, what "change" has occurred, and how can both these quantities be precisely defined and measured?

Answers are not readily forthcoming. First, while the direction of organizational change dictated by NEPA is clear, the actual magnitude of the change demanded is not. NEPA's environmental goals are not absolutes, but must be balanced against nonenvironmental goals. Second, the actual magnitude of change occurring is hard to assess, due in large measure to the decision-making bias of social science measurement. It may be possible to examine how well the environmental impacts of a proposed action have been evaluated by a governmental agency preparing an impact statement, but one has no way of knowing how many environmentally harmful actions were deferred for fear their exposure to the impact statement process would subject an agency to considerable outside criticism. Moreover, in cases where an agency has made clear its decision-making processes in an environmental impact statement, clearly revealing environmental trade-offs, this may fulfill NEPA's procedural goal of making agency reasoning explicit. However, this may mean only that what has always been implicit now has become explicit, without any substantive change being made in the balancing of environmental and nonenvironmental considerations.

Despite these conceptual problems, several indicators are available that provide insight into administrative willingness to comply with NEPA. The discussion below shows how they may be interpreted.

INDICATORS OF AGENCY RESPONSE TO NEPA

Agency Procedures: Timing of Issuance

The legislative history of NEPA conveys throughout it a sense of urgency. The lag time between NEPA's enactment and the promulgation of implementing rules and regulations by individual federal agencies provides one measure of the extent to which this sense of urgency has been felt by the federal bureaucracy.

A CEQ list prepared in November 1971 contained the names of 22 nondepartmental entities and 39 components of 10 departments for which the council was able to obtain apparent agency agreement that formal agency procedures implementing NEPA should be prepared.[14] The council has produced an annual summary of agency implementation procedures; these figures are presented in Table 20.1.[15]

TABLE 20.1

Numbers of Agencies Preparing
NEPA-Implementing Procedures

Date	Departments	Components of Departments	Nondepartmental Agencies
August 1970	8	1	8
December 1971	9	12	16
October 1972	9	34	22
CEQ implemental goal*	10	39	22

*This row refers to number of entities that CEQ believed required NEPA-Implementing Procedures.

Sources: "Comment: Agencies' Revised NEPA Procedural Compliance Guidelines Near Completion, Months After Deadline for Submission to CEQ," Environmental Law Reporter, October 1971, 1 ELR 10167; "Council on Environmental Quality," Hearings before the Subcommittee on Fisheries and Wildlife Conservation of the House Committee on Merchant Marine and Fisheries, 91st Cong., 2d sess., 1970, pp. 69ff; 36 Fed Reg. 23666 (December 11, 1971); 37 Fed. Reg. 22668 (October 20, 1972).

CEQ first reported in August 1970, noting that some implementation procedures had been adopted or tentatively drafted by eight departments, one departmental component, and eight independent agencies. This record of the seven months following NEPA's enactment is noteworthy in several respects. First, three departments to which the NEPA requirements were held applicable by CEQ did not prepare any guidelines whatsoever—the Justice Department, the Post Office Department, and the State Department. Second, one agency not renowned for its environmental sensitivity, the Corps of Engineers, promulgated procedures that predated even the CEQ's interim guidelines. Third, virtually no procedures were prepared by subdepartmental components. Many of the latter may have been relying on departmental procedures. Nevertheless, the absence of subdepartmental procedures may also suggest a lack of urgency on the part of most of these offices to comply with NEPA.

By December 1971 the procedural situation had improved substantially. In the December 1971 CEQ compilation of procedures, 9 departments, 12 departmental components, and 16 nondepartmental entities were shown to have guidelines. However, the Justice and State Departments had still not developed procedures, nor had 6 nondepartmental entities. Although the 16 months between the first and second CEQ summaries saw a marked increase in agency procedural preparation, much of the stepped-up activity occurred only in the latter 4 months of this period, 19 to 23 months after NEPA's enactment.

By October 1972 most of the entities listed by the CEQ had filed environmental impact statement preparation procedures, including the six independent agencies that by December 1971 still had not done so. Missing from the 1972 compilation were a number of subdepartmental entities that were, in all probability, adequately covered by departmental regulations. But also included were four agencies that had not been listed in the November 1971 CEQ memo.

The record of agency procedural promulgation reveals that there was often a considerable lag between the preparation of departmental and subdepartmental NEPA procedures. For example, in early October 1971, the Interior Department published departmental procedures, a section of which ordered bureau heads to prepare bureau-specific procedures.[16] Of the 13 Interior Department bureaus affected by the order, only three had complied by December 1971. Two more filed in January, one in February, and three more in March. It was not until six months later in April 1972 that three additional offices complied, and not until June 1972 that the

Bureau of Land Management published its procedures. All the delays, according to a knowledgeable Interior Department official, were attributable to "bureaucratic inertia."[17]

Agency Procedures: Content

The existence of procedures and the timing of their promulgation provides one perspective on agency implementation, but it provides but a very incomplete view. On the one hand, agency regulations can be concrete signals to administrative subordinates that a particular congressional enactment must be adopted as agency policy. But on the other hand, regulations can merely be symbolic gestures of statutory implementation structured in such a way as to muffle the impact of a new law on an agency's decision-making processes. Since CEQ, in keeping its own guidelines vague, placed primary responsibility on the agencies for detailing the manner in which NEPA applied to their actions, the extent to which the agencies' guidelines promoted and elaborated upon NEPA provides some measure of agency willingness to adapt decision making to NEPA's environmental demands.

Regulations of the Corps of Engineers

The Corps of Engineers' rules stand out as being the best of all those prepared within 12 months of NEPA's enactment by federal agencies.[18] They elaborated upon the environmental statement content requirements and upon the requirement for considering alternatives, called for the consideration of environmental impacts from the outset of project planning, and demanded the objective, detailed evaluation of proposed projects. The rules specifically addressed the matter of responding to outside critiques, stating that statements should include and comment on the views of those opposing a project on environmental grounds. The 1970 Corps regulations also anticipated interpretations of NEPA that would not become part of the CEQ guidelines until the following year.

Regulations of the Department
of Transportation

DOT's initial set of regulations, like the Corps', are quite impressive when compared to those of other agencies.[19] Among their admirable features were the following: First, they provided for the preparation of "negative declarations," documents to be developed by administrators when a decision was made not to prepare an environmental impact statement.

Decision makers would thus be put on record as having decided that no impact statement was required for a particular
action. Virtually no other agency regulations contained
such "negative declaration" provisions at the time. Second,
the regulations recognized the importance of citizen input
into the decision-making process, suggesting that final impact statements must discuss, where appropriate, problems
and objections raised by citizens. Third, the departmental
rules underscored the urgency of meeting the NEPA requirements by demanding within two weeks of their promulgation
preparation of agency-specific NEPA regulations (for example,
Federal Aviation Agency rules for airport grants and Federal
Highway Administration rules for highway plans). Fourth and
last, the DOT regulations declared that if a decision maker
had any doubt as to whether an impact statement should be
prepared, a decision was to be made in favor of statement
preparation.

Regulations of the Atomic Energy Commission

The initial regulations of the AEC were challenged in
court by environmentalists and were declared by a federal
judge to have made a mockery of NEPA.[20] They delayed implementation of NEPA until 14 months after the statute's enactment and postponed consideration of partially constructed
nuclear plants' environmental impacts until a late stage of
AEC action. They also precluded the consideration of environmental impacts through every stage of AEC decision making,
and they shifted a considerable environmental analysis burden onto nuclear power opponents intervening in AEC licensing proceedings.

Reguations of the Federal Power Commission

Prior to having its regulations overruled by the courts,
the FPC had declared that its routine practice would be to
circulate for comment by other agencies the draft environmental statements prepared by applicants for commission licenses.[21] By refusing to prepare its own statements and by
relying on those of applicants, the FPC was shirking the responsibility imposed on it by NEPA of conducting environmental evaluations. As the Second Circuit Court of Appeals observed, applicants' statements were likely to be comprised
of "selfserving" assumptions.[22]

Comparison of Four Agencies' Regulations

The Corps, DOT, AEC, and FPC are considerably different
from one another. The Corps is a public-works agency

concerned with the planning, design, and construction of its
own projects. DOT is a grant-giving agency, overseeing federally financed projects planned and constructed by state
agencies. AEC and FPC, in contrast, are regulatory agencies
whose function is to license projects planned, designed,
constructed, and paid for by utility companies.

Despite these agencies' functional differences, comparisons between their regulations may legitimately be made,
because the gross variations among the regulations could
have been much reduced if the AEC and FPC had taken their
NEPA obligations seriously. In brief, the regulations represent competing philosophies as to what the agency's role
should be in implementing NEPA. On the one hand, the Corps
regulations advocated the application of the NEPA requirements to the fullest extent possible and the DOT rules
stressed the urgency of compliance. The FPC's rules, on the
other hand, sought to evade the law's requirements, while
the AEC's rules sought to delay their implementation. Furthermore, the Corps guidelines took a liberal view of an
agency's analytical responsibilities, requiring the evaluation of a broad range of alternatives to proposed actions.
In contrast, the AEC regulations, by delaying consideration
of environmental impacts until a late stage of plant licensing proceedings, permitted the de facto foreclosing of alternative energy and site alternatives. Further comparisons
can be made among these and other agencies' regulations, but
space does not permit an extended discussion here.

Numbers of Impact Statements

It was left to federal agencies to decide which of
their actions merited environmental impact statements, that
is, which were major and had a significant impact on the
human environment. Some agencies conduct more environmentally impacting activities than others, and as a result produce more impact statements. Therefore, an agency's output
of impact statements does not provide a reliable indicator
of its response to NEPA. An analysis of the extremes of
agency action in this regard nevertheless furnished constructive insight into agency NEPA implementation

Many Statements: The Case of the
Federal Highway Administration

Since NEPA's enactment, the Federal Highway Administration (FHWA) has prepared approximately 45 percent of all the
impact statements written.[23] This large number is partly

the result of the FHWA's ill-defined guidance to state highway departments writing impact statements and may partly be
the product of state highway officials' effort to clog NEPA
review channels.

The FHWA's initial effort to implement NEPA was a November 1970 memorandum specifying in an overly broad manner
those actions likely to require impact statements.[24] Following the memorandum's issuance, the federal government was de-
luged with highway impact statements. The flow of statements was so great that it was sometimes represented in
terms of pounds of paper or linear feet of shelf space.

One interpretation of this outpouring is that it might
have represented an earnest effort on the part of environmentally conscious state highway officials to comply with
NEPA. A recent study of highway impact statements by the
Center for Science in the Public Interest (CSPI) calls this
conclusion into question.[25] Ideally, an impact statement
should provide a discussion of the pros and cons of proposed
actions, and where a controversy exists, both sides should
be fairly reported. The CSPI sampled highway impact statements and concluded that they contained arguments rather
than findings, opinions rather than studies, and generalities rather than facts. The generalities, according to CSPI,
appeared repeatedly, precluded further data seeking, and
ended inquiry by affirming the notion that a safer, more
efficient highway facility has a positive effect on man's
environment.

A second interpretation of the many statements is that
they represented an attempt by state highway officials to
undermine NEPA. The large number of impact statements would
clog interagency review channels, producing administrative
cries for relief from an onerous paper burden. The division
of lengthy highway projects into multiple impact statements
would also enable highway officials to promote projects that
individually might not have much environmental impact, but
that cumulatively might have enormous land use, air, and
noise pollution implications. Outside reviewers, swamped by
impact statements describing highway segment X's impact on
40 redwoods, highway Y's impact on 30 oaks, and so on, might
lose a forest for the trees.

A third interpretation is that state highway officials
were merely being cautious. Anxious to avoid lawsuits charging them with not writing impact statements and having received inadequate guidance from the FHWA, state highway officials, unsure when statements should be prepared, developed
them for a host of actions for which they were not necessary.*

---

*The heavy stream of impact statements became the sub-
ject of consultations between CEQ and FHWA. While FHWA

Few Impact Statements: The Case of
the Department of Housing and
Urban Development

HUD is a large decentralized department administering
thousands of federal housing grants, but through September
1973 it had prepared only 74 impact statements.[26] The low
number is attributable in part to the content of HUD's NEPA-
implementing regulations, which in their initial form directed HUD regional offices to prepare statements solely for
precedent-setting or controversial projects. Thus, the bulk
of HUD's daily decision making was exempted from the impact
statement requirement. HUD subsequently revised its guidelines to subject a larger number of actions to the impact
statement process, yet it has continued to produce relatively few statements; their dearth is attributable to HUD's reluctance to apply NEPA retroactively.[27] Even as late as
August 1972, this reluctance on HUD's part was still in evidence. In a letter to HUD Secretary George Romney, CEQ
Chairman Russell Train commented:

> We are concerned that eight suits have been
> filed so far this year alleging failure to
> comply with NEPA in [urban] renewal actions.
> In part, the problem is related to compli-
> cated issues of retroactivity upon which
> there is some disagreement between the Coun-
> cil's legal staff and HUD attorneys.[28]

Train also commented in his letter that HUD's revised regulations had taken more than one year to develop and had not
been finalized as of August 1972 and that HUD needed to as-
sign more personnel to NEPA-related matters, reallocating
existing manpower if necessary.

SUMMARY AND CONCLUSIONS

The timing and content of agency regulatory issuances
and the numbers of impact statements prepared provide merely three indicators of administrative response to NEPA.

---

still produces the major part of all impact statements written, the flow has lessened somewhat since FHWA revised its
administrative regulations so as to indicate in a more meaningful manner which highway projects merited impact statements.

They can be used to identify instances of begrudging, incremental implementation of the statute. Additional insight into the implementation process can be provided by a host of other indicators, though considerable care must be exercised in making assumptions concerning their validity.[29] Political scientists, in their quest for quantitative indicators of agency response, should recognize that such response is multidimensional; its assessment must be based on an evaluation of multiple indicators whose validity has been closely scrutinized.

NOTES

1. 42 U.S.C. Sec. 4321 et seq. Pub. L. No. 91-190, 83 Stat. 852, ELR 41009 (January 1, 1970).

2. Peter Harnik, "Testing the Movement. It's Time to Save NEPA," Environmental Action 3 (April 15, 1972): 3.

3. Senator Henry Jackson, "Environmental Policy and The Congress," Natural Resources Law 11 (July 1971): 407.

4. Cited in Robert Gillette, "National Environmental Policy Act: Signs of Backlash Are Evident," Science 176 (April 7, 1972): 30.

5. Cited in Claude Barfield and Richard Corrigan, "Environment Report/White House Seeks to Restrict Scope of Environmental Law," National Journal 4 (February 26, 1972): 347.

6. Harnik, op. cit., p. 4.

7. Esther R. Schachter, "Standards for Evaluating a NEPA Environmental Statement," Public Utilities Fortnightly 90 (August 31, 1972): 29.

8. Hanly v. Mitchell, 460 F.2d 640, 2 ELR 20216, 20217 (2d Cir. 1972).

9. City of New York v. U.S., 337 F. Supp. 150, 2 ELR 20275, 20276 (E.D. N.Y. 1972).

10. For a detailed examination of NEPA's legislative history, see Terence T. Finn, "Conflict and Compromise: Congress Makes a Law, The Passage of the National Environmental Policy Act" (Ph.D. dissertation, Department of Government, Georgetown University, 1972). See also Chapter 3 of Richard N. L. Andrews, "Environmental Policy and Administrative Change: The National Environmental Policy Act of 1969 (1970-71)" (Ph.D. dissertation, Department of Civil and Regional Planning, University of North Carolina, 1972). The discussion here draws from Chapter 2 of the author's dissertation "NEPA and Its Aftermath: The Formulation of a National Policy for the Environment" (Ph.D. dissertation [in progress], Department of Political Science, Northwestern

University), wherein all the assertions above are fully documented.

11. See, for example, Frederick R. Anderson, NEPA in the Courts (Baltimore: Johns Hopkins University Press for Resources for the Future, 1973).

12. This discussion draws from material in the author's "The Council on Environmental Quality," Environmental Law Reporter, August 1973, 3 ELR 50051. Citations to source material and elaborations on the points made here can be found in the original.

13. See the discussion of incremental decision making in Andrews, op. cit., pp. 14-20. See also the author's discussion in "Administrative, Judicial and Natural Systems: Agency Response to the National Environmental Policy Act of 1969," Loyola University Law Journal 3 (Winter 1972): 25-29. The discussion here draws on material from Chapter 4 of Liroff, "NEPA and Its Aftermath," op. cit.

14. See "Comment: Agencies' Revised NEPA Procedural Compliance Guidelines Near Completion, Months After Deadline for Submission to CEQ," Environmental Law Reporter, October 1971, 1 ELR 10167.

15. The August 1970 summary is printed in "Council on Environmental Quality," Hearings before the Subcommittee on Fisheries and Wildlife Conservation of the House Committee on Merchant Marine and Fisheries, 91st Cong., 2d sess. (1970), pp. 69ff.; 36 Fed. Reg. 23666 (December 11, 1971); 37 Fed. Reg. 22668 (October 20, 1972).

16. 36 Fed. Reg. 19343 (October 2, 1971). Promulgation dates can be found in the 1972 CEQ list of agency procedures.

17. Interview with the author.

18. E.C. 1120-2-56 (September 25, 1970). They have continually evolved to remain among the best.

19. DOT Order 5610.1 (October 7, 1970).

20. Calvert Cliffs Coordinating Committee v. United States Atomic Energy Commission, 449 F.2d 1109, 1 ELR 20346 (D.C. Cir. 1971), cert. denied, 404 U.S. 942 (1972).

21. Greene County Planning Board v. FPC, 455 F.2d 412, 2 ELR 20017 (2d Cir. 1972).

22. Ibid.

23. See the figures and discussion in Council on Environmental Quality, Environmental Quality (Washington, D.C.: Government Printing Office, 1973), p. 245.

24. Draft Instructional Memorandum dated November 30, 1970. Reprinted in "Red Tape-Inquiring into Delays and Excessive Paperwork in Administration of Public Works Programs," Hearings Before the Subcommittee on Investigations and Oversight of the House Committee on Public Works, 92d Cong., 1st sess., 1971, pp. 41-45.

25. James B. Sullivan and Andrew S. Farber, "NEPA: Getting Citizens into the Act," Environmental Action 5 (September 1, 1973): 13-15.

26. 102 Monitor (Council on Environmental Quality) 3 (October 1973): 176.

27. See Anderson, op. cit., Chapter 5, for a discussion of the retroactivity questions.

28. Letter in author's files.

29. Andrews, op. cit., pp. 421-37, uses seven criteria to compare four agencies.

EPILOGUE:

UNRESOLVED POLITICAL SCIENCE ISSUES

IN ENVIRONMENTAL PROTECTION

Stuart S. Nagel

      This book on the politics of environmental protection
has discussed many political science issues from the perspective of the fields of political science. That format
has involved treating environmental protection from the perspective of such fields as normative political philosophy,
empirical political analysis, international relations, comparative government, American national government, state and
local government, parties and political dynamics, the legislative process, public law, and public administration.
      The purpose of this epilogue is to discuss some rela-
tions between political science and environmental protection
from the perspective of unresolved policy issues in environmental protection rather than from the perspective of fields
of political science. By "policy issue" in this context is
meant a question of which of two or more alternatives is the
best or most effective way for a government to handle a given
problem. A policy issue can be contrasted with a legal issue
that asks the question whether a given statutory provision,
judicial decision, or administrative action conforms to some
law such as constitutional law. In other words, a policy
issue asks what should a government do to maximize a given
set of goals excluding the goal of compliance with past law;
and a legal issue asks what can a legislator, judge, or administrator "legally" do if he is going to comply with past
law, especially constitutional law as discussed in Chapter
17 of this book. Both policy issues and legal issues can be
contrasted with technological issues that ask what can physically be done given the funds available with regard to creating nonpolluting facilities, monitoring devices, or other
relevant equipment.
      Policy issues can be approached from a political sci-
ence perspective that emphasizes the role of governmental

persons, groups, and institutions in resolving those issues. Such a perspective can be contrasted with an economics perspective that emphasizes the role of scarce resources, or a psychological perspective that emphasizes the role of individual motivation, or other social science perspectives. Political science policy issues can be divided into what is appropriate to reduce pollution with regard to (1) government structures, (2) government and private procedures, (3) government controlled incentives, and (4) what weights should be given to conflicting environmental policy values especially in regard to protecting innocent third parties. Environmental policy issues can also be classified in terms of the type of pollutant or environment-improving activity involved. That classification refers to water pollution, air pollution, solid wastes, radiation, conservation, land use planning, and development of energy sources.

This epilogue will emphasize water and air pollution in its examples, but what it says is generally applicable to other pollution and environmental activities as well. The epilogue, however, is only designed to describe what some of the main political science issues are under the four issue groupings given above. It is not designed to describe all political science environmental policy issues. It is especially not designed to resolve the issues. That is a matter to be undertaken hopefully through a fruitful collaboration among environmental political scientists, other scholars, policy makers, policy appliers, and the general public.

GOVERNMENT STRUCTURES TO REDUCE POLLUTION

A key political science issue with regard to government structures concerns the respective roles to be played by central governments versus local governments. In other words, should the government structures to reduce pollution be primarily federal or centralized or primarily local or decentralized? Those arguing for more centralization emphasize that the federal government is generally less subject to pressures from local business polluters and local governmental polluters and that it can promote better coordination and uniformly high standards. Those arguing for more decentralization emphasize that local governments are more aware of and possibly more responsive to local needs and conditions.

As with many of these political science issues, there are many compromise positions that can be taken. One can, for example, simultaneously have (1) federal control with decentralized field offices, (2) local control with interlocal agreements and commissions, (3) federal standard setting with local enforcement, (4) federal standards for newly built sources of pollution facilities with local standards for already-built factories and automobiles, and (5) federal control for air pollution and local control for water pollution, which tends to be more local. All of these arguments and compromises can apply whether we are talking about federal versus state control, state versus local control, or federal versus local control. In that sense, state control represents a compromise between federal and local control.

A second key political science issue with regard to governmental structures concerns the respective roles to be played by administrative agencies versus legislatures and the courts. Administrative proceedings provide the advantage of greater expertise and time to devote to specialized environmental activities. Unlike the courts they can also take the initiative rather than have to wait for cases to be brought to them. Unlike the legislatures, they can also act more flexibly in light of changing conditions. Courts, on the other hand, provide more formal due process for protecting the innocent than administrative agencies do, and have more power to issue enforceable orders. Legislatures also have the advantage of being elected and thus are generally more responsive to the public will in their lawmaking work. As a compromise, power is increasingly going to administrative agencies but with strings attached whereby they are required to provide more due process in their proceedings and be subjected to both judicial review by the courts and changing guidelines by the legislatures.

If administrative agencies are to be set up to fight pollution rather than rely heavily on legislatures and the courts, how should these agencies be structured? More specifically, should they consolidate all governmental anti-pollution activities, be independent of the regular cabinet agencies, and have heads with fixed tenure such that they are not subject to political removal? Those advocating stronger agencies argue that without these devices, there would be conflict, gaps, and undesirable duplication between the existing agencies. They also say that otherwise the antipollution effort would be too subject to business pressures and pressures from polluting governmental bodies. On the other hand, these devices might tend to make administrative agencies less responsive to those who might be unjustly adversely affected by their decisions. The agencies might also be less responsive to the popular will, which manifests itself through the political channels that these independence devices are designed to constrict.

In structuring the system, one might question the appropriateness of the use of advisory boards consisting of representatives mainly from industry, but some from labor,

consumers, and conservation groups. On the one hand, such
boards might provide useful informational input, and they
can also carry back information and thereby help industry to
comply more with environmental standards. On the other hand,
they may either become too powerful such that industry domi-
nates the pollution control agencies, or else if they are
very weak boards, then they are virtually useless.

An increasingly important issue is to what extent
should the federal government encourage interstate, interlocal, and international antipollution activities. Such cooperation produces greater uniformity and consistency across
governmental units especially with regard to common rivers
and other bodies of water. Without such cooperation, the
work of one government might be nullified by another government. In spite of those considerations, one might argue
against intergovernmental activities (from a decentralized
perspective) by arguing that interstate agencies undesirably
decrease the sovereignty of the participating states. One
might also argue against intergovernmental activities (from
a centralized perspective) by arguing that interstate agencies undesirably decrease the likelihood of establishing
needed national-level standards and enforcement. The same
arguments from opposite central-versus-decentral motivations
can be made against agreements between nations on the grounds
they decrease the sovereignty of the participating nations,
and they simultaneously decrease the likelihood of establishing possibly needed world government standards instead of
fragile agreements between a few sovereign nations.

GOVERNMENT AND PRIVATE PROCEDURES
TO REDUCE POLLUTION

An important procedural issue that slowed the passage
of the 1972 federal water pollution legislation was the issue of what should be the relative weight given in an environmental protection program to private suits as contrasted
to governmental action. It seems that governmental action
needs to be emphasized because only the government generally
has the personnel and the funds to monitor continuously and
litigate skillfully major pollution violations. On the
other hand, it also seems that private suits should be encouraged because the government itself is often a polluter
or is unduly influenced by the polluters, and because the
government's heavy workload may prevent it from getting to
a pollution situation that some private individuals or organizations are willing and able to litigate. Along with
encouraging or facilitating private suits, private informers

can be encouraged by being given bounties or commissions
from fines collected as under the 1899 Refuse Act.

As an important procedural issue, what should be the
relative weight given in an environmental protection program
to prospective standard-setting as contrasted to a more ad
hoc case-by-case approach? Standard setting informs potential polluters, government regulators, and potential victims
in advance and more clearly what constitutes liability. A
case-by-case approach, however, allows for greater flexibility to adapt to changing situations. By dealing with concrete cases, the case approach is also more likely to lead
to more realistic precedents than trying to prepare abstract
standards. Minimum standards may also cause those above
the minimum to drop to the minimum so that the required minimum becomes the observed maximum. If standard setting is
used, a much-debated related issue is whether the standards
should be placed on regional quality, pollution discharges,
or on equipment and materials. The 1972 water pollution
legislation, for example, emphasizes effluent discharge
standards rather than regional water quality standards.

To what extent should the system provide for permits to
begin or to continue certain operations and to what extent
should there be periodic inspections? The permit system is
defended as a meaningful preventative program since otherwise sanctions have to be imposed when the damage is already
done, and when changes are harder to institute. Inspections
are defended to check on continued compliance. The permit
system, however, is attacked as too difficult and expensive
to administer to prevent the few bad pollutions that might
otherwise occur. Permit systems and frequent inspections
are also attacked as harassing to legitimate businessmen and
private citizens. Permit systems for already-existing facilities like factories or automobiles may be particularly burdensome to the persons regulated, including low-income owners of automobiles and small businessmen.

To what should time extensions and exceptions be
granted for polluters to comply with new standards especially where economic or technological hardships are involved?
Some environmentalists argue that business firms can generally comply if they want to, but that given the profit mo-
tive, business firms will tend to ask for more exceptions
and longer extensions than they really need. In the meantime, the public may be subjected to lengthy, unnecessary
pollution. On the other hand, some business groups argue
that legitimate businessmen should not be unreasonably
pushed to the detriment of themselves, their employees, and
their consumers. They argue that stays should especially be
granted while litigation is pending in view of the presumption of innocence until guilt is proven.

310

Should the system provide for vigorous antitrust action and compulsory licensing of patents in order to prevent one or a few firms in an industry from monopolizing the antipollution devices of the industry? The environmentalist position is that unless antipollution devices can be freely adopted by all firms in an industry, pollution will not be adequately fought. On the other hand, some people argue that to preserve incentives to invent, inventors should be able to control their inventions; and to obtain the benefits of large-scale operation, antitrust actions should not be taken against an efficiently operating firm that is the only firm producing a certain antipollution product.

Should the government be actively involved in research and development of new water filtration techniques, auto propulsion systems, smokestack filters, and other antipollution devices? Some argue that private industry is not likely to move fast enough in this kind of research and development because of low profitability, disruption to present industry, and inertia. Those with more of a conservative taxpayer's orientation, however, might argue such a research and development program is too costly to the taxpayer and runs contrary to the notion that in a capitalistic system the development of new products should be left to private enterprise. Those with more of a liberal or less business-oriented perspective might also argue against such a research and development program, but on the grounds that such programs lead to turning expensively developed products over to private industry as a taxpayer's handout to big business.

Should the system tend to hold polluters liable in quasi-criminal or civil litigation if they violate certain standards regardless what reasonable precautions or efforts they are making to reduce pollution? Those advocating strict enforcement might say that allowing for the subjective defense of "we took reasonable precautions" makes it very difficult to ever prove any violations, and thus difficult to invoke deterrent incentives or get changes made. Those advocating more flexible enforcement, however, might say that only those who are negligent should be held liable in accordance with our traditional law of liability and in order to give businessmen more freedom to operate.

GOVERNMENT-CONTROLLED INCENTIVES TO REDUCE POLLUTION

In this section we are concerned with issues that relate to incentives that governments can manipulate as part of an environmental protection program in order to reduce pollution. One such issue that has been widely discussed is whether the program should include charges or taxes on pollution emissions or effluents. Such charges are defended mainly on the ground that they will deter polluters from polluting because they become a part of the polluter's business expenses that he would prefer to reduce. If he does not thereby reduce his pollution, the charges collected can be used for a clean-up fund or for related research and development. Such charges, however, are attacked on the grounds they become a license or a payment to pollute, they are too difficult to assess equitably, and they tend to be passed on to the consumer.

To what extent should the system provide governmental rewards to polluters for reducing their pollution such as accelerated tax depreciation, tax credits, tax exemptions, low-interest loans, or outright subsidies? If such rewards are made high enough, they should be capable of getting pollution reduced more effectively than negative penalties or pricing charges will. It seems wrong to many people, however, to reward a polluter for not violating the law. To such people, a polluter should pay for antipollution devices out of his profits, not out of public tax money. Business itself may also resist outright subsidies as too much like welfare payments rather than have a more subtle indirect subsidy by means of special tax considerations.

To what extent should negative sanctions be imposed upon polluters like stiff fines, jail sentences, high damage awards, and injunctions backed with severe contempt of court possibilities? Those who are punishment-oriented or who believe strongly in deterrence through punishment argue that such sanctions are needed to decrease pollution and that lighter penalties are readily absorbed or passed on. Others argue that severe negative sanctions breed resentment, evasion, and cast a stigma on legitimate busines. Such sanctions may also result in abandonment of some business ventures, thereby adding to unemployment and wasted capital. They may also greatly decrease the likelihood of obtaining convictions or antipolluter judgments, thereby defeating the purpose that the severe sanctions are designed to achieve.

To what extent should the federal government make substantial grants and services available to state and local governments to fight pollution and to cut down their own pollution? Like the reward system to private business, the more money without strings attached the federal government makes available, the more effective state and local governments can be in fighting pollution given their own limited financial resources. Such a program might be objected to by conservatives as too costly to the taxpayer and too likely to increase inflation. Such a program might also be objected to by liberals who tend to be profederal government in their orientation as pouring money into inefficient state and local governments that could be better spent by the federal government.

Should the federal and other governments use their buying power to discourage pollution? If the federal government goes out of its way to buy from firms with relatively good pollution records and refuses to buy from firms with bad records, this will have a substantial impact on business practices. On the other hand, one can argue that governments should buy from sellers who can sell least expensively the products the government needs. Any other criteria will waste money and encourage inefficient business practices.

Should the system provide for strong publicizing of pollution wrongdoers? Such publicity would probably cause the business firms affected to decrease their pollution activity, especially if they sell brand-name products. Such publicity, however, will have little effect on business firms not selling brand-name products, and it may stigmatize legitimate business entrepreneurs. In some cases, casting stigma on wrongdoers may decrease their likelihood of being rehabilitated and may result in more negative behavior if adverse publicity is the only sanction. Related to the partly psychological and partly economic weapon of adverse publicity is the weapon of conference persuasion. It minimizes conflict between the complainant and the polluter and thus may be helpful where the complainants are employees of the polluter and both sides need to preserve rapport. Conference persuasion, however, tends to result in long delays and ineffective results if it has nothing to back it up other than rational discussion or the ethics and good will of the polluter.

WEIGHING CONFLICTING VALUES AND PROTECTING INNOCENT THIRD PARTIES

The set of policy issues in this section are quite fundamental and perhaps these should have been stated first. These issues, however, are especially oriented toward the subject matter of environmental protection, whereas the earlier political science policy issues cut across many political policy problems besides environmental protection.

Possibly the most fundamental policy issue in the environmental protection controversy is whether the effects of water, air, and other pollution are socially detrimental enough to merit large-scale regulatory and grant programs. Water pollution is damaging to public health, recreation, aesthetics, commercial fishing, and industrial water

supplies. Air pollution is damaging to public health, plant
life, materials, visibility, and climate. The high monetary
and nonmonetary costs have been documented by the Council on
Environmental Quality and by other scholarly studies.

On the other hand, at least five arguments are sometimes made against a more vigorous environmental protection
program. First, in random order, massive environmental programs use resources and human effort that could be better
devoted to problems of domestic and worldwide poverty or
other social problems. Second, such programs interfere with
industrial production and the raising of standards of living.
Third, such programs tend to emphasize middle-class aesthetics and recreation. Fourth, the basic health problems have
already been controlled via water filtration plants and anti-
smoke ordinances. Fifth, an overly vigorous environmental
protection program against water pollution and air pollution
can interfere with the development of energy resources by
hampering oil transportation, slowing the adoption of nuclear energy, and by decreasing the use of abundant fuels
that do not burn as cleanly as less abundant fuels do. Perhaps governments can be vigorous in fighting water and air
pollution in view of the extensive damage that such pollution causes, but perhaps they can also show flexibility in
order to take into consideration the above counterarguments.

A basic policy problem in the water and air pollution
field involving some fundamental conflicting values is the
problem of what should be the guiding principles in a dispute where an upstream or upwind person, firm, or city
causes pollution to a downstream or downwind person, firm,
or city. The basic alternatives that have been developed in
different places, times, and degrees are (1) protect land
owners from harm or at least award them damages if they are
harmed, (2) allow the first user of the water or the air to
win so long as he is not wasteful, and (3) maximize the total social or community well-being in accordance with a community plan administered by a regulatory agency. The emphasis in the past has been on protecting private property
rights and business interests as emphasized in the first two
alternatives. These alternatives are justified on the
grounds that otherwise people will not do well in their work
in order to raise their incomes so as to acquire private
property, and that business firms will not be as willing to
take business risks. The trend, however, is toward the
third alternative. Courts, legislators, and administrative
agencies are increasingly considering the total public interest, not just the property or business interests of the
immediate parties. This trend reflects expansion of the
electorate, increased pressure group power of unpropertied

and nonbusiness forces, and more egalitarian philosophical values that possibly stem from contemporary American society becoming more affluent.

Innocent third parties in the battle against pollution include victims, workers, and consumers. First, should the government somehow provide for compensation to victims of pollution? Those advocating governmental compensation of pollution victims argue that when pollution occurs, society is in a sense responsible for not having adequately regulated the polluters. The compensation fund can come from permit fees, effluent charges, and fines rather than from general taxes. Often the injured victim himself cannot determine or collect from the polluter. Contrary arguments emphasize that the injured person should sue for damages if he really has a good injury case. Under such circumstances he can possibly obtain a free lawyer who will collect his fee as a percentage of the damages awarded. Those making such arguments also emphasize that a compensation fund would be too expensive to business or to the taxpayers.

Should governments establish programs for relocating, reeducating, and temporarily subsidizing workers who are displaced by pollution crackdowns? Such programs would help win labor over to the antipollution side. They would also enable displaced workers to be more productive, and they can be justified on humane share-the-burden grounds. Opposition arguments emphasize that such programs are costly, unduly paternalistic, unnecessary in times of full employment, and unrealistic in times of high unemployment when there is no place to readily shift the workers to.

Should consumers be protected from business polluters by (1) prohibiting the passing of penalties onto the consumer, (2) requiring the business firm to remedy at its own expense products that are defectively polluting like old cars, and (3) regulating the price of filters and other antipollution products? Those who successfully advocated including provisions like these in the California air pollution legislation emphasized that the manufacturer rather than the ultimate consumer is the cause of the pollution and should thus bear the cost, that the manufacturer is still probably making a profit, and that the public will support antipollution more if the cost to the public is minimized. On the other hand, one can argue that it is too difficult to detect the passing of costs on to consumers, that it is unfair to hold manufacturers responsible for a good product that goes bad years later, and that price controls run contrary to a free market.

It is hoped that this descriptive list will help in the preparation of agendas for research on environmental policy

issues from a political science perspective. It is especially hoped that this total book on environmental politics will
interest more political scientists in doing work in the area
and will interest other scholars, policy makers, policy appliers, and the general public in the roles that political
scientists can play in environmental protection problems.

economics, 4, 15, 22, 240, 278, 281
energy crisis, 34, 40, 152–153, 286, 287
engineering, 25
engineers, 4
Environmental Action, 181
environmental activists, 15
environmental concern, 10, 178, 196–217; arguments against, 314; arguments for, 313; correlates of, 203–205; dimensions of, 178–203; explanations of, 205–209; social bases of, 203–205; value conflicts raised by, 314–315
environmental impact statements, 31, 91, 128, 187, 260, 263, 265, 266, 285, 292, 293, 294–302 (see also NEPA)
environmental interest groups, 163–164, 238
environmental law, 108
environmental lawsuits, 227
environmental lawyers, 28
environmental policy-making (see also environmental politics); administration of, 278–289; aggregate measures of, 15; basic concepts, 127–128; basic references on, 14–22; causal relationships in, 74–75; defining, 14–15, 109, 125–126, 131–133, 140–141, 177–179, 279, 289–290; facilities for studying, 24–33
    research centers, 129
    university programs on, 24–29;
federal legislation, 233–240; fellowships for, 27; incrementalism in studies of, 24–25; journals and other publications on, 28–31; legal issues involved in, 254–258,

306–307; policy analysis and, 61–66, 136–138; political institutions and, 177–305; political science research on, 3–10, 14–15, 139–153, 289
    air pollution, 20; attitudinal studies, 21, 56–57, 195–217; comparative case studies, 162–163, 165–167; institutional analysis, 15–16, 64–65, 110, 129; international relations, 20–21, 90–123, 306; normative political theory 34–60, 150, 346; state and local governments, 17–18, 160–168, 228–234, 242–244; water policies, 18–20;
research designs for studying, 67–91; rich versus poor nations and, 108; state legislation and, 180, 228–233; short- versus long-term, 8–10; unresolved policy issues 306–316
environmental politics (see also environmental policy making); assumptions about, 54–57; Congress and, 233–238; congressional attitudes toward, 234–235; the courts and, 188; dimensions of, 5–10, 108; environmental interest groups, 163–164, 180–184; international law and, 103–123; the legislative process and, 225–253; literature on, 139–154, 289–290
    basic issues in, 143–149;
    critique of, 141–142; research needs of, 149–154, 237–238;
normative political philosophy and, 34–60; party identification and, 210–215; political parties and, 177–178,

210-217, 228-229; public
opinion and, 180-186, 195-
217; reforms suggested for,
186-192
environmental problems, 126-
128 (see also environmental
policy making and environmental politics); causes of,
280-281; effects of governmental action on, 7, 51-57,
160-168; effects of tech-
nology and economic development on, 6-8, 14, 36-37, 40-
42, 108-109; expertise and,
53-54; explanations for,
128, 283-286; political
philosophy and, 34-60; research by engineers and
scientists on, 4; research
by political scientists on,
3-10, 14-23; short- versus
long-term strategies and,
7-8
Environmental Protection
Agency, 162, 167-168, 185-
186, 187, 191
equality, 189
equal protection, 256
evaluation research, 75, 89
executive behavior, 247
experimental designs, 75-91
ex post facto laws, 256

Federal Highway Administration, 300-301
federal legislation, 233-240
Federal Power Commission, 186,
268, 291, 299
federalism, 232, 242-244, 247,
255, 307-308
Ford Foundation, 232
foreign policy, 14
Fourteenth Amendment, 255
freedom, 51-52, 58, 110-115

Gallup polls, 196-197, 199,
201
geographers, 20, 21

Harris polls, 196-200, 200-201

ideology, 21, 22, 133, 210,
214-215
impact statements (see environmental impact statements)
incentives, 22, 311-313
incrementalism, 37, 42, 50,
227
individual rights, 37, 110
industrialization, 75
injunctions, 258
interest groups, 178, 232, 306
intergovernmental structures,
309
international law, 103-123
international relations, 20,
97-123, 306
"interrupted time-series" design, 76-77, 80-82
interstate commerce clause,
254
Interstate Commerce Commission, 183
interstate compacts, 19
Izaak Walton League, 180

judicial process, 188, 260-
275, 306 (see also courts)
justice, 52, 58

laissez faire, 37, 40, 42
land use, 229-230, 307
law schools, 27-28
lawyers, 15, 30 (see also environmental lawyers)
League of Conservation Voters,
181, 255, 237
legal issues, 254-258, 306
legislatures, 225-253, 306,
308-309, 314
liberalism, 57, 134, 209-210,
214-215, 286
liberty, 40, 133, 189
licensing, 311
local government, 160-168,
242-244 (see also state and
local government)

319

medicine, 25
methodology (see research design)
military policy, 14
Minnesota poll, 197
multicollinearity, 68-69, 74

National Air Pollution Control Administration, 162
National Audubon Society, 180
National Environmental Policy Act of 1969 (see NEPA)
National Wildlife Federation, 237
natural resources, 14-15, 26, 27
natural scientists (see physical scientists)
necessary and proper clause, 255
NEPA, 18, 30, 32, 146, 177, 183, 185, 226, 234, 260-275, 287, 291-305; agency response to, 294-303; compliance with, 264-271; congressional backlash, 270-271; court interpretations of, 263-274, 292-293; delay caused by, 261; guidelines implementing, 293-294
New Deal, 145
normative political philosophy, 34-60, 150, 306
nuclear energy, 41

Office of Management and Budget, 185-186, 293
oil pollution, 19-20
Opinion Research Corporation, 197

permits, 310
pesticides, 22
physical sciences, 3-5, 25, 133
planners, 15
policy analysis, 61

policy issues, 306-316; contrasted with legal issues, 306; defined, 306-307; governmental and private behavior, 309-311; government incentives, 311-313; government structures, 307-309
policy outputs, 67, 69-70, 71-74
political economists, 15
political myths, 178-179, 189-190
political parties, 178, 211-217, 306
political science, 3-10, 14-15, 26, 45-46 (see also specific subfields); American government, 139-168, 209-223; comparative politics, 124-138, 306; constitutional law, 254-259, 306; empirical political analysis, 61-93, 306; general political science, 3-33; international law, 103-123; international relations, 97-123, 306; judicial process, 188, 260-275, 306; legislatures, 225-253, 306; normative political philosophy, 34-60, 150, 306; public administration, 17, 278-305, 306; public opinion, 10, 177-178, 306; political parties, 177-178, 210-217, 306; state and local government, 160-168
polls, 195-217, 235
pollution, 6, 14, 16, 17, 38, 97-99, 108, 109, 111-112, 113-114, 115, 209, 234, 307 (see also specific types of pollution)
population, 141
pork barrel politics, 241-242
presidency, 263-264
public administration, 17, 27, 278-305, 306

public health, 25
public opinion, 9-10
Pure Food and Drug Law, 182

quasi-experimental research
  designs, 75-91

radiation pollution, 22, 307
rational-comprehensive model,
  16
recreation, 20
Refuse Act of 1899, 161
regional governmental structures, 242
regression analysis, 69, 75
regulatory agencies (see administrative agencies)
Republicans, 211-214, 229
research design, 67-91

search and seizure clause,
  256
seniority system, 234
separation of powers, 255
Sierra Club, 180
Soil Conservation Service,
  183
solid waste pollution, 307
sovereignty, 104, 106-107,
  110, 115
standard setting, 9, 310
state and local government,
  17-18, 160-168

state of nature, 39-40
"steady-state" society, 34,
  56
subgovernments, 20
Survey Research Center surveys, 197, 200, 211, 212,
  215
systems analysis, 16

taxing and spending clause,
  255
technology, 40-42, 44
Tennessee Valley Authority,
  183
Tenth Amendment, 255
Tragedy of the Commons, 38,
  54, 65
transnational institutions,
  133

United Nations, 99-100

Voting Rights Act of 1965,
  163

water pollution, 18-19, 161,
  307-315
Water Pollution Control Amendments of 1965, 164
Water Quality Act of 1965,
  161, 163

LYNTON K. CALDWELL is a professor in the Political Science Department and the School of Public and Environmental Affairs of Indiana University. He has been a consultant to the Senate Committee on Interior and Insular Affairs on the drafting of the National Environmental Policy Act of 1969 as well as national land use planning legislation and was chairman of the Panel of the National Academy of Sciences Committee on International Environmental Programs. He is the author of Environment: A Challenge to Modern Society and In Defense of Earth.

EDMOND COSTANTINI is associate professor and chairman of the Department of Political Science, University of California, Davis. He received his Ph.D. at the University of California, Berkeley. He has published widely on political leadership and related topics and is coauthor of California Parties and Politics. His current research interests include selected aspects of political party structures and functions, public opinion, and environmental politics.

EUGENE E. DAIS is a professor in the Political Science Department of the University of Calgary in Alberta, Canada. He has contributed articles to such journals as Human Rights, Legal Reasoning, and ARSP (Archiv für Rechts- und Sozialphilosophie), and to "Law, Value and Validation in Basic Social Change," in Validation of New Forms of Social Organization, ed. G. L. Dorsey and S. I. Shuman (1968).

CHARLES M. HARDIN is a professor in the Political Science Department of the University of California, Davis. He is the author of The Politics of Agriculture, Freedom in Agricultural Education, Food and Fiber in the Nation's Politics, and Presidential Power and Accountability: Toward a New Constitution.

MICHAEL E. KRAFT is an assistant professor of political science at Vassar College. His major research and teaching interests are in the areas of American politics, political behavior, and the politics of ecology. His recently completed dissertation, "Congressional Attitudes Toward the Environment: Attention and Issue-Orientation in Ecological

Politics" (Yale, 1973), is an empirical study of congressional behavior and the environment and he is the author of several articles and papers on ecology and politics, most recently as a contributor to Richard L. Clinton, ed., Population and Politics: New Directions in Political Science Research and as a coauthor with Peter G. Stillman of "Toward a Political Theory of Ecological Survival," a paper presented at the 1973 Annual Meeting of the American Political Science Association.

RICHARD A. LIROFF is a member of the staff of The Environmental Law Institute in Washington, D.C., and a Ph.D. candidate in Northwestern University's Political Science Department. He is the author of articles on NEPA and environmental policy appearing in Environmental Law Reporter, Loyola University Law Journal, and The Politics of Ecosuicide, edited by Leslie L. Roos, Jr.

LENNART J. LUNDQVIST is currently research assistant in the Department of Political Science of the University of Uppsala, Sweden. He served for one year (1972-73) as visiting assistant professor of the Department of Political Science and the School of Public and Environmental Affairs at Indiana University. He is the author of Miljövårdsförvaltning och politisk struktur (Environmental administration and political structure) and several articles in professional journals. His field of interest includes comparative and environmental public policy and administration.

DEAN MANN is a professor and chairman of the Political Science Department at the University of California, Santa Barbara. He is the author of The Politics of Water in Arizona, Offshore Oil Pollution, Uncooperative Federalism and the Public Interest, and Political and Institutional Analysis of Interbasin Transfers (1972 Report to the National Water Commission).

STUART S. NAGEL is a professor of political science at the University of Illinois. He is the secretary-treasurer of the Policy Studies Organization and coordinator of the Policy Studies Journal. He is also a member of the Committee on Water Quality Policy of the National Research Council and National Academy of Sciences. Among other books, he has authored The Legal Process from a Behavioral Perspective and Improving the Legal Process: Effects of Alternatives. His relevant articles include "Incentives for`Compliance with Environmental Law," American Behavioral Scientist.

WILLIAM OPHULS is an independent writer on political and environmental affairs. Formerly a Foreign Service Officer stationed in Africa and Asia, he obtained a Ph.D. in political science from Yale University in 1973. He is the author of several articles on the politics of environmental issues.

VINCENT OSTROM is a professor in the Political Science Department of Indiana University. He is the author of The Choice of Institutional Arrangement for Water Resource Development and The Political Theory of a Compound Republic.

ROBERT RIENOW is a professor in the Political Science Department of the State University of New York at Albany. He is the author of Moment in the Sun: A Report on the Deteriorating Environment, Man Against His Environment, and the forthcoming To Rescue Earth: The Path to International Stewardship.

LESLIE L. ROOS, JR. is associate professor of administrative studies at the University of Manitoba in Winnipeg, Canada. He has previously taught at Brandeis, Northwestern, and Indiana Universities. He is the coauthor of Managers of Modernization, editor of The Politics of Ecosuicide, and co-editor of Quasi-Experimental Approaches.

WALTER A. ROSENBAUM is an associate professor in the Political Science Department of the University of Florida. He is the author of The Politics of Environmental Concern (Praeger, 1973) and "The Year of Spoiled Pork: Comments on the Role of the Courts as Environmental Defenders," Law and Society Review 7 (1972): 33.

PAUL A. SABATIER is assistant professor of environmental studies at the University of California, Davis. He is presently completing a manuscript on the role of environmental interests groups on air pollution policy in Illinois, Indiana, and Michigan.

J. FRED SPRINGER is a postgraduate research scientist with the Institute of Governmental Affairs, University of California, Davis. His current research interests include comparative administrative systems and comparative research methods.

HAROLD AND MARGARET SPROUT are research associates in the Center of International Studies of the Woodrow Wilson

School of Princeton University. The Sprouts are coauthors
of numerous books and shorter writings in naval history,
international relations, and, more recently, the political
aspects of environmental repair and protection. Their most
recent major work, written from an explicitly ecological
perspective, is Toward a Politics of the Planet Earth. They
are scheduled to complete an essay entitled "Environmental
Politics: Objectives, Costs, Resources, Priorities, Dilemmas," to be published in the monograph series of the Princeton Center of International Studies in the early spring of
1974.

    PETER G. STILLMAN is at present an assistant professor
at Vassar College, where he teaches political philosophy and
modern political thought. He has articles accepted for publication in the American Political Science Review, Polity,
Journal of the History of Philosophy, and other journals,
and he delivered a paper, coauthored with Michael E. Kraft,
on ecological political theory at the 1973 Annual Meeting
of the American Political Science Association.

    GEOFFREY WANDESFORDE-SMITH is assistant professor and
vice chairman in the Department of Political Science and the
Division of Environmental Studies, University of California,
Davis. He is coeditor of and contributor to Congress and
the Environment and is the author of articles in Policy
Studies Journal, Public Administration Review, Stanford Law
Review, and other journals. He is also a member of the
Tahoe Research Group at Davis and a member of the Science
Advisory Panel created by the National Science Foundation
to review research on environmental problems in the Lake
Tahoe Basin.

    CLIFTON E. WILSON is director of the Institute of Gov-
ernment Research and professor of international law and relations in the Department of Government at the University of
Arizona. He is author of Diplomatic Privileges and Immunities and Cold War Diplomacy, coauthor of Law and Politics in
Outer Space: A Bibliography, and has contributed to journals
and collections in international law and politics.

ENFORCING AIR POLLUTION CONTROLS: Case
Study of New York City
> Esther Roditti Schachter

ENVIRONMENTAL POLICY: Concepts and
International Implications
> edited by Albert E. Utton
> and Daniel H. Henning

INTERNATIONAL ENVIRONMENTAL LAW
> edited by Ludwik A. Teclaff
> and Albert E. Utton

THE INTERNATIONAL POLITICS OF MARINE
POLLUTION CONTROL
> Robert A. Shinn